P9-CQE-661

BREAKING OPEN
THE WORD OF GOD

Resources for Using the Lectionary for Catechesis in the RCIA
Cycle A

Karen M. Hinman and Joseph P. Sinwell

PAULIST PRESS
New York/Mahwah

DEDICATION

To those who founded the North American Forum on the Catechumenate and all those who help to unfold the vision of the RCIA throughout North America.

Paulist Press gratefully acknowledges the use of: excerpts from TAKE LORD, RECEIVE by John B. Foley, S.J. Copyright © 1975 by John B. Foley, S.J. and North American Liturgy Resources, 10802 N. 23rd Ave., Phoenix, Arizona 85029. All rights reserved. Used with permission; the English translation of the opening prayers and the "Universal Prayer" from *The Roman Missal* © 1973, International Committee on English in the Liturgy, Inc. (ICEL); excerpts from the English translation of Rite of Penance © 1974, ICEL. All rights reserved; excerpts from *Seasons of Your Heart* by Macrina Wiederkehr, O.S.B. © 1979 Silver Burdett Company, are used by permission; "The Offer" and "The Find" by Anthony de Mello from *Wellsprings*, copyright © 1984 by Anthony de Mello, are reprinted by permission of Doubleday & Company, Inc.

Copyright © 1986 by
Karen M. Hinman and Joseph P. Sinwell

All rights reserved. No part of this book may be reproduced or transmitted in any form, or by any means, electronic or mechanical including photocopying, recording or by any information storage and retrieval system without permission in writing from the Publisher.

Library of Congress Cataloging-in-Publication Data

Breaking open the word of God.

    1. Bible—Study. 2. Lectionaries. 3. Christian education. I. Hinman, Karen M., 1953–
II. Sinwell, Joseph P.
BS592.B74 1986   268   86-15051
ISBN 0-8091-2822-5 (pbk.)

Published by Paulist Press
997 Macarthur Boulevard
Mahwah, New Jersey 07430

Printed and bound in the
United States of America

CONTENTS

Preface

Some eight years ago I was introduced to the Rite of Christian Initiation of Adults when I took part in a week-long seminar in Pineville, Louisiana. I shared this happy experience with some eighty persons—clergy, religious, laity—and I saw then the great potential of the RCIA for the renewal of the Church in our time.

I have not been disappointed! Since then I have visited a number of parishes to give talks at the RCIA meetings. Each time I am impressed by the enthusiasm and dedication of both candidates and sponsors. I rejoiced to see them receive a good spiritual formation based principally on the word of God in the weekly use of the lectionary.

What a joy to see the catechumens and candidates assemble with the people of God every Sunday morning! They were nourished by the word which was shared as a community that day. I witnessed that wonderful family spirit grow and mature as well as the bonds of friendship and fellowship.

I heartily recommend this new book by Karen Hinman and Joseph Sinwell. The lectionary is a rich source or font for catechesis in the catechumenate. I know from my own personal use and daily meditation on the Scripture readings as found in the lectionary. St. Jerome reminds us that to search and to know the Scriptures is to discover Jesus with his riches of the Spirit. I believe that this book serves as a convenient and helpful instrument in that direction. This work is unique as it represents the combination of authors from all Christian lifestyles: single, married, religious, priest from different parts of the country.

Among the holy and remarkable disciples of Jesus living in our time is Mother Teresa of India. She begins her day with her hearing of God's Word at Holy Mass. After receiving Holy Communion and making a fervent thanksgiving, she goes out into the world with the light and joy of Jesus within her heart. I am confident that catechumens and candidates will find also rich food for their spiritual formation in the lectionary and in the helpful insights found in this work.

Stanley Joseph Ott
Bishop of Baton Rouge

November 30, 1985

Foreword

In *What Can You Say About God?* (Paulist Press, 1971), William Luipen writes:

> A child is born and the believer exclaims "God!"
>
> In health or illness that believer shouts "God!"
>
> He sexually unites with another person and in his ecstasy the believer calls "God!"
>
> She is dying and her lips whisper "God!"
>
> At the rising and the setting of the sun, in the pale of the sea, at the undulating of the wheat stalks, the threat of a storm and the menace of a flood, at the welling up of a spring and the germinating of the seed, the believer exclaims "God!"
>
> Conquering in battle or suffering defeat, living in poverty or in prosperity, suffering injustice or finding justice, the believer calls "God!"
>
> When they are reduced to slavery in Egypt, rise against their oppressors and when they overcome the terrible risk of their revolt against their masters, believers exclaim "God!"
>
> When, while wandering through the desert with their people, they meet ethical demands imposing themselves . . . as inescapable conditions of humanity, believers shout "God!"
>
> And when they must go into exile, they complain "God!"
>
> When they can again return from . . . exile, they joyfully shout "God!"

The *Rite of Christian Initiation of Adults (RCIA)* says much the same thing in this way:

> Together with the catechumens, the faithful reflect upon the value of the paschal mystery, renew their own conversion, and by their example lead the catechumens to obey the Holy Spirit more generously (#4).

That "churchy" language of paschal mystery summons us to reflect in community on all the ways we die and all the ways we rise—precisely in those moments of agony and ecstasy when a child is born, when we sexually unite, before suns, stars, wheat and storm, in slavery and exodus, in exile and homecoming when believers meet their God. In the pain which we can't bear alone, in the gift which we can't create alone, believers meet the God who carries us through death to life.

Christian believers meet that God by following Christ among us. He who became flesh of our flesh and bone of our bone that he might enter those times of agony and ecstasy is risen and still enfleshed in his people. Wherever two or three gather in his name he journeys with them through death to life (cf. #7, *Constitution on the Sacred Liturgy*).

But the privileged times to reflect upon and celebrate that paschal mystery are in liturgy. Every sacrament invites us into the dying and rising of Jesus, in birth and initiation, in vocation and married love, in reconciliation and healing and death, in Communion meal. That's what's right "about the rite." It's not the program nor class nor instruction of Christian initiation. It's the *rite*. It thrives in chapel, not classroom. It proclaims that *the* sacrament of Christ among us is not a book but a people journeying through death to life in liturgy.

For catechumens, when that people does gather around a book, *the* book is not catechism and not even the Bible, but the word proclaimed and prayed in the lectionary at worship (again, cf. #7). That word is not just doctrine nor truth *about* God. It is real presence. It is the real presence of the God who is enfleshed in Jesus Christ journeying with the "two or three gathered in his name," uniting the stories of Hebrews and Jesus to our stories.

Recall the encounter between Nathan and David (2 Sam 12:1–15). Nathan tells a story of a rich man defrauding a poor man. David's anger flares up against the man. Nathan proclaims, "You are the man!" You are the one. That is the proclamation of every Scripture—in our times of passage through death to life, when a child is born, when we sexually unite, in slavery and exodus, exile and homecoming, the lectionary proclaims that we are the men, we are the women. We are the prodigals welcomed home. We are sinking in waves of despair; Jesus is with us in the storm. We are the outcasts and sinners; we are Zacchaeus and the sinful woman whom Jesus welcomes to table. We are the paralytic forgiven and healed. We are the disciples journeying with Jesus to Emmaus, recognizing him in shared brokenness at table. We cry from the cross, "Why have you abandoned me!" We hear the good news of Easter—they are not here; they are risen!

That is the goal of this guide through the lectionary—to invite us into the stories and the message of the Sunday readings. The goal is not to exegete texts but to exegete lives—to look deeply into our personal and communal lives and to see them in the light of the persons and communities who have journeyed with the Lord before us and who are still with us in the real presence of the word. We enter not an abstract discussion of data but dialogue with stories and persons through putting ourselves into their stories and their journey, knowing that they are risen and present to our story and journey. All those risen into Christ Jesus invite us into real presence through the word.

If that happens, enter doctrine. Doctrine is the result of theological reflection on the *meaning* of those stories, in pithy one-liners or encapsulized paragraphs. Dogma is an official summary of the meaning of the communal religious experience of our people. We trust that catechumens in an atmosphere of freedom will raise piercing questions about doctrine and the meaning of marriage today, for example, after hearing a word which calls us to faithfulness till death. They will want to explore the doctrine of reconciliation and all the possibilities of how the Church reconciles today after hearing stories of Jesus eating with sinners. But if catechumens do not first hear a word of fidelity and reconciliation in their own lives and stories, there is danger that doctrine and dogma touch head but not heart, rendering information not transformation, instruction not conversion. Indeed, catechists should have a multitude of good catechisms and theological commentaries on their shelf to help explore the meaning of Scripture and our historical heritage in relation to contemporary signs of the times. But this guide listens to the word proclaimed through the lectionary and resounding in our lives as the starting point for doctrinal reflection and the search for meaning.

Kudos to Karen Hinman and Joseph Sinwell for gathering resources which will invite us into real presence through the word. In this volume they offer the assistance of other ministers in the catechumenate who in practical ways have invited catechumens to join their stories to the big story. These catechists and catechumens are with us as we enter the dialogue. We are grateful to them, and they are with us when we gather in God's name.

Rev. James B. Dunning

Introduction

What books are suitable for use with adult catechumens in the period of catechesis? How do catechists explain and share the Catholic faith and tradition with catechumens? These are common questions among ministers on adult catechumenate teams throughout the United States and Canada. This volume is a pastoral attempt to respond to these concerns and to the use of the lectionary for catechesis in the implementation of the Rite of Christian Initiation of Adults [R.C.I.A.].

The foreword to the book highlights the importance of catechesis in the R.C.I.A. The book focuses on using the lectionary in catechesis throughout the entire liturgical year. Articles on the liturgical year, the importance of adult religious education principles, the role and basic use of the lectionary, and the integration of prayer into catechumenal catechesis precede the commentary on cycle A readings and outlines of sessions for each liturgical season, including major feasts.

The outlines of the sessions have been authored by ministers active in adult catechumenates in the United States and Canada. The session outlines offer a variety of models. Catechumenate teams can use these sessions as springboards and resources for adapting the lectionary to local needs; the sessions are not intended to be used as lesson plans for a text in the catechumenate. Flexibility and adaptability are the key to creative catechesis. Other resources are suggested in the sessions and bibliography.

The use of the outlines presumes:

1. That the parish offers on-going catechesis for catechumens throughout the liturgical year.
2. That the parish has extended the period of catechesis with adult catechumens for one to three years. (Rite of Christian Initiation of Adults No. 19 & 20)
3. That the parish celebrates the rite of dismissal for catechumens in a Eucharistic liturgy. (Rite of Christian Initiation of Adults No. 19)
4. That the parish catechumenate teams promote the principles of adult religious education in the catechumenate.
5. That catechumens and team members have available their own copy of the Sacred Scriptures during catechetical sessions.

These assumptions represent the development of catechumenal catechesis in North America.

Although this volume is primarily intended for use in parish adult catechumenate, Church educational leaders could easily adapt it for use with Scripture sharing, post-RENEW, ministerial support, prayer groups and others. Hopefully, a variety of pastoral ministers will utilize this practical resource.

We wish to gratefully acknowledge the contributing authors for their cooperation and creativity; Mr. Robert Hamma of Paulist Press for his support and advice and Mrs. Marie White and Mrs. Michelle Kelly for their diligent typing and assistance.

This resource can be a practical, pastoral tool for adults who are breaking open the word of God in the catechumenate and other forms of adult religious education. By praying, reflecting and sharing God's word as broken in the community, each adult will continue to grow in his or her journey of faith in response to the challenge of actively building the reign of God.

INTRODUCTORY ARTICLES

The Liturgical Year: Memory and Promise

By J. Michael McMahon

The passing and marking of time shapes our experience of belonging to a community. My sense of belonging to a family, for example, was nurtured and strengthened by events that took place at regular times during the day, the week and the year. Our family gathered at the dinner table each evening to share a meal and to review the events of that day. Sunday afternoons usually were spent visiting relatives or friends. Annual events were important as well. Picnics on Memorial Day, the Fourth of July, and Labor Day, along with crowded family dinners on Thanksgiving and Christmas, helped me to experience our extended family, including grandparents, uncles, aunts, and cousins.

These special times are important for the life of any family. They are occasions for *gathering*, for bringing together family members of all generations for a common celebration. The times of celebration are opportunities to share *memories* of the family's history, as older members recount important events and draw younger members into them. Stories are passed from generation to generation, and become the common experience of the whole family. Hopes for the future are shared as well. As new members are added to a family, there is a shared sense of the *promise* that awaits them and the whole family.

Just as the marking of time shapes our experience of belonging to a family, so does it help to form us as persons belonging to the Catholic Christian community. Week to week and year to year, the Church marks the passing of time by celebrating and reflecting on the mystery of Christ.

Christians mark the passing of time by a cycle of Sundays, seasons and feasts. These events, occurring at regular times, shape our experience of belonging to Christ and to the Christian community. They are times of *gathering*, as Christians come together for worship. In the liturgies that we celebrate, *memories* are evoked as the great stories of Scripture are recounted and savored. We also look forward with joyful hope to the fulfillment of God's *promise* to bring the saving work of Christ to completion in the establishment of God's reign of truth, justice, and peace. We live in this present time, aware of God's presence and action among us in the past, and looking forward to the fulfillment of God's promises in the future. We look both backward and forward as we live in Christ today.

The cycle of Sundays, seasons, and feasts continues to meet us as we pass through the events of life that shape us, change us, and challenge us to keep growing. Each year on December 25, we celebrate the feast of Christmas once again, but each year we are not quite the same as we were the previous year. The same feasts may recur year after year, but because we are a living community, the celebrations are not simply repetitions of the past. Christmas this year is not the same as Christmas last year, because *we* have changed.

A View of the Church Year

It is tempting to understand the liturgical year simply as marking various *events* in the life of Christ: his birth, his baptism, his ministry, his miracles, his teaching, his death, his resurrection, his ascension, his gift of the Spirit, his coming again in glory. This view leads us to view the Church year as a travelogue, beginning with the expectation of the Messiah's birth during Advent, and concluding with the gift of the Holy Spirit at Pentecost.

The trouble with approaching the Church year as a travelogue is that we can too easily remain spectators, merely watching past events go by once more. Instead of looking at the Church's cycle of Sundays, seasons and feasts as a tour of Christ's life, we might understand it as celebrating a single *person-event*, Jesus Christ. Because we have been baptized into Christ, his history has become our history. Each celebration in the Church's calendar not only recalls that history, but makes it present for us now. Every feast, every season, every Sunday opens us up, not only to past events, but to the ways that Jesus Christ is present and active in the Christian community today.

As the Church marks time through the day, the week, and the year, we celebrate our union with Christ. The focus of our celebration is different at different times because the mystery of Christ is so rich. In the Christmas season, we remember that God became human in Jesus the Christ; and yet we also celebrate that in Christ, God has made us sharers in divinity! On Pentecost Sunday as we recall the gift of the Holy Spirit to the apostles, we also affirm the outpouring of God among us, members of Christ's Church.

Sunday, the First Holyday

The Church regards Sunday as the primary festival of its calendar:

> The Church celebrates the paschal mystery on the first day of the week, known as the Lord's Day or Sunday. This follows a tradition handed down from the apostles and having its origin from the day of Christ's resurrection. Thus Sunday must be ranked as the first holyday of all.[1]

Long before Christians observed any annual feasts, they assembled on the day of Christ's resurrection, the first day of the week. It was for them the day of assembly, when the whole community gathered together to celebrate the Lord's supper, to recognize the abiding presence of Christ in their midst in the breaking of the bread.

Just as families gather to share meals and to remember their stories, so have Christians from the earliest days assembled to keep the memory of Jesus Christ in word, in Eucharist—in shared stories and in the common meal. When could it be better for these gatherings than that first of days, when the disciples found an empty tomb, when Jesus appeared in their midst, when he came walking toward them on the shore, when he sent upon them the gift of the Holy Spirit? Like the disciples on the road to Emmaus on another Sunday, they too recognized his presence among them in the Scriptures they read and in the bread they broke.

Sunday is the first day, and at the same time is the eighth day, which points beyond our own time to God's promised future. It is a day of memory, but it is also a day of promise. We look forward to that day when we will rise and be taken up to God as Jesus was. The earliest Christians expected that Christ would return—when else?—on the first day of the week! The first day is thus the eighth day, the day of promise.

In its Constitution on the Sacred Liturgy, the Second Vatican Council directed that Sunday be restored to its place as the first holyday of the Church's calendar. Sunday after Sunday, we gather as the early Christians did to celebrate in word and Eucharist our share in the death and resurrection of Christ. Each week our assemblies proclaim that we are a people plunged into the paschal mystery, and that we are a people of the promise, working for God's reign of peace and justice as we live in joyful hope.

The Seasons

The mystery of Christ is savored over the course of the year. The seasons of the liturgical year give expression to different facets of this mystery, and allow us to enter into it more deeply. Figure 1 presents a thumbnail sketch of the seasons.

Figure 1: Seasons of the Liturgical Year

Season	Focus	Length	Time of Year
Advent	Coming of Christ (Past, Present, Future)	4 weeks	Late November to December 24
Christmas Season	Incarnation, Manifestation and Mission of Christ	2–3 weeks	December 25 to early or mid-January
Lent	Baptism, Reconciliation	40 days	Ash Wednesday (mid-February or early March) until Holy Thursday (late March or early April)
Easter Triduum	Death and Resurrection of Christ	3 days	Late March or early April
Easter Season	Abiding Presence of the Risen Lord	50 days	Easter Sunday to Pentecost (April, May)

Easter Triduum

The first of the annual feasts to be celebrated by Christians was Easter. This feast has many parallels with the Jewish Passover, in which the people of Israel remembered their deliverance from slavery in Egypt and the covenant that God made with them. Christians began to celebrate their own Passover, recalling how in baptism we have passed with Christ from death to life, and through Christ have entered into a new covenant with God. The early celebration of Easter observed not only the resurrection, but the whole paschal mystery of Christ's dying and rising, his passing from death to life.

Even though we remember and celebrate Christ's death and resurrection every Sunday, the Easter Triduum is a time for even deeper reflection on this paschal mystery. It begins on the evening of Holy Thursday with the Mass of the Lord's Supper, reaches its climax in the celebration of the Easter Vigil, and concludes with evening prayer on Easter Sunday. Even though it lasts for three days, it is really one continuous celebration.

As in the early Church, the Easter Vigil is the normative time for celebrating the great sacraments of initiation (baptism, confirmation, and Eucharist). As Paul taught in Romans (see chapter 6), we are baptized into the death of Christ so that we might rise to a new life in him. As Christ died, so our old selves are destroyed. As Christ rose again, so are we called to walk in newness of life.

Lent

Lent originated as a time of final preparation for those who were to be initiated at Easter. As the practice of public penance developed in the Church, this season was also a time for preparing penitents for reconciliation on Holy Thursday.

In the early Church, catechumens were called to intensive preparation for the sacraments in these weeks before Easter, which were a time of purification and enlightenment. The element of purification was stressed in the scrutinies, solemn exorcisms celebrated by the bishop to assure that the lives of the elect had truly changed and that they were free of any demons that might keep them from following Christ wholeheartedly. The presentation to candidates of the Gospels, the profession of faith, and the Lord's Prayer were intended to enlighten candidates, to lead them to see things in a new way.

Lent was also in early churches a season for penitents to prepare for reconciliation with the Christian community. By allowing themselves to be marked with ashes, penitents gave evidence of their sincere desire to do penance. Fasting, prayer and almsgiving were the three great ways of penance that these Christians were called to embrace.

In the Roman calendar today, Lent has been restored to its baptismal and penitential character. Conversion, however, is not the calling of only a few among us, but rather of the whole community. Thus, as the elect prepare for initiation at the Easter Vigil, all of us are called to reflect on the meaning of our baptism. Marked with the sign of penance on Ash Wednesday, every member of the Christian assembly is called to the practices of prayer, fasting and almsgiving. The conversion to Christ that we celebrate in baptism is to be renewed constantly, and especially during our yearly observance of Lent.

Easter Season

Our Easter joy does not end with the close of the Easter Triduum, but continues for fifty days. In the Roman calendar today, this season is to be "celebrated in joyful exultation as one feast day, or better as one 'great Sunday.'"[2]

This season is a time of post-baptismal catechesis or mystagogy for the neophytes, who have just for the first time shared in the community's sacramental life. The Scripture readings of these Sundays speak with special power to them about their new life in Christ and in the Church community.

The images of these weeks all point to the abiding presence of the risen Christ. The crucified one who rose from the dead has not left us orphans; he is with us! We meet him in the community itself, in the word that is proclaimed, in the bread that is broken. He cares for us as a shepherd tends the flock, and he sustains us as a vine nourishes its branches. This risen Lord now sends us out to make the good news known to others, and has given us the Holy Spirit as the pledge of his continued presence with us.

Even though the Easter season embraces the great feasts of Easter, Ascension and Pentecost, it is indeed one great feast in which we celebrate that Christ is risen and with us.

Christmas Season

Just as Easter Sunday is the pivotal feast of the Lent-Easter cycle, so is Christmas the focal point of the Advent-Christmas cycle. Beginning then on the evening of December 24 with the celebration of the vigil of Christmas, the Christmas season continues to the Sunday after January 6, the feast of the Baptism of the Lord.

The first celebration of Christmas took place in Rome during the fourth century. This feast came about long after Easter had become a time-honored tradition among the Christian churches. Falling at the time of the winter solstice, Christmas incorporated the elements of darkness and light which figured so prominently in the pagan festival of *Sol Invictus* ("the unconquered sun"). As pagans celebrated the birth of the sun, so Christians remembered the birth of the "Sun of Justice," Jesus Christ.

The historical development of this season is very complex, since it incorporates a variety of feasts that originated in different parts of the Christian world, some of which were interpreted differently in different places. Today, however, the feasts of Christmas time all focus our attention on the mystery of God-made-human, the incarnation.

A close reading of the readings and other texts of this time give evidence of a surprisingly unsentimental approach to this mystery. The Gospel for the Mass of Christmas Day, for example, is the very beautiful, but highly theological, prologue from John (chapter 1). The Sunday after Christmas, observed as the feast of the Holy Family, proclaims that the Word-made-flesh was part of an amazingly ordinary human family which experienced misunderstanding and even conflict.

The Christmas season celebrates not only God-made-human, but also the Word accessible and made known to people of all nations. This dimension is particularly evident on the feast of the Epiphany—in Greek, "manifestation".

God took flesh in Jesus Christ not to remain an innocent child, but to fulfill his mission of proclaiming the reign of God. The mystery of the incarnation is ultimately understood in light of Easter. At his baptism in the Jordan, the true meaning of Christ's birth is revealed as he begins the ministry that will eventually lead to his death and resurrection.

Advent

Advent, the first season of the Church year, is a time of prayerful preparation. The coming of Christ is our constant concern during this period. As in the last weeks of ordinary time, Advent begins by directing our attention to the future. We who live two thousand years after Christ still wait for his coming! The Gospel calls us to be watchful in prayer and to change our hearts so that we may be prepared to meet him.

As Advent unfolds, the focus gradually but perceptibly changes from the future coming of Christ to his coming among us today and his historical coming in the past. As Christmas draws closer and closer, John the Baptist and Mary are introduced because of their roles in preparing the way for Christ. At the same time, our Advent preparation becomes more and more joyful and expectant. It is as though the Church were itself pregnant, ready to give birth to its Lord and make him present and known to the whole world.

Ordinary Time

The great cycles of Lent-Easter and Advent-Christmas take up less than half the year. The rest is called Ordinary Time, and yet no time is really ordinary, since we live now between the time of Christ's life, death and resurrection and the time of his return in glory and the fulfillment of God's reign.

On the Sundays of Ordinary Time, we focus on the basics. We continue to gather both to remember the dying and rising of Christ and to celebrate the promise that he left us. The paschal mystery is our constant concern, the continuing pattern for our liturgy and our life.

Feasts

This chapter has focused on Sunday as the first holyday and on the "temporal cycle," or the seasons of the year. The Church also observes many days which are not related to the Sunday celebration or to the liturgical seasons. Among these are annual celebrations of the Lord, of Mary, and of the saints. Only a very few of these are important enough to be ranked as "solemnities." Other major observances, ranking below solemnities, are called "feasts." In addition to solemnities and feasts, the Church also observes "memorials" of many saints.

These celebrations are also an important part of the community's memory, remembering those in our tradition who serve as examples of life in Christ. They also draw our attention to the promise of the future, when we and all of creation will join the saints in God's reign of unending peace and justice.

Conclusion

The experience of the Church's time is an important element in our formation. By baptism, confirmation and Eucharist, we are initiated into the mystery of Christ, a mystery that is far too rich to be fathomed all at once, and is in fact inexhaustible. Just as we come to belong to our families and other human communities by participating in the times of their lives, so we come to belong to Christ and the Church by journeying through liturgical time. The cycle of Sundays, of seasons, and of feasts gradually open us to a deeper appreciation of the Christ who joins us to himself.

Each year as we celebrate these cycles, we evoke the memories once again and look forward anew to the promise. And as we ponder the mystery of Christ, we are transformed more and more in his image.

Notes

1. Congregation of Rites (Consilium), General Norms for the Liturgical Year and the Calendar, no. 4, in *Documents on the Liturgy 1963–1979: Conciliar, Papal and Curial Texts* (Collegeville, Minnesota: The Liturgical Press, 1982), p. 1156.

2. *Ibid.*, no. 22.

Teaching Liturgical Prayer to Catechumens

By Victoria M. Tufano

In the recent movie "Starman," a young widow and the extra-terrestrial who has taken on the form of her late husband undertake a cross-country automobile ride in order to rendezvous with his space vehicle. After several hours in the passenger's seat, the alien offers to take over the driving. He assures the woman that he has internalized the operation of the car and the rules of the road by watching her drive. After he runs a stoplight and narrowly misses being hit by a semi-trailer truck, she screams "I thought you said you knew the rules." "I do," he replied. "Red light means stop; green light, go; and yellow, go faster." He had indeed learned to do just as she had done.

Liturgical prayer is learned in much the same way as the alien learned to drive. We observe those who seem to know what they are doing and we imitate their action. The various rites of the catechumenate provide many opportunities for the catechumens to observe how the Catholic community prays in common.

First and foremost among the rites of the catechumenate is the celebration of the word of God. The Rite of Christian Initiation of Adults in paragraphs 106–108 refers both to those celebrations of the word which constitute the first part of the Sunday Mass and to those special celebrations which may be held after catechesis or in conjunction with the minor exorcisms and other blessings.

Celebrations of the word celebrated in the context of the parish community's Sunday Mass are the ordinary means of the catechumens' gradual incorporation into the worship life of that community. They are the occasion at which the community as a whole teaches the catechumens, the newest members of the household of faith, what it means to be a member of this body. This places some demands on all those participating in these celebrations, and in particular on those who are concerned with the planning and other ministries of the liturgy.

After some deliberation on what exactly these demands are, one may conclude that they are exactly those which the liturgy of the word makes even in the absence of catechumens. Those who plan are always charged with seeing that such celebrations are prepared in accordance with the season of the liturgical year, the particular Scriptures to be proclaimed, and the needs of the celebrating community. Musicians must always take into consideration these same realities in performing their primary ministry of leading and supporting the assembly in sung prayer. Ministers of hospitality welcome all who come to the Church's house and see that they have whatever is needed to participate in the celebration. Those concerned with the physical environment take care that the space is clean and decorated in a way that enhances and assists the celebration. Ministers of the word (lectors, deacons, priests) always strive to proclaim the Scriptures in such a way that the assembly is moved to faith.

The presence of catechumens does place an extra demand on homilists. They must attempt to preach the word in such a way that it will be understandable to those whose faith is new and to whom the ways of Catholic Christians may still be unfamiliar. At the same time, they must not neglect the needs of those whose faith has been tested and those who struggle to continue to live the word. One might argue, however, that this is so in any parish congregation. In any case, homilists must be particularly aware that their words constitute a major part of the formation of catechumens.

Finally, through their willingness to welcome catechumens into their midst, both through their ritual actions and through very ordinary actions (e.g., introducing themselves, helping find a place in an unfamiliar pew book, inviting a catechumen to sit with them, smiling, etc.) members of the assembly participate in and effect the integration of the catechumens into the community's worship. The assembly's example of "full, conscious, and active participation"[1] in the celebration is the principal teacher of liturgical prayer to catechumens.

Celebrations of the word celebrated in the smaller contexts of catechumenal sessions contain the same elements as those above, but they are more easily adapted to the needs of the catechumens. Care must be taken that these celebrations retain the character of liturgical prayer in the Catholic tradition. One important goal of these celebrations is to lead the catechumens into the worship of the whole assembly.[2] To add elements foreign to Catholic worship to these services runs counter to this goal.

While the primary locus of learning liturgical

prayer is the liturgical assembly, specific instruction is still necessary. The catechumens first instruction on the Church's liturgical tradition probably occurred during the precatechumenate stage. Since many people are initially attracted to the Catholic faith through the liturgy, it is likely that inquirers would have asked questions concerning it prior to making the decision to seek membership in the Church.

This first teaching concerning liturgical prayer is expanded during the catechumenate. Instruction and experience of the many elements of the Church's liturgical tradition, along with the opportunity to reflect on them, provide the fullest approach to learning about liturgical prayer.

Some elements, however, are best experienced with only a minimum of instruction beforehand. Recently, in a midwestern parish, the members of the congregation were invited to extend their hands over the newly-admitted catechumens while the intercessory prayers for them were prayed. After their dismissal, several of the catechumens reflected that they felt the strength and power of the community's prayers surround them. They felt supported and embraced by this gesture. No instruction beforehand could have better taught them the gesture's meaning.

Many elements of liturgical prayer can be introduced during the catechumenal sessions following the dismissal from the Sunday assembly. The format for the catechumenal session described below as based on that proposed by Karen M. Hinman in "Catechetical Method: A Model for Sunday Catechumenal Session," a paper published by the North American Forum on the Catechumenate. Basically, that format consists of a period following the dismissal from the larger assembly during which the catechumens continue to focus on the Scriptures until the liturgy ends. At that point, spouses and sponsors join the catechumens for a catechetical session which ends in a period of prayer. The time from the beginning of Mass until the end of the session is two and a half to three hours.

The first element of concern for teaching prayer in a catechumenal session is the environment in which the session is to take place. Fortunate is the catechumenate which has a clean, well-lighted, flexible space to call its own! Whatever the space, it should invite the catechumens to participate in prayer and discussion. A few minutes spent before Mass arranging chairs, passing out any needed songbooks and sheets and making coffee will be greatly rewarded with a smooth transition from the liturgical assembly to the catechumenal session. Soft (non-fluorescent) lighting, no desks, an attractively bound Bible enthroned on a simply decorated stand, perhaps a candle or two and the smell of fresh coffee and tea create a pleasant environment. At different seasons, a cross, an Advent wreath, or some fresh or dried plant arrangements might be added. Refrain from inventing symbols which will have to be explained and from using those which belong to other religious traditions. Bread and wine, water, oil, and strong contrasts of light and darkness are most closely associated with the initiation sacraments and are best left for that stage of the catechumenal process.

Once the place is prepared, and the catechumens and catechists have arrived, a variety of sequences may follow.

Music, an important element of liturgical prayer, may be used to regather the catechumens. A hymn of praise, a seasonal hymn, the setting of the responsorial psalm used in the larger assembly, or even some instrumental music might be used.

The one invariable element of these sessions is the proclamation of the Scripture which will form the basis for catechesis. Usually it will be the day's Gospel, although one of the other two readings might occasionally be chosen. Invite the hearers to stand for the Gospel. Use the customary beginnings and endings. The catechumens may wish to know the significance of the crossing of the forehead, lips, and breast. Invite them to use it, if they desire.

Following the proclamation, music might be used to respond to the reading, or a guided meditation might be led by a catechist. Some aspect of the homily might be discussed, or a bit of quiet time for meditation or journaling might be provided. However that period is spent, it is brought to a close with prayer.

Prayers of intercession following the pattern used at Mass may be prepared, with time for the catechumens to formulate their own petitions. "Lord, have mercy" or "Lord, hear our prayer" generally work better than long, easily forgotten responses.

Whether petitions are prayed or not, a collect-type prayer is most appropriate to conclude this portion of the session. Such a prayer usually follows the you-who-do-through pattern,[3] that is, an address to God (the first person of the Trinity), a brief stating/remembering/praising of God's activities, a petition, and a doxology of praise in Jesus Christ. A prayer composed by the catechist or the opening prayer of the day's Mass might be used.

Note that the sacramentary prayers usually end "now and forever" or "through Christ our Lord"; most Catholics will automatically respond "Amen." Note also that these prayers usually exhibit an economy, beauty, and simplicity of language. They make use of the traditional imagery, and they avoid flowery phrases, obscure language, and jargon. For the catechist who chooses to compose prayers for these moments, they provide excellent models.

When the Mass has ended, and sponsors and spouses are ready to join the catechumens, a coffee break is a good way to integrate the newcomers.

The catechetical session which follows the coffee break is also based on the day's Scriptures and homily. A period of prayer completes the entire session.

This period of prayer may incorporate various liturgical elements. If the Lord's Prayer has already been presented, the group may pray it together, perhaps using the gesture of raising the arms or simply turning the palms upward in prayer. In Lent, the gesture of kneeling may be used to accompany a prayer of repentance. Catechists may use one of the prayers of blessings found in the rite and invite sponsors to join in the laying-on of hands or the signing with the cross. The gathering may conclude with the sign of peace.

Whenever a new element is to be introduced in the closing prayer, a brief explanation of the element and its use in liturgical prayer may be offered. Sponsors may wish to mention the new element at some point after its introduction to allow the catechumens to react and to ask questions.

When a new element is introduced, it is wise to incorporate it into several succeeding sessions. Like a new piece of music, any new liturgical element takes some time to work its way into the memory. Repetition is the essence of ritual prayer. Catechists need not reinvent prayer forms each week. As time passes, the catechumens will have a sizable liturgical repertoire which can be incorporated into these prayer sessions.

Other elements which may be introduced at these times include the gesture of bowing, particularly at the doxology at the end of a psalm and the litany of saints (at the Feast of All Saints, for example). Other liturgical elements may first be met at the larger assembly's Sunday gathering, including the genuflection, incense, processions and acclamations. These may need to be explained and some may be adapted for use in the smaller group. Beware of smoke detectors if you decide to use incense somewhere other than in the church.

Some elements will only be experienced on particular occasions. These include the prostration of the ministers at the beginning of the Good Friday service, the entrance and veneration of the cross at the same service, the washing of the feet on Holy Thursday, and the extinguishing of candles at Tenebrae. Catechumens may also have occasion to participate in a Catholic funeral, wedding, or even an ordination. Introduction of elements unique to these celebrations may be made beforehand and more fully discussed afterward.

The Catholic tradition of liturgical prayer is one of the great treasures that the Church has to present to its newest members. Care must be taken that they are formed in this tradition throughout the catechumenate. In addition, liturgical prayer must be experienced as integral to the life of faith, along with the practice of charity and the moral teachings of the Church.

In addition to liturgical prayer, the Church's tradition includes a wealth of other prayer forms. The various methods of private prayer and such devotional practices as the stations of the cross, novenas and the rosary are also part of the inheritance which catechumens receive, but they must be seen as being rooted in the Church's liturgical prayer life. Sponsors, catechists, and spiritual directors will want to see that these practices are shared and placed in the proper perspective.

By providing a structure in which catechumens participate regularly in the liturgy of the parish community, the Rite of Christian Initiation of Adults encourages the gradual internalization of the practices of liturgical prayer. Catechists, sponsors, and spiritual directors have the particular duty to support that internalization through instruction and reflection, but it is the responsibility of the entire welcoming community to examine what it will be observed doing in liturgical prayer.

Notes

1. *Constitution on the Sacred Liturgy*, paragraph 14.

2. *Rite of Christian Initiation of Adults*, paragraph 106d.

3. Credit for this phrase is given to the Rev. Patrick Byrne, editor of *The National Bulletin on the Liturgy*, published by the Canadian Conference of Catholic Bishops.

The Lectionary as a Source Book for Catechesis in the Catechumenate

By Karen M. Hinman

The catechumenate is "an extended period during which the candidates are given pastoral formation and are trained by suitable discipline." Paragraph 19 of the Rite of Christian Initiation of Adults (RCIA) provides insight into the formation of candidates for membership in the Roman Catholic Church. The formation of these women and men is to be "pastoral." This formation is achieved through four elements: catechesis, community, liturgy, apostolic works. This article will unfold these elements of the formation process pointing to the fact that the Sunday morning dismissal and the use of the lectionary is the way to achieve this pastoral formation.

Catechesis is "given in stages and presented integrally, accommodated to the liturgical year enriched by celebrations of the word," which leads catechumens to a "suitable knowledge of dogmas and precepts and also to an intimate understanding of the mystery of salvation in which they already share" (RCIA #19). This catechesis is rooted in the celebrations of the word of God. The lectionary is one way to open men and women to this word of God. I propose the lectionary as "the way" for the catechumenate.

Human experience in dialogue with the word and our living tradition (as we do celebrate this word each week) leads catechumens to a rich understanding of dogmas and Church teachings. Using the lectionary as sourcebok for catechesis, more than one catechumen has said: "I have learned a great deal about the Catholic Church—its teachings and way of life—but I have also walked a way of faith where I have been given the tools to live and continue learning and growing as a Catholic Christian the rest of my life." Catechumens learn dogmas and precepts, Church teachings using the lectionary as sourcebook for catechesis. Catechesis accommodated to our liturgical year means living and reflecting on the word in the midst of our major celebrations and feasts—our Catholic celebrations: Christmas, Assumption, Easter, Ascension Thursday, Advent, Lent, All Saints Day, Immmaculate Conception, Corpus Christi, Trinity Sunday, Epiphany, to name a few of the major celebrations to say nothing of other daily feasts which can be found in our lectionary and liturgi-

cal year. It is the use of the lectionary *in the midst* of the liturgical year! What better way to learn our Catholic truths than to experience them with us. Do we not learn more about a community by what they do and who they are than what they say! This applies to our Catholic truths as well. Catechumens learn about our major truths as they are dismissed each week from the Sunday celebration to reflect upon these truths to make them their own.

The lectionary is the best tool for catechesis because it provides for the fact that catechesis can then be given in stages and the "unique spiritual journey of candidates" (RCIA #5) can be reverenced. As Catholics we have three years of readings. This means we have three years of catechetical material—liturgical Year A, Year B, Year C—with enough material for three years of different sessions in the journeys of the men and women who seek membership with us. Men and women can respond to the word of God uniquely and can then be called to the sacraments of initiation some Easter as they are ready. The three year cycle allows for time, for change. This cycle opens up a variety of Christian truths in our Catholic way of life providing time to the catechumens to integrate these truths and to respond uniquely to the call of God in their life as they live it with us.

Community: Pastoral formation is achieved by catechumens "becoming familiar with the Christian way of life" (RCIA #19). This means that catechumens are formed as Catholics by being in relationship with other Catholic Christians. Through these relationships catechumens learn about the Christian way of life. They will "learn to pray to God more easily, to witness to the faith, to expect Christ in all things, to follow God's inspiration in all their life deeds, and to exercise charity toward all" (RCIA #19). Sunday mornings when the community assembles together is the primary time for the community as a whole to share in this formation process. On Sunday mornings the community hands on our tradition of liturgical prayer where catechumens can be drawn to pray to God more easily by our praying together. Sponsors, spouses, other members of the Christian community are readily available on Sunday morning as witnesses of faith. This is *the* community gathering of the week, a very appropriate time for pastoral formation. This is not to say that Sunday mornings are the only times the catechumen is formed by the community but to point to the fact that it is the primary time.

Implied in the community as a dimension of pastoral formation are hints at who the catechists and members of the catechumenate team may be. Women and men in our parish who can break open the word are the best catechists. Catechists will be skilled in sharing faith, in listening to others, in enabling the faith of the community to be handed on to the catechumens. Catechists are, as one person in Texas said, "the BLP's: The Basic Lay People." Pastors, catechumenate directors, pastoral ministers, directors/coordinators of religious education, are enablers of the community, are model catechists; however, they are the ones who need to let go and enable the community to be the primary catechist in this formation process. The best catechists with whom I have worked in three parishes directly and around the United States and Canada are women and men who are serious about their faith, have *no* degree in religious education or ministry, and who are persons of prayer and commitment to their own conversion journey. These women and men hand on a faith they have lived for many years. Selection and training of these catechists is essential; however it is not the topic of this article. There are other resources available for assistance here.

Liturgy: "Catechumens are cleansed and strengthened through celebrations of the word with the faithful" (RCIA #19). The pastoral formation of catechumens occurs in liturgy. Throughout the Rite the importance of catechumens gathering with the assembly of the faithful for the liturgy of the word is repeated. Likewise it is repeated that catechumens, except in *extreme* situations, are dismissed. The liturgy of the word, once known as the Mass of catechumens, is essential to their pastoral formation. Many catechumenate directors and pastors throughout the United States and Canada say: "But we can't dismiss because. . . . " Why can't you? What are you afraid of? The rite points to its importance. Pastoral practice of dismissal indicates that they are dismissed to be nourished by the word, that this experience of dismissal is a rich experience for both the candidate (who deepens in hunger for the Eucharist and who in the meantime is nourished by the "real presence of Jesus in the word") and a valuable experience for the community (who begins to question why the process takes as long as it does, what Eucharist means for them if they are able to stay, and what being a Catholic means today). Dismissal is not a negative experience as most people fear it will be. Rather it is an enriching moment for all involved. What better catechetical moment for

both candidate and the faithful when questions begin to emerge about the process as it becomes visible on each and every Sunday! Pastoral formation in the liturgy on Sundays especially with dismissal also better prepares the catechumens to celebrate, to receive and become Eucharist. Sunday dismissal after the liturgy of the word is *the* time for catechesis.

Apostolic Works: Pastoral formation in this area is to assist the candidates to live and spread the Gospel in family, neighborhood, work, church and all areas of their life and world. This formation does not necessarily include extra service projects or "churchy" ministries such as those involved in religious education, liturgy, etc. Rather this formation develops an apostolic way of life. Apostles are formed in the breaking open of the word.

Summary: Paragraph #19 of the Rite points to the fact that catechumens are to confront their human experiences in order to discover in that experience divisions, contradictions of values, and anything in themselves and in their world that separates them from life with God. Thus, the bottom line of this pastoral formation is conversion—a continually changing person: someone who is passing as a catechumen from an old self to a new self; someone who is learning that to live as a Catholic Christian is to live in response to a Gospel each and every day of his or her life confronting divisions and contradictions in values, in relationships, in beliefs which separate one from God and from other women and men; someone who can celebrate the changes that have already occurred—the signs of new life—the ways that he or she has already grown close to God and others. The pastoral formation pointed to in paragraph #19 is one of conversion of the whole person. The way to conversion is through the Gospel. Catechesis during the catechumenate is thus conversion catechesis. Such catechesis can be built on our Sunday lectionary. The tradition which we hand on to catechumens is a "living" tradition—experienced in word and community celebration on Sunday. The lectionary and homily in the midst of our liturgical year will raise issues of life, issues of doctrine significant to our Catholic Christian tradition. These issues can and will be dealt with throughout the catechumenate period. The agenda, however, is set by the lectionary and the experience and searching of catechumens in response to this lectionary agenda. In using the lectionary where conversion is the norm, catechumens may not learn "everything *we* always wanted them to know about the Catholic Church." However, if we believe that growth in faith, understanding and knowledge of our faith is a lifelong process, then by using the lectionary we are giving catechumens the skills they need to live this life the rest of their life. Is this not the goal of all Christian formation?

Sample Method for Sunday Morning Catechumenal Session Following Dismissal

Sunday morning arrives! What does it look like when we have our catechumenate sessions on Sunday mornings? A typical Sunday agenda is provided below. The structure provided is a sample; it is not "Gospel." It is the agenda on an average week in any parish.

9:00 a.m.	Gather with the assembly for liturgy of word Dismissal after the homily
9:30 a.m.	Coffee/rolls as catechumens and catechist(s) gather
9:40 a.m.	Time for prayer with catechumens only
10:00 a.m.	Sponsors and spouses join catechumens (Mass is over) Catechetical session
11:20 a.m.	Closing prayer and dismissal

Allow me to elaborate on the various elements of this schedule.

The gathering of the assembly for the liturgy of the word and dismissal of candidates is self-explanatory. This happens *every Sunday* as long as there are catechumens! After the homily the candidates are sent forth by the assembly with the words: "Go in peace to reflect upon the word and to make it your own."

Once settled in the gathering place a catechist reads the Scriptures of the day (one or all three). It is best to select the word upon which your catechetical session is built. Following the rereading of that text one of several activities may be done: a guided meditation (whereby catechumens are invited to place themselves in the text or in a similar situation); a journal exercise recalling a life event similar to the readings; a time of spontaneous prayer or prayer based on the psalm response; quiet meditation; reflection and/or discussion of some point of the homily. Vicky Tufano's article in this book gives some helpful guidelines for this prayer time with catechumens.

When sponsors and spouses arrive there are as many options for catechetical sessions as there are persons and Scriptures. This book is filled with sample sessions and methods so I need not deliberate more about this here.

The closing prayer and dismissal can be as simple or as complicated as you would like. Again samples are provided in this book. Some parishes I know ask a sponsor/candidate team to prepare the closing prayer for each week based on that week's readings. Creativity leaves open all sorts of possibilities here.

In general the structure of Sunday morning is simple. The process is simple when the lectionary is used as the basis. The sessions in this book are good guide-lines for creating a process which will work best for your people.

Method for Catechist to Prepare for Sunday Morning Dismissal Session

Preparation for the Sunday morning session is essential for effective use of time and materials. There are many ways a team member may prepare to be the facilitator for Sunday morning. The method I present is the one I have used and have shared with team members for their use. There are seven steps to this method. ALL seven are essential!

First, find the readings for the given Sunday in the lectionary. Read all three readings slowly and thoughtfully at least three times, preferably one time aloud. Underline thought patterns, significant words and phrases in all the readings. Jot down connections you notice between the readings. The purpose of this step is to become familiar with the texts for the given Sunday.

Second, work with the Gospel. Read the Gospel slowly and deliberately one more time. Visualize the Gospel. Where is this text taking place? At what time of day or night? What season of the year? Ask yourself: Do time and place make any difference in the reading? Name all the characters. With whom do you identify? Of these characters, who is the principal person in the Gospel? What is their problem? Find a passage from the text which articulates the problem of the principal person—from his or her perspective. Finding the problem in the text of the Gospel is essential. What is Jesus' response? How does Jesus deal with the problem? Again find the answer in the text. How do the other characters respond to the situation? Situate the text by visualizing it—sensing it (feeling, seeing, smelling, hearing that passage). Place yourself in the text.

Third, once you have done the work of visualizing the text (and only then), read commentaries about the passage. Helpful resources are *Unfinished Images* available through Wm. H. Sadlier Company and *Share the Word* from the Paulist Evangelization Center. Commentaries assist in stretching beyond our own images, understandings, and interpretations of this passage. Note any connections between the commentaries, your reflections, and readings. How do commentaries enlighten, challenge, affirm your understanding of this passage?

Fourth, set all readings, visualizations, commentaries aside and go before God to pray with this Gospel. Questions you may sit with are: What meaning do these readings offer for my life? for the life of the catechumens? for the Church? for the world? Where do you find yourself in the Gospel (e.g., are you the man born blind, the family, his neighbors, the Pharisees, Jesus)? What similarities and/or differences do you find in your world and the world of the principal character? Does this passage recall for you a concrete example or situation in your life? If so describe that time in detail. In what ways do the readings call you to growth? to new awareness? How do you meet this challenge? What is the hard word that the Gospel calls you to hear? How do you or will you respond? These are just some ways of being with the Gospel. There are many ways to pray with the word. Methods of praying with the Scripture are left to your creativity.

Fifth after reading texts, visualizing, attending to commentaries, and praying with the Gospel, call the pastor/presider for the liturgy at which the catechumens will be present. Ask him to share with you briefly the focus of his homily. The catechumenal session builds upon the word and upon how that Word is broken open by the homilist. Therefore, it is helpful to speak with the presider in the planning stages.

Sixth, with all of the data gathered, list the questions about the Catholic Christian tradition which could emerge. For example from the Feast of the Baptism of Our Lord questions about baptism could emerge. Readings on the call of the disciples could lead to questions about the origin of the Catholic Church and/or what it means that Peter is the rock of the Church. On Sundays when a letter is read (e.g., from the bishop, about reconciliation, peace pastoral, economic pastoral), questions could emerge about these issues. The issues raised about our tradition emerge as candidates live this tradition with us on each and every Sunday of the year. These issues and concerns emerge from our living and being together.

Seventh and last, realizing the wealth of information in word, in experiences, in homily, the team member sets aside preparation materials and designs a process to be used with catechumens on Sunday morning. The team member decides how to use the Gospel, what other texts of the day will be used, what symbols can be used effectively from the Scriptures for prayer or reflection, what context needs to be addressed, and what catechetical issues may emerge based on his or her experience with the catechumens.

With all this in mind the team member designs a process to be used on Sunday. This process will vary as do the readings from Sunday to Sunday.

Concluding Image: Alcoholics Anonymous

James Dunning and others have recently been making analogies between RCIA and Alcoholics Anonymous (AA) or any twelve-step program: Overeaters Anonymous, Gamblers Anonymous, Adult Children of Alcoholics, etc. The analogy is as follows: AA is peer to peer recovery. RCIA is Church handing on tradition: adult to adult. The Big Book is the guide for the Re-covering Alcoholic. The Big Book is a book of stories of the lives of other alcoholics. The lectionary is the sourcebook and guide for RCIA containing the many stories of our tradition. AA members attend weekly and sometimes daily meetings. RCIA attends our Sunday morning dismissal. Both groups gather to share stories, strength, hope. In AA the recovering alcoholic selects a sponsor to help him or her work the program. RCIA provides each catechumen with a sponsor to support him or her through the journey: "to work the program!" "Let Go and Let God" is a theme of the twelve-step programs. Conversion is the heart of the catechumenate—is that not "letting go and letting God?" Twelve-step programs have for the fourth step a moral inventory of their life and later in the steps they make amends to all they have hurt. In RCIA we have scrutinies, major and minor exorcisms, sacrament of reconciliation, blessings. AA claims to be a way of life forever! In RCIA we are led to profess vows—to make a commitment forever! The promise of AA is life! The promise of RCIA is eternal life!! The final step of AA is to "share the message with all who still suffer." The final stage of RCIA: is to proclaim the good news. The unique parallel about RCIA and AA is that twelve-step programs are meetings of peers with each sharing strength, weakness, changes, growth in his or her life. It's a spiritual program with no leader. The marvelous mystery is that it works. If it works with AA, why not with RCIA? I suggest that AA offers us a model for our Sunday morning dismissal sessions, for the structure of our catechumenates. The mystery, I believe for us, is that it will work!

Catechumenal Catechesis and Adult Religious Education

By Joseph P. Sinwell

A prospective convert makes an appointment at the rectory to talk with someone who will help her understand the Catholic Church. She has been discussing and sharing her faith with a small group of people regularly; she knows that she is ready to become a member. When she arrives, she is welcomed and joined by the priest or pastoral associate who says, "Why not come to the adult religious education class?" She agrees to attend.

The woman attends the hour and a half class—a lecture on some Catholic dogma and a time for questions. She has unanswered questions; she is hesitant to ask at the question period because they don't pertain directly to the lecture. Why is she there? What does she believe? She feels lost and out of place.

No one, unfortunately, has asked her what her issues, interests or questions are. No one asked why she wanted to become a Catholic. In short, no one asked what her story was—no one discussed with her her story, her relationship with others and with God, her readiness for the period of catechesis. The basic principles of adult education have been overlooked. These principles apply to all periods of the catechumenate, especially the period of catechesis.

The period of catechesis in the Rite of Christian Initiation of Adults needs to be implemented not for, but with adults, following principles of adult religious education. This period emphasizes the sharing of the story of Catholic faith as a living tradition with those who are catechumens. According to the Rite of Christian Initiation of Adults (n. 191,2), "Catechesis is to be shaped by the liturgical year, enriched by the celebrations of God that lead catechumens to a knowledge of doctrine and precepts, intimate understanding and the integration of how each individual lives as a Catholic." Some catechists and directors plan this period as an induction into the dogmas of the Church; the emphasis is on learning the Catholic faith through information. Because the fundamental thrust of the adult catechumenate is conversion, the goal in catechesis is not information, but transformation.

If the emphasis in catechesis is placed on being transformed, a legitimate concern is the question of instruction. How will the truths be communicated? What book or program will be used? In the period of cate-

chesis the basic book is the lectionary. Adults are to be initiated into the on-going life of the parish community. The parish community joins to listen to the word of God each week and in reflection tries to live the Gospel. The lectionary readings and homily are the stimulus and common gathering point for the entire parish community.

Some say, "What about creedal statements? Those are not contained in the lectionary." Creedal statements originated from the community reflection on its belief together. The doctrines contained in the creedal statements exist because human beings needed to give meaning to how God touched their lives. The approach of initiating adults into the faith is to help them realize what it means to be Catholic. The Catholic experience is sacramental, personal and life-giving.

Adults need to raise and will raise their own questions and reflections. How can individuals discuss Jesus' calming the storm at Galilee and not raise questions about the divinity and humanity of Jesus? Or discuss the angel's appearance to Mary (Lk 1:26–28) and not raise issues concerning Mary and her role? Through discussion of and reflection on the lectionary, the truths/mysteries will be raised, explored and become integrated into the lives of catechumens. The study of doctrines or the "basics" will be not an experience of dry bones, but an experience of someone who is dynamic and alive in each of us. The goal of all catechesis is to lead individuals not only to an informed faith, but to a living, conscious, active faith.

The journey of adults is on-going; the word of God and the living Catholic tradition challenge each person to pray, witness and serve with others in a community of believers.

The question for catechumenate team members becomes how to plan and implement catechesis in the process of initiating adults. *Serving Life and Faith: Adult Religious Education and the American Catholic Community*, a document developed by adult religious educators and approved by the United States bishops, provides descriptions of the elements characteristic of adult religious education: relational, life-centered, actualizing, communal, liberating, continual, integrative and transcending. Each of these elements has its application to catechesis in the catechumenate.

Relational

Catechumens come from a variety of social, psychological and economic levels of development, as well as diverse cultural and faith perspectives. Together, they bring a richness to the initiation process. They are to be invited to tell their stories in the catechumenate; their thoughts and feelings are to be respected. Central to the catechumenal process is the growth of individuals in relationship to the Lord and others. This approach, therefore, will build relationships among teams, sponsors, parish community and others. Individuals will be encouraged to learn from the stories and reflections of others. These valuable and precious learning stimulators and modes are invaluable to the faith growth process.

Life-Centered

The challenge for catechists is to enable catechumens and sponsors to experience the Gospel within Catholic tradition as dynamic. Adults are motivated by felt needs experienced in life. To apply the readings of the lectionary to everyday life and global events is a crucial task. In this way, each person involved in the process will enhance his or her critical faith reflection and realize that on-going conversion demands a conscious response.

Actualizing

All adults in catechesis are involved in a process which embraces the total person; all participants can shape this process of self-actualizing. Some argue that catechesis aims only at the intellect; an affective process aims sometimes at intellect, other times at emotion, others at action. The catechetical process is involved with all these, with the totality of the human person within a Christian community. The element of actualizing incorporates processes that aim at both right lobe and left lobe of the brain functions. Research in brain function has led religious educators to point out that left lobe religious education has received the most attention. The left lobe emphasizes information, logic, creedal statements, and apologetics. The right lobe is the locus of primary experiences in stories, myths, symbols, memories and poetry. The right lobe is where primary relationships form and where primary images of God enter our consciousness.

Catechists encourage the right lobe experience through storytelling, the use of visual aids, the reading of poetry. Indeed, if catechetical ministers listen to the needs of individuals, catechesis also requires some lecture and formal presentation. The goal is to achieve a balance of both right and left brain approaches, suitable to the needs of catechumens.

Communal

The Rite of Christian Initiation of Adults clearly states that initiation takes place within the community. The experiences of the community through story, symbol, ritual and structure effect the catechesis. Individuals from the community may be asked to share their richness of faith and ministry; liturgies and prayer experiences may lead catechumens to a deeper realization of their faith journey. The parish community and family communities can learn from those involved in the process. The nurturing of catechumens can lead others to examine how they are being called to participate more deeply in the ministry of Jesus Christ.

Liberating

The catechumenal process emphasizes the call of the Gospel and the free response to the Gospel. Jesus preached a freedom from fear and sin and a response of wholeness and growth. Catechists can help catechumens and sponsors to embrace the liberating power of the Gospel by promoting an atmosphere of openness, trust and communication.

The process of catechesis can lead toward Christian freedom and its concomitant responsibility by encouraging critical thinking, clear presentation of doctrine, and reflective dialogue.

The opinion that there is only one way to view the Gospel and tradition must give way to the respect for healthy, theological pluralism. The stories and perspectives of catechumens in dialogue with the stories of the tradition of the Church enable individuals to think and act freely as Catholics in an expanding world and universe. Catechists need to be conscious that the Church is pluralistic. It is multi-lingual, multi-ritual and multi-cultural. The Church upholds a deep respect for each individual within a community. Adults do not learn by being constantly ignored or berated for their opinions. A spirit of listening with respect and tolerance for diversity communicates this plurality and fosters relationships within the community.

Continual

The period of catechesis has a definite time frame; it is initiatory because topics and issues are presented as introductions to full understanding of the implications of the Gospels in one's life. The attitude of some is to crowd "everything one always wanted to know about Catholicism" into the framework of the catechetical period. If catechumenal ministers are honest about their own learning and growth in faith, they will readily admit that growth is an evolving process. Learning about the Gospel and tradition is a lifelong endeavor. The answers sought may be too complex and elusive; the questions raised may be open-ended. Aware of this, those involved in directing catechesis should have the view of learning as continual. Future opportunities for learning are present in the periods of illumination, mystagogia and beyond—learning to be disciples of Jesus cannot be limited to any time frame.

Integrative

The process of preparing catechumens is meant to be collaborative. As indicated in the *National Catechetical Directory*, "From its earliest days the Church has recognized that liturgy and catechesis support each other. Prayer and the sacraments call for informed participants; fruitul participation in catechesis calls for the spiritual enrichment that comes from liturgical participation" (#36). The catechumenate team should cooperate with other ministries: liturgical committee, religious education committee, social justice and family life committees and others, so that the period of catechesis can be holistic and intertwined with the entirety of parish life. This approach reinforces the principle that the whole community welcomes the catechumens and prepares them for initiation. Hopefully, it also eliminates any sense of "turf fighting" in the catechumenal process.

Transcending

The process of catechesis leads beyond itself. Those involved in the catechumenate are not simply teaching, sharing and learning for themselves or for only the parish community. Rather, catechesis leads to conversion and conversion leads to a realization of mission to family, community and world. The catechumenate is not an end in itself. It is meant not to simply build a small community of ministers, sponsors and catechumens. It is meant to serve as a symbol for the community itself; through the different stages of the Rite of Christian Initiation of Adults each and every member should be challenged to extend the reign of God by preaching, teaching, serving, celebrating, and building community for others.

Conclusion

The period of catechesis centers on the Gospel, broken and shared in a community of disciples and catechumens; this catechumenate period, as the other periods of catechumenate, fosters the building of the reign of God within this world.

The period of catechesis demands a process which is open and flexible. This process must be relational, life-centered, actualizing, communal, liberating, continual, integrative, and transcending. Implicit in these characteristics is that catechists and catechumenate di-

rectors be or become comfortable with working with adults and examining their own learning styles and attitudes.

If these elements of adult religious education are incorporated, the catechesis will be creative and life-giving for the whole parish community. Adult Catholics will request a similar process for themselves. If the process is evaluated, it may lead to the formation of critical reflection and action groups willing to listen to the Word of God and enflesh the word in people's lives so that conversion, teaching, initiation, celebrating, and mission become real marks of the parish community.

ADVENT AND CHRISTMAS

The History of Salvation

By Eugene A. LaVerdiere

The Gospel readings for Advent and Christmas draw our attention to the history of salvation and its dramatic tensions between the absence and presence of God, sin and divine love, the promise of salvation and its fulfillment, hopeful yearning for the Lord and rejoicing in his presence. Even as the Gospel proclaims Jesus' birth, it announces his passion and death.

One of the readings connects the history of salvation with the life of God and creation (Jn 1:1–18). Another looks to the new creation and the fulfillment of salvation history when the Lord comes in glory (Mt 24:37–44). Most of the readings explore the course and meaning of Jesus' life and mission, their relationship to biblical history, the Jewish people, the Gentiles and the life and mission of Christians, who share in Christ's life and continue his mission in history.

The Coming of the Son of Man

Advent and the liturgical year open with a reading from a discourse of Jesus to his disciples on the unfolding and climactic ending of salvation history (Mt 24:37–44). In Matthew's Gospel, the discourse was addressed to a young Church of Jewish Christians contemplating the future in turbulent times. Read in the liturgy, it is now addressed to us as we too look for the full manifestation of Jesus in glory.

The passage speaks of Jesus as the Son of Man coming at the consummation of history and creation and tries to instill in us an appropriate Christian attitude regarding his coming. The Son of Man will surely come, but no one knows the day of his coming. Indeed he will come at the time we least expect. Therefore, Christians must always be prepared for his coming. They will thus avoid the fate of those who were unconcerned in the days of Noah or who lack vigilance now and in the future.

For the present context, the title "Son of Man" was drawn from the rich imagery of Daniel 7:13–14 (see Mt 24:30) and applied to Jesus the risen Lord in his full manifestation. In Jesus, Lord and Son of Man, humanity is born anew and recreated in the image of God.

Preparing the Way of the Lord

Vigilance does not mean passivity. It is not enough to be prepared for the Lord's coming. We must also prepare his way (Second Sunday of Advent). In this we have John the Baptizer as a model (3:1–12).

John was an historical figure, of course, and Matthew, along with the other Gospels, presents him as the prophetic reformer who prepared Jesus' first coming and the inauguration of a new period of history. In his work and message (3:3), he fulfilled the word of Isaiah (Is 40:3). In his person and garb (3:4), he represented Elijah (2 Kgs 1:8).

While Matthew respected John's historical mission, he was even more interested in him as a model for Christians. This is apparent in the summary of John's message, which is identical to that of Jesus: "Reform your lives! The reign of God is at hand" (3:2; 4:17). Further, John's message to the Pharisees and Sadducees presupposes that the mission of the Church is not limited to the Jewish people but open to all: "God can raise children to Abraham from these very stones" (3:9). Christianity transcends all considerations of ethnic origins. Finally, John's distinction between the two baptisms, his own and that of Jesus, refers much more to Jesus' final coming than to his first coming.

He Who Is To Come

We are then to prepare the way for the coming of the Lord. But how shall we recognize him at his coming? How shall we distinguish false messiahs from the true Messiah, and true prophets, those who really prepare the way for his coming, from the false (see Mt 7:15–23; 24:23–28)? A dialogue between Jesus and John's disciples (11:2–6) and part of a short discourse of Jesus about John (11:7–11) show the way (Third Sunday of Advent).

John had expected the Messiah to come with fiery judgment. Jesus had come as a gentle prophet, a healer and reconciler, one who raised the dead to life and who preached good news to the poor. And so from prison John sent his disciples to inquire whether Jesus was "he who is to come" (11:3). In response, Jesus draws their attention to what they have actually seen and heard, and in doing so describes his entire work as well as that of his disciples in terms drawn from Isaiah (29:18–19; 35:5–6; 25:8; 61:1–2). The order in which the signs are given indicates that preaching the good news to the poor was viewed as the most important of them all. The dialogue shows how faith recognition comes from seeing and hearing, from experience, and from the illumination of that experience by the word of God.

In his discourse, Jesus shows how the one who prepares the way for his coming is not a weakling without convictions nor one who moves in luxury with royalty but a prophet and a very special prophet, one who comes like Elijah as God's messenger (Mal 3:1). Even so, the Christian prophets, those born into the kingdom of God and who prepare the way for his definitive coming, are greater than he.

They Shall Call Him Emmanuel

The Gospel for the Fourth Sunday of Advent (Mt 1:18–24) focuses on another of Jesus' theological titles, Emmanuel, which means "God is with us" (see Is 7:14). The title does not refer to a static presence, as when a thing is said to be present, but to a personal, creative and liberating presence. God's covenant relationship with Israel was often summed up in these terms. "I will be with you" and "You will be with me" are statements of mutual solidarity.

The covenant presence of God was realized in Jesus in an unprecedented manner. Never before had God come so close to sinful humanity. To express this newness as well as the grounds for it, the Gospel shows how from the instant of his conception Jesus' life was from the Holy Spirit. He was thus virginally conceived. At the same time, however, Jesus was very much a human being. The Gospel consequently shows his relationship to Joseph, his human legal father through whom Jesus became a member of the family of David. In and through Jesus, Emmanuel, the kingdom of David would become the kingdom of God.

As Christians, prepared at every moment for the coming of the Son of Man, actively preparing the way for the Lord's coming, and proclaiming the good news to the poor, we work for the full establishment of God's kingdom and the definitive coming of Emmanuel.

Jesus Christ, Son of David, Son of Abraham

At the Christmas Vigil, we read the entire first chapter of Matthew (1:1–25), which includes the passage read on the Fourth Sunday of Advent (1:18–24) and whose first section recapitulates the biblical history of salvation in the form of a genealogy of Jesus (1:1–17). This genealogy, like that in Luke 3:23–38, is a theological statement. However, whereas Luke emphasized Jesus' relationship to Adam and creation, Matthew stressed his identity as the Christ and his relationship to King David and Abraham. As the Son of David, Jesus is a messianic king. As the Son of Abraham, he ful-

fills the promise made to Abraham that in his seed all nations would be blessed (see Gen 22:18). So it is that in the concluding verses of Matthew's Gospel, Jesus commissions the eleven remaining disciples to "make disciples of all the nations."

Tidings of Great Joy

Matthew helped us see Jesus' relationship to the biblical history of salvation (Vigil). At the Midnight Mass of Christmas, Luke helps us see his relationship to Caesar Augustus and the Roman Empire. It is through Caesar's decree that Jesus came to be born in David's city of Bethlehem, which did not provide hospitality at the time of his birth. Even the Roman emperor could be God's instrument in the unfolding of salvation history (2:1–7).

The shepherds were the first to hear the Gospel, the tidings of great joy that a Savior has been born to them, the Messiah and Lord. Here was the good news of salvation. It came from heaven, from God through an angelic messenger, just as Jesus himself was born Son of God through the power of the Holy Spirit. After they were given a sign in which they would be able to see the good news, a chorus of angels responded with a hymn of praise (2:8–14).

Seeing and Understanding

The shepherds had been given a sign: "in a manger you will find an infant wrapped in swaddling clothes" (Lk 2:12). In the Christmas Mass at Dawn, we read of how they went to Bethlehem, saw the baby lying in the manger and believed (2:15–20). A manger is a place where nourishment is given to the flock. The shepherds, who evoke the leaders of the early Church, saw how Jesus' life and person was offered as nourishment to the little flock (see Lk 12:32) of the Church. They saw, and on the basis of this concrete experience they understood the gospel they had heard. The story ends with a series of reactions to the event and its Gospel.

Much of the same text, but without 2:15 and with the addition of 2:21, is read on January 1, the Solemnity of Mary Mother of God. This second reading invites us to focus on how "Mary treasured all these things and reflected on them in her heart." Here is how we are to hear the Gospel. At the end of the passage, the circumcision is mentioned to introduce the naming of Jesus (2:21). Just as his very life came from God and the Gospel of salvation came from heaven through God's messenger, so also his name, Jesus, which expressed his very identity (see Lk 1:31).

The Word Became Flesh

At Christmas Mass During the Day and on the

Second Sunday after Christmas, the magnificent prologue of St. John (1:1–18) is our Gospel reading. The basic form of this prologue is a hymn, which most likely was written independently of the Gospel. It sings the story of the word, a term which gathers up much of the biblical reflection on God's self-expression and communication from creation, and, even before, to the sharing of divine life. Although the Greek term used for this, *logos*, came from popular Greek philosophy, its meaning is closer to wisdom, *sophia*, as developed in works such as the Book of Wisdom.

The hymn opens with the first words of Genesis, "In the beginning," to introduce the word in God's own life prior to creation (vv. 1–2). It then shows how the Word burst into creation (vv. 3–5), entered the world, the cosmos, a human reality (vv. 10–12), and even became flesh, taking on our human condition (vv. 14–16).

Several prose passages were added to the hymn when it became John's prologue. These verses speak of the person and role of John the Baptizer (vv. 6–9, 15), explain the meaning of "children of God" in terms of virginal conception (vv. 12b–13), and comment on God's enduring love which came through Jesus Christ (vv. 17–18). The hymn had referred to the Father's only Son without actually naming Jesus. The prologue's editor named him directly. Jesus Christ, the only Son, is the revelation of the Father.

He Shall Be Called a Nazorean

One of the differences between the infancy narrative of Luke and that of Matthew has to do with Jesus' relationship to Nazareth and Bethlehem. In Luke, the holy family lives in Nazareth and travels to Bethlehem where Jesus was born. In Matthew, the family lives in Bethlehem and eventually moves to Nazareth because of persecution (2:13–15, 19–23). For Matthew, this is how the prophets came to be fulfilled that Jesus would be called a Nazarene. It may be that in this Matthew did not have particular prophetic passages in mind. The passage, which we read on the Second Sunday after Christmas, the Feast of the Holy Family, is based not only on the story of Joseph in Genesis but also on Jewish traditions concerning Moses and Israel. Jesus, the new Moses and the new Israel, is threatened by Herod, the new Pharaoh. While recapitulating biblical history, the passage also announces the eventual rejection of Jesus.

Magi from the East

On the feast of Epiphany, we celebrate the manifestation of Jesus to the magi, who alone see the special star of Jesus at its rising among all the lesser personal stars in the heavens. King Herod and all Jerusalem, including the chief priests and the scribes, failed to see the star of Jesus.

The magi, religious Gentiles from the East, prefigure the eventual proclamation of the Gospel to the Gentiles, all the nations, after Israel's rejection of Jesus. Prostrating themselves before Jesus in homage, as they would before God himself, they offered the two gifts mentioned in Isaiah 60:5–6, gold and frankincense, and they added myrrh, an aromatic substance used in anointing a body for burial (see Jn 19:39). In Matthew 2:11, the myrrh may well symbolize the passion and death of Jesus. Jesus was offered gifts worthy of a king, but his kingdom was not of this world.

This Is My Beloved Son

Jesus was baptized by John (3:13–17), an event we celebrate on the Sunday after Epiphany, which closes the Christmas season and at the same time is the First Sunday in Ordinary Time. We tend to take the event for granted. Jesus has already been manifested as divine in the Gospel's prologue, and we forget that John's baptism was for the sake of reform. Others confessed their sins as they were being baptized.

In his baptism, Jesus who was sinless, humbly showed solidarity with sinful humanity and most especially with the mission of John the Baptizer. The passage thus shows Jesus in his humanity, but it also reveals him in his divinity as the Spirit of God descends upon him and he is proclaimed God's beloved Son.

Introduction to Advent and the Christmas Season

Each session in this section contains the following parts:

    Gathering Prayer
    Reflection
    Summary
    Closing Prayer

The gathering prayer consists of a song and a psalm. The song may be listened to or sung together if familiar to the catechumens. The psalm may be read meditatively by the catechist, or may be recited antiphonally by the group. This is done by dividing the group into two parts, each part praying a section of the psalm in turn. The catechist could also select a verse from the psalm as a response, thus praying the psalm as is done in the liturgy of the word. A brief closing prayer is offered for each session. This may be used simply as presented, or combined with shared prayer and song.

The reflection section often contains two parts. Each part develops a theme from the Gospel and the other readings. The catechumens will often be invited to use a journal. They could be encouraged to begin a journal as we begin the new liturgical year, and to keep it throughout their journey.

The summary contains directions and reminders for the catechist to use in concluding the session. At the end of the material for each session, some doctrinal and pastoral issues are highlighted. These can assist the catechist in preparation and can serve as a guide for further reading or study by the catechumens. References to these issues should be made in a way which builds on the Scriptures and the faith that is expressed during the session.

First Sunday of Advent

Isaiah 2:1–5
Romans 13:11–14
Matthew 24:37–44

GATHERING PRAYER

Song

"Wait on the Lord" (On the album *Daniel Vail*)

Pray together Psalm 119:33–40

REFLECTION

Part 1

Two men will be out in the field. One will be taken and one will be left. Two women will be grinding the meal; one will be taken and one will be left. Stay awake therefore! You cannot know the day your Lord is coming. The Son of Man is coming at the time you least expect.

Today is the First Sunday of Advent and we begin our preparation to celebrate the Lord's coming. For the early Christian community the Scriptures we hear today had an added emphasis in that many were expecting the risen Lord to return at any day to establish his kingdom on earth. Two thousand years later we continue to look forward to that day.

Journal exercise (5–10 minutes quiet reflection and writing) followed by group discussion (approximately 15 minutes) on the following questions:

1. How might we differ from the early Christian communities who anticipated the Lord's coming during the first century?

2. How might we be similar to those who expected to see the Lord return shortly after his death and resurrection?

Part 2

The readings today call us to prepare ourselves to stay awake (Matthew 24), to cast off the deeds of darkness, and put on the armor of light (Romans 13). After a brief moment of silent reflection and writing, in small groups of three or four discuss the following (approximately 25 minutes): If the Lord were scheduled to return next month, what would you need to do to be prepared? After gathering the group back together, invite some sharing of the preparation needed.

SUMMARY

Catechist should take key points from the readings—preparation, anticipation, invitation to put on Jesus—and link them with key points noted during the group discussion and sharing.

CLOSING PRAYER

Lord, God of power and mercy, open our hearts to welcome you. Help us in our preparation for your coming. Take away those things that hinder us from receiving your light. Let us share in your wisdom and joy. We ask this through Christ our Lord who lives and reigns with you and the Holy Spirit, one God, for ever and ever.

Doctrinal and Pastoral Issues: "Son of Man," The Day of the Lord, Eschatology, Parousia

John T. Butler

Second Sunday of Advent

Isaiah 11:1–10
Romans 15:4–9
Matthew 3:1–12

GATHERING PRAYER

Song

"Come to the Water," (John B. Foley, S.J., North American Liturgy Resources)

Pray together Psalm 25:1–7

REFLECTION

In the Gospel reading today we see John the Baptizer admonishing the Pharisees and Sadducees, who were coming forward to be baptized, to give some proof that they intended to reform their lives. Just as John the Baptizer confronts the Pharisees and Sadducees, this Scripture confronts us here today. Last Sunday we shared with each other what we needed to do to prepare for the Lord's coming. I invite you to consider for a moment your own need for reform and to record in your journal or on a sheet of paper your responses to the following:

1. Name an area or behavior in your life that you feel the Lord is calling you to change.

2. Why would a change be beneficial?

3. What might be standing in the way of your changing?

4. What/who could help you to change?

Allow several minutes of quiet so that adequate thought can be given and time allotted to write responses. It is suggested that the catechist lead the groups through the exercise by giving the group only one question at a time.

Invite the group to pair off with another catechumen/candidate whom they feel they know the least and share reponses.

Reassemble for large group discussion on baptism. What is your view of baptism—those who are already baptized and those who are preparing for baptism.

SUMMARY

Catechist should be prepared to contrast the ministry of John the Baptizer, baptizing with water and calling for reform and repentance, with that of Jesus' baptism with water and the Holy Spirit.

Catechist should further be prepared for some discussion on: infant baptism, the Catholic Church's present sacramental practises, the Holy Spirit.

PRAYER

Lord, we are continually challenged by your word. Help us to remain always open to you and continue to call us closer to yourself. Teach us your way, O Lord. Give us a new strength. Encourage our hearts and our minds so that we may respond more and more with love each day. We ask this through Christ our Lord who lives and reigns with you and the Holy Spirit, one God, for ever and ever. Amen.

Doctrinal and Pastoral Issues: Baptism, Initiation, Repentance, Conversion

John T. Butler

Third Sunday of Advent

Isaiah 35:1–6, 10
James 5:7–10
Matthew 11:2–11

GATHERING PRAYER

Song

"Soon and Very Soon" (Andre Crouch and Lexicon Music Inc. in *Songs of Zion Supplemental Worship Resources 12*, 1981)

Pray together Psalm 63:1–9

REFLECTION

Part 1

See how the farmer awaits the precious yield of the soil. He looks forward to it patiently while the soil receives the winter and the spring rains. You too must be patient. Steady your hearts because the coming of the Lord is at hand (Jas 5:7–8).

How difficult it is sometimes for us to wait, especially in this society where everything is instant and automatic. We grow to expect immediate responses to our questions, needs and desires. This season of Advent calls us to wait with anticipation on the Lord's coming.

1. Can you recall a time in your life when you have waited for something or someone to respond to a need of yours?

2. What was the event? How would you describe the period of waiting?

3. Were your expectations met when the response finally came?

Allow 10–15 minutes quiet reflection on the questions. Candidates may want to write in their journal.

Invite catechumens/candidates to share experiences with the entire group (approximately 10–15 minutes). As the sharing proceeds, help the group to shift its focus from experiences of waiting for something or for a response from someone, to that of waiting for a response from God.

Part 2

The Jewish community of Jesus' time hoped for a Messiah who would bring divine judgment on the unrepentant and establish a new kingdom. Jesus' continuing call for repentance prompted John the Baptizer to ask: "Are you he who is to come, or do we look for another?" Not only are we called to wait on the Lord, but also to be prepared for his coming in ways that we might not expect. The response that we look for from the Lord might inevitably prove to be very different.

How might the Lord have already come into your life in ways or in some manner that you did not expect or readily recognize? Invite sharing/discussion in either large or small groups after a time of quiet reflection.

SUMMARY

Encourage the catechumens/candidates to continue to look for signs of the Lord's presence in their lives as they go throughout the coming week. Reiterate the faithfulness of the Lord. The Lord's promise to his people is always fulfilled. Those who wait on the Lord will not be left alone.

PRAYER

Lord, with hope and anticipation we continue to look to your coming. Renew our strength and help us to turn more toward you every day. Draw us nearer to your light, O Lord; open our eyes, clear our ears, free our tongue so that we might sing you praise all the days of our lives. Amen.

Doctrinal and Pastoral Issues: Repentance, Messiah, Advent (Waiting), Kingdom of God

John T. Butler

Fourth Sunday of Advent

Isaiah 7:10–14
Romans 1:1–7
Matthew 1:18–24

GATHERING PRAYER

Song

"O Come, O Come Emmanuel" (Adapted by Thomas Helmore, 1954, World Library Publication)

Pray together Psalm 111:1–10

REFLECTION

Part 1

Invite the group to listen to the Gospel reading and to take mental note of the words, phrases, images and questions that come to mind for them. At the end of the reading allow a minute of silence. Then ask the group to write down all of the words, phrases and images about this reading that stood out for them. Next invite the group to list all of the questions that are raised for them on hearing this Scripture.

On a blackboard or newsprint list on one side "Mary, Virgin Mother," and on the other side "Emmanuel—God with us." Collect the group's reflections (not the questions) and place them under one or the other category. As you collect the reflections, ask the group to determine which category to place each word, phrase, image. Some of these reflections (words, phrases, images) will be attributed to both Mary, Virgin Mother and Emmanuel—God with us. Help the catechumens/candidates to see the rudiments of Marian theology growing from the fulfillment of the prophecy:

> The virgin shall be with child and give birth to a son and they shall call him Emmanuel. (Isaiah 7:14)

Part 2

In fulfillment of the prophecy, Mary is favored. She is raised up by the divine power of the Holy Spirit and through her own openness to the activity of the Lord in her life. Direct the group to Luke 1:26–55, especially Mary's canticle, verses 46–55. Read aloud.

Blest is she (he) who trusts that the Lord's word would be fulfilled. Both Mary and Joseph in their openness to the Lord placed themselves in opposition to the culture of their time. To have a child outside the bonds of marriage and to accept a woman as wife under such conditions were radical actions for Mary and Joseph.

How are you called to be like Mary and Joseph, to trust the word of the Lord and act even in a radical way? Discuss in small groups of three to four after a time of quiet reflection on this question.

SUMMARY

Catechist should be prepared to speak on Marian devotions (novenas, rosary, appearances, local churches, practices, or shrines such as the Shrine of the Immaculate Conception in Washington, D.C.).

PRAYER

Hail Mary, full of grace, the Lord is with you.
Blessed are you among women,
    and blessed is the fruit of your womb, Jesus.
Holy Mary, Mother of God, pray for us sinners
    now and at the hour of our death.
Amen.

Doctrinal and Pastoral Issues: Role of Mary, Virgin Birth, Emmanuel

John T. Butler

Christmas

(During the day)

Isaiah 52:7–10
Hebrews 1:1–6
John 1:1–18

GATHERING PRAYER

Song

"Jesus the Light of the World" (Leon Robert, Roberts Production, Washington, D.C.)

Pray together Psalm 8:1–10

REFLECTION

Part 1

To "give one's word" is a phrase that is heard from time to time. A person's word is his/her bond. "I will," "I do" are words that bind us to something or someone. "I am" precedes the description of oneself. "I was," and "I will" speak to where one has come from and where one plans to go. The spoken word is a dynamic entity, it forms us, defines us and orients us. Throughout time we can trace the importance of the spoken word, especially for those cultures which write little or not at all. As for those more literate cultures, the permanence which the written word takes is reinforced by the belief in the continuing reality of the spoken word.

Think for a moment of words which are active in your own life. What words of your own or words from others to you have served to form you into the person that you are now? Allow time for reflection and ask the catechumens/candidates to record these words, phrases and people (if other than themselves) on a sheet of paper or in their journal. Invite the group to share in small groups of three or four.

Part 2

The reality and power of words are rooted in the personality who speaks them. In the Old Testament, the personality and power of Yahweh creates (Genesis 1), calls (Genesis 12:1, Exodus 3, Isaiah 3), elects (Isaiah 9:17, 10:17–24) and rejects (Isaiah 15). Yahweh puts his word in the mouth of the prophets Jeremiah (1:9) and Ezekiel (2:9).

In the New Testament, Matthew, Mark, Luke and the Acts of the Apostles use "word" to signify the Gospel, the message proclaimed by Jesus. In the writings of John, however, a different concept and emphasis is used: that of Jesus speaking the words of the Father. Jesus and the Father are one:

The word became flesh and made his dwelling among us.

It is for this that we might share in everlasting life. Jesus brings light to the world and all who open themselves to him walk in the light that flows from the word of God.

With this image of God's word through Jesus forming us and bringing us out of darkness into light, recall some Scripture passages where the word of God has had a particular impact on you. Invite sharing with the entire group after a time of quiet reflection. Provide Bibles for candidates reflection.

SUMMARY

Catechist should help the catechumens/candidates see the power that God's word can have in their lives. The rite of becoming a catechumen celebrates their openness to the word and calls them to be nourished by the Word week after week.

Catechist should emphasize the real presence in the word.

PRAYER

Lord, by your Son we have been called to a more intimate relationship with you. By your words we are formed. A holy day has dawned upon us. The glory of an only Son coming from the Father, filled with enduring love, calls us out of our darkness and brings us into the light of day.

Glory be to the Father, the Son and the Holy Spirit, as it was in the beginning, is now and ever shall be, world without end, Amen.

Doctrinal and Pastoral Issues: Real Presence of Jesus in the Word, Incarnation

John T. Butler

Holy Family Sunday

Sirach 3:2–6, 12–14
Colossians 3:12–21
Matthew 2:13–15, 19–23

GATHERING PRAYER

Song

"Let There Be Peace on Earth" (Sy Miller and Jill Jackson, Jan-Lee Music)

Pray together Psalm 103:1–8, 11–13

REFLECTION

Part 1

In the first reading this morning we are reminded of the fourth commandment (Ex 10:12): "Honor your father and your mother that you may have a long life in the land which the Lord, your God, is giving you." Discuss with the entire group the following (approximately 20 minutes) after a time of quiet reflection on the following questions:

1. Why do you think there was a need for the Lord to give this commandment as one of the ten commandments?

2. Why do you think the connection is made here between honoring one's parents and having a long life?

3. How are parents honored or not honored in today's society?

Part 2

Paul in his letter to the Colossians tells us today to bear with one another, to forgive whatever grievances we have against one another ("put on love"), for Christ's peace must reign in our hearts.

Take a moment to think about your family, your parents, brothers and sisters, and your spouse and children if applicable. In our relationships and shared lives together as family we sometimes find ourselves at odds with those we love deeply. As you review your various family relationships, list in your journal or on a sheet of paper those relationships or areas in relationships where some attention might need to be given to reflect more fully Christ's message of love and peace. Invite catechumens/candidates to share with *one* other person some of these situations. Allow 10–20 minutes for sharing.

Bring the group back together. In the Gospel reading today, Matthew states that Herod is searching for the child Jesus to destroy him. Christ comes to bring peace to all the earth and this peace is threatened with destruction.

Group discussion (approximately 15 minutes): Name some of the major threats to our living peacefully as family together.

SUMMARY

Catechist should be prepared to speak about the cultural milieu from which the fourth commandment grew, as well as the reference in Paul's letter for wives to be submissive to their husbands.

Some input on forgiveness and reconciliation should also be applicable given discussion on family and possible dissidence.

PRAYER

Lord, on the feast of the holy family, help us to clothe ourselves with mercy, kindness, humility, meekness and patience. To put on love and let the word of your Son Jesus Christ dwell deep within our hearts. Lord, protect us from those things that threaten us, our families, our relationships. Always mindful that we are members of your one body, we pray: Our Father, who art in heaven, hallowed be thy name. Thy kingdom come, thy will be done on earth as it is in heaven. Give us this day our daily bread and forgive us our trespasses as we forgive those who trespass against us. And lead us not into temptation but deliver us from evil. For thine is the kingdom, the power and the glory forever and ever. Amen.

Doctrinal and Pastoral Issues: Fourth Commandment, World Peace, U.S. Bishops' Peace Pastoral, Sexism

John T. Butler

January 1—Solemnity of Mary, Mother of God

Numbers 6:22–27
Galatians 4:4–17
Luke 2:16–21

GATHERING PRAYER

Song

"Sing of Mary" (Anonymous, *Worship II*)

Pray together Psalm 34:2–11

REFLECTION

Part 1

If you were asked to count your blessings, how many would you be able to list?

Invite catechumens/candidates to list as many good things that have happened for them as they can in four minutes.

As you look over your list, which items would you say are accidental or incidental to your life as opposed to those that you would call blessings from God. Place a one (1) next to those you would say are accidental and a two (2) next to those that you feel are blessings.

Invite the group to share their list and categories with the person sitting next to them (approximately 15 minutes).

Part 2

In the first reading, the Lord gives words of blessing to the Israelites:

> The Lord bless you and keep you.
> The Lord let his face shine upon you
>   and be gracious to you.
> The Lord look upon you kindly
>   and give you peace.
>
> (Numbers 6:24–26)

These words spoken through to the time of Christ, down to our present age, speak to all of us here today. We celebrate during this season the fulfillment of that blessing in Christ's coming.

Close your eyes for a moment and reflect with me on these words. Catechist should repeat the words of blessing slowly, with care and certainty, guiding the imagination of the group as follows:

> The Lord bless you and keep you . . .

Think of all of the blessings the Lord has bestowed on you and how God has kept you.

> The Lord let his face shine upon you
>   and be gracious to you . . .

Can you see the face of the Lord smiling on you? Picture God extending abundant grace on you.

> The Lord look upon you kindly and give you
>   peace.

Now feel the calm and the comfort of the Lord's presence; feel the peace and the joy of the Lord.

One blessing that we all have received is that of being made adopted sons and daughters of the Lord (Gal 4:7). God has called us into an intimate relationship.

Can you imagine how the parents who seek to adopt a child must feel as they anxiously await the process to reach fruition? The love that they harbor awaiting the moment to openly share it with that special one. Invite sharing on this theme with the entire group.

SUMMARY

The catechist should be prepared to speak also about this feast of Mary, Mother of God with some reference to the early councils that spoke about our Marian doctrine. The link can be made between Mary, the Blessed Mother, and the blessing God bestows on humanity through Jesus Christ.

CLOSING PRAYER

Lord with a parent's love you have brought us into a fuller relationship with you. As we continue to celebrate the joy of you coming, keep us mindful of your abiding love for us. Help us as we dedicate our lives to you, Lord. Let this new year find us growing more in the example of your Son Jesus.

May the Lord bless you and keep you.

May the Lord let his face shine upon you and
    be gracious to you.
May the Lord look upon you kindly and give
    you peace.

*Doctrinal and Pastoral Issues: Marian Devotion, Mary,
Mother of God, Blessing*

John T. Butler

Epiphany

(Sunday between January 2 and January 8)

Isaiah 60:1–6
Ephesians 3:2–3, 5–6
Matthew 2:1–12

GATHERING PRAYER

Song

"We Three Kings," John Hoplius

Pray together Psalm 138:1–8

REFLECTION

Part 1

With today's Gospel we celebrate the feast of Christ's manifestation to the wise men of the East. We see peace and light threatened by darkness and destruction. The wise men are presented with the option of following the call rising in their hearts, this light that leads to Christ, or following the command of King Herod which threatens to destroy the light.

As we enter this new year and near the close of our Christmas celebration, I cannot help but wonder what continues to threaten our own embracing of the light that Christ brings to the world. The first reading provides an opportunity for vivid imagery:

Invite catechumens and candidates to relax, close their eyes, and reflect on the words of Isaiah. Read aloud slowly and with inflection Isaiah 60:1–4:

> Rise up in splendor, Jerusalem.
>> Your light has come,
>> the glory of the Lord shines upon you.
> See, darkness covers the earth and thick
>> clouds cover the peoples;
> But upon you the Lord shines,
>> and over you appears his glory.
> Nations shall walk by your light,
>> and kings by your shining radiance.
> Raise your eyes and look about;
>> they all gather and come to you:
> Your sons come from afar,
>> and your daughters in the arms of their
>> nurses.

As you reflect on these words what images come to mind? What is this thick cloud that covers the people? Can you name the cloud that threatens to cover you?

Ask the group to slowly open their eyes and then invite sharing in small groups (approximately 20 minutes).

Part 2

Reassemble group and invite sharing with the entire group on verse 2b:

> But upon you the Lord shines,
>> and over you appears his glory.

How does the Lord shine upon you?

In the second reading, Paul's letter to the Ephesians, he states: "In Christ Jesus the Gentiles are now co-heirs with the Jews, members of the same body and sharers of the promise through the preaching of the Gospel." (Ephesians 3:6)

What implication does this early Christian message have for us today?

Help the catechumens and candidates see the Epiphany as a celebration of the unversality of the Church:

> Nations shall walk by your light,
>> and kings by your shining radiance. (Isaiah 60:3)

How are nations walking by the light of the Lord? How are nations still covered by a thick cloud?

SUMMARY

Catechist might discuss the tension that existed in the early Church with the spread of Christianity, especially the conflict between Peter and Paul regarding criteria for membership in the Judeo-Christian community. The cultural tensions that a universal message of salvation confronted in early Church history also continue today.

Some attention might also be given to the U.S. bishops' pastoral letter on peace.

CLOSING PRAYER

Lord, you sent your Son so that we might be called out

of our darkness into your light. The darkness that once covered us ceases to hide us, for your light has broken forth and has redeemed the world.

Lord, let your light dispel all of our darkness. Continue to call us to yourself and give us your peace. Amen.

Doctrinal and Pastoral Issues: Christ as Light of World, Universality of Church, U.S. Bishops' Peace Pastoral, Epiphany

John T. Butler

Baptism of the Lord

Isaiah 42:1–4, 6–7
Acts 10:34–38
Matthew 3:13–17

GATHERING PRAYER

Song

"Come to the Water" (John B. Foley, S.J., North American Liturgy Resources)

Pray together Psalm 113:1–9

REFLECTION

Part 1

> I the Lord have called you for the victory of justice, I have grasped you by the hand. I formed you and set you as a covenant of the people, a light for the nations. (Isaiah 42:6)

These words of Isaiah as well as the entire passage we heard today in our first reading is thought by various Scripture scholars to be a reference to the historical Israel or an Old Testament historical character before or during the lifetime of the prophet. Some also believe these Scriptures refer to Isaiah himself. Through the New Testament and Christian tradition we have come to see a fulfillment of these prophecies in Jesus Christ.

If we take Isaiah's words and apply them to ourselves, what does it mean for us:

To be called by the Lord?

To have the Lord grasp us by the hand?

To be formed by the Lord and set as his covenant and as a light?

Invite quiet reflection followed by sharing in small groups of three to four. (Approximately 20 minutes.)

Part 2

The importance of these words of Isaiah in connection with Matthew's account of the baptism of Jesus not only illustrates that God was with Jesus, but also illuminates the divinity of Christ.

As Jesus began to minister after his baptism, the apostles and others gradually came to discover who Jesus really was. Only after his death and resurrection would the early Christian community come to see him fully as Lord.

How has Jesus been revealed in your life? What meaning does the divinity of Jesus have for you?

Invite large group discussion using these or similar questions.

SUMMARY

Catechist should be prepared to direct catechumens through an exploration of the early Church's growth toward the doctrine of the divinity of Christ. Important to note would be the early Church councils and the controversies that led to them (e.g. Nicea, Chalcedon, etc.).

These readings also provide an opportunity to appropriately move into some catechesis on our Trinitarian doctrine.

Some connection might also be explored between Jesus' baptism, mission, and ministry, and that of our own impending sacramental celebration.

CLOSING PRAYER

Lord, through your Son Jesus you have revealed your love for us. You have taken us by the hand and by your word you continue to form us. Send us your Spirit, Lord, to strengthen and guide us as we grow in our love for you. Amen.

Doctrinal and Pastoral Issues: Call of God, Divinity of Christ, Christology, Development of Doctrine

John T. Butler

LENT

The Work of Redemption

By Eugene A. LaVerdiere

Lent is a very special season in which we see Jesus' teaching and other activities in the light of his passion and death. We also see what his passion and death implied for our redemption and how by learning from his life and following his teaching we open ourselves to salvation.

The Gospel readings begin on Ash Wednesday with a call to enter into the season devoutly and generously as people willing to translate the first century demands of the Gospel into those of the twentieth (Mk 6:1–6, 16–18). On the First Sunday, we hear of the most basic challenges Jesus received and of the way he responded to them. Those challenges are now ours. We enter into the mystery of redemption by responding as Jesus did (Mt 4:1–11). On the Second Sunday, we read of the transfiguration, an anticipated glimpse of Jesus' risen life and glory (Mt 17:1–9).

From the Third to the Fifth Sundays, we join John's Gospel and explore the most basic issues for Christians in any age, conversion and baptism (4:5–42), the opening of our eyes in faith (9:1–41), and the promise of new life in the resurrection (11:1–45). Finally on Passion Sunday, we hear how, at the climax of a life which always gave of itself, redemption came through the complete gift of Jesus' life (Mt 21:1–11; 26:14–27:66).

Almsgiving, Prayer, and Fasting

The Lenten season opens on Ash Wednesday with a Gospel reading on the three practices characteristic of a good person in a religious and cultural world such as that of the Bible. The passage, which is drawn from Jesus' Sermon on the Mount (Mt 5—7), includes a general principle (v 1) and its application to almsgiving (vv 2–4), prayer (vv 5–6) and fasting (vv 16–18). The parallel structure of these sub-units indicates that they formed a rhetorical whole before being included in Matthew's Gospel, when 6:7–15 was inserted and broke up the pattern. The same three practices are considered in Tobit 12:8–10.

The purpose of the passage is to warn against inappropriate attitudes and behavior in each of these areas. Alms should be given discreetly, not in order to be applauded by others. Prayer should be done quietly or privately, not in order to be noticed. One's fasting should not be advertised to draw attention to oneself.

Response to Temptation

The Gospel reading for the First Sunday of Lent presents the temptations of Jesus by the devil (Mt 4:1–11). To appreciate Matthew's message in the passage, we should recall that it follows the account of Jesus' baptism, where he is declared God's beloved Son (3:13–17). This provides the context for the devil's statement: "If you are the Son of God." Three times the devil tries to tempt Jesus to act in a manner contrary to his Sonship of God.

Although we commonly describe the event as a series of temptations, a better translation sees them as a triple test. We are then able to view the scene in relation to the last petition of the Lord's Prayer, "Lead us not to the test" (Mt 6:13), that is, to the passion, the supreme test of Jesus' Sonship of God, and in relation to Jesus' warning to the disciples at Gethsemane: "Be on guard, and pray that you may not undergo the test. The spirit is willing but nature is weak" (26:41).

Transfiguration

On the Second Sunday of Lent, the transfiguration of Jesus (Mt 17:1–9) anticipates his appearance to the disciples as risen Lord and the coming of the Son of Man in his kingship (see 16:28), and it recalls the heavenly manifestation at Jesus' baptism. Appropriately, the event takes place on a high mountain. As with the Sermon on the Mount (Mt 5–7), the nourishing of the four thousand (15:29–38), and the final commission (28:16–20), the mountain is the symbolic place for divine revelation, and it is pointless to try to identify it geographically. With Jesus in glory are Moses and Elijah, the law and the prophets, which are being fulfilled in Jesus.

Earlier, Simon Peter had confessed his faith in Jesus as "the Son of the living God." Jesus' heavenly Father, we are told, had revealed this to him (16:16–17). Now the Father confirms Peter's faith: "This is my beloved Son on whom my favor rests."

The Samaritan Woman and the Waters of Eternal Life

The First and Second Sundays of Lent placed the

entire season in the context of the testing of Jesus and his manifestation as Lord. They thus pointed ahead to the passion and resurrection and announced the mystery of our redemption. On the Third Sunday of Lent, attention focuses on the baptismal experience and commitment through which Christians enter this mystery (Jn 4:5–42).

The setting is a Samaritan town and by a well where Jesus speaks to a Samaritan woman. The account's main theme is the new life, symbolized by the water which Jesus provides. Literally, one should notice that the woman and Jesus refer to the water on two different levels of discourse. The woman thinks of physical water and the way it quenches thirst. Jesus speaks of water symbolically. For him the thirst it quenches is a deep spiritual thirst for eternal life.

The Man Born Blind and the Vision of Faith

The Fourth Sunday of Lent builds on the Third. Its Gospel reading, the story of the man born blind in John 9:1–41, deals with the blindness of those who have no faith and the sight of faith which is given by Jesus, the light of the world. The passage also deals with important questions regarding the origins of physical evil. It was assumed that the man's blindness had come from sin. Jesus disassociates blindness from sin. Those who have physical sight can also be filled with sin. They thus remain in the dark, unwilling to open their eyes to the light of the world, and so are truly blind.

As in the story of the Samaritan woman, where water was referred to on different levels, so here with blindness and sight. Those who challenge Jesus remain on an earthly, physical level. Jesus speaks on a spiritual or symbolic level, akin to what we now call sacramental.

Lazarus and the Resurrection

The Third and Fourth Sundays of Lent focused on the baptismal water of eternal life and the sight of faith. The Gospel for the Fifth Sunday dwells on resurrection from the dead. The story of the raising of Lazarus (Jn 11:1–45) presents a physical resuscitation from the dead as a symbol for the resurrection which will take place when we enter into eternity. Unlike the resurrection of Lazarus, through which he was able to resume life at the point where it had been interrupted, the raising of Christians to eternal life through belief in Jesus, who is the resurrection and the life, involves a transformation into a whole new way of being and relating.

The passage reveals Jesus as Lord of life and death, but at the same time it shows him profoundly human. Few passages in the New Testament bring out his humanity so forcefully as the moment of grief he experiences as he meets Mary, the sister of his friend Lazarus who had died (11:32–35).

Triumphal Entry into Jerusalem

The Passion Sunday celebration begins with a procession with palms at which we read the account of Jesus' entry into Jerusalem (Mt 21:1–11). From Jesus' point of view, this entry must be humble. He does not come astride a horse like a conquering warrior, but humbly and peacefully astride an ass, a peasant's beast of burden (see Is 62:11 and Zec 9:9). However, from the crowd's point of view, Jesus' entry is triumphal. He comes as David's royal Son. This limited vision, which cannot foresee the humiliation of the passion, is reflected in the way the people describe Jesus: "the prophet Jesus from Nazareth in Galilee."

The Passion and Death of Jesus

The Gospel reading for the Passion Sunday liturgy is Matthew's account of the passion, death and burial of Jesus (26:14–27:66). With the passion, Jesus' struggle with evil and the work of redemption come to a climax. Judas' role in Matthew's passion is greater than in the other Gospels (Mt 26:14–16, 20–25, 47–50; 27:3–10). Only Matthew recounts how the blood money was returned and the betrayer hanged himself (27:3–10). And only Matthew describes the death of Jesus as an earth-shaking event (27:51–54).

The passion story is filled with irony. At the trial before Pilate, the people shout: "Let his blood be on us and on our children" (27:25). Jesus already had said: "This is my blood, the blood of the covenant, to be poured out in behalf of many for the forgiveness of sins" (26:28). Wrapped in scarlet, crowned with thorns, and with a scepter in hand, the King of the Jews calmly listens to the soldiers mock him: "All hail, King of the Jews" (27:28–29). The people, the chief priests, the scribes, the elders, and those who were crucified with him all challenged Jesus to save himself by coming down from the cross. But is is by remaining on the cross to the end that Jesus entered into his glory and opened the doors of salvation for all human beings. The Son of David, the King of the Jews, was the Son of God, the Son of Man and the King of all people.

Introduction to Lent

Each session for the Lenten season contains the following parts:

Opening Prayer
Reflection
Integration
Closing Prayer

In each session there are a number of reflection and integration sections. Note that these sessions are for use with catechumens rather than the elect.

The opening prayer begins with a song chosen from familiar liturgical music. These hymns may be listened to reflectively or sung together if a musician is available. The leader then prays the opening prayer. The closing prayer usually revolves around a meditative reading of the Gospel of the day. Various ways are suggested to enhance the environment for prayer. The cate-chist should also be mindful of the need to vary the group's posture while at prayer.

The method for this section is one of reflection and integration. The catechist is called to lead the group in reflecting first on some aspect of their experience, then on the Scriptures. After each reflection, the integration section poses questions for reflection or discussion. The method is thus based on a dialogue between the cate-chist and the catechumens. The catechist should be careful to allow time for quiet reflection when posing the integration questions. At times, a small group discussion or exercise is called for as a way of responding to the questions. Note too that there are a variety of questions from which the most appropriate may be selected.

Once again, doctrinal and pastoral issues have been highlighted for the catechist's use.

Ash Wednesday

Joel 2:12–18
2 Corinthians 5:20–6:2
Matthew 6:1–6,16–18

OPENING PRAYER

Song

"Turn to Me" (*Glory and Praise*, Volume One) or other appropriate song

Leader: Good and gracious God,
        we gather together in trust and hope
        to break open your word for our lives.
        As we begin this most holy season of Lent,
        we pray your Spirit will lead us
        to a deepened awareness of our gifts and
            our limitations
        so that we can come before you in all hon-
            esty
        and recognize you as our God, full of love
            and compassion.
        We make this prayer in the name of Jesus,
            the Lord,
        through the power of the Spirit.

All: Amen

REFLECTION

(Material for leader to develop)

Recognition and praise are important for most of us. We need the public support and approval others give us: the pat on the back, the applause, the words of encouragement. Such recognition gives us a good feeling about ourselves, that we're worthwhile and what we have to say and do is important. We sense that our deeds are appreciated. Recognition and approval are necessary for good mental health.

INTEGRATION

(Choose appropriate exercises/discussion questions)

1. Remember the most recent time you experienced recognition or approval. What did it feel like to you? How did you feel afterward?

2. Discuss the importance of recognition and approval for good mental health and its impact on spiritual development.

REFLECTION CONTINUES

Recognition and approval are free and spontaneous gifts given to us. They are not earned or else they become programmed gestures. Sometimes, because we try to program the recognition, we distort the importance of recognition and approval. They become ends in themselves. And so we start "doing things" to get approval, to be praised. The focus becomes us and what we want and do. The formal recognition of our service to the community, our achievement in the arts, our development of something only become important because they build us up. Therefore we donate the west wing of the hospital so that it will be named after us, or we contribute new uniforms to the youth baseball team so that our picture can appear in the newspaper, or we spend a lot of time preparing a text for publication or a lecture so that the audience will acclaim us. The focus is lost. Or perhaps we have more subtle ways of gaining recognition. We wear the right animal on our shirts, or the right name on our pants; we join the right club, are seen with the right people at the right time in the right place. Or perhaps we are even more subtle: we have God on our side. So we let everyone know how holy we are: we carry the Bible around prominently, we remind everyone we are going to pray, we are sure everyone knows the great fasts and spiritual disciplines we undergo—all, of course, for the greater glory of God.

INTEGRATION

(Choose appropriate exercises/discussion questions)

1. What are some of the more subtle and accepted ways of gaining recognition, of "blowing oneself up"?

2. Identify ways in which adults seek religious recognition (as an end in itself) and how this recognition can be destructive.

REFLECTION CONTINUES

Today we celebrate the inauguration of the great season

of Lent. Lent means "springtime," the opportunity for new life and new possibilities. Lent is the season of renewed hope because it affords us the opportunity to examine more carefully our way of life, our grappling at recognition and praise. Today's Gospel text stands as an examination for each of us. If we truly want to turn our lives around, truly want to repent and seek the Lord, then we must be careful not to make a "show" of it, or else we are again building up our own kingdom.

INTEGRATION

(Choose appropriate exercise/discussion questions)

1. Reread the Gospel text. List for yourselves the ways of seeking recognition in the text, and the way of life prescribed for those who sincerely choose repentance.

2. Discuss the importance of Lent as a new springtime.

REFLECTION CONTINUES

Lent is a time to "turn around," repent, be changed by the proclamation of the Gospel as it roots itself in our hearts. The change of Christian discipleship is a change of attitude, of heart. The actions are only expressive of a deeper commitment of following the Lord, of choosing the Lord's values. Our recognition of our sin leads us to want to change. Therefore, as the first text tells us, "rend your hearts, not your garments." It was common for repentant persons to rip their clothes and wail in repentance. But so often this became more of a show than a sign of repentance. The real change must happen in our hearts, where in the silence we meet our God.

INTEGRATION

(Choose appropriate exercise/discussion questions)

1. What can we do to facilitate our hearts being "rendered"?

2. What does this reflection (rend your hearts not your garments) tell us about our relationship with God?

REFLECTION CONTINUES

Why do we choose to be showy? Why do we hunger for other persons' approval? Why do we need their applause? Because we have lost touch with our center, we have become off-balanced and therefore are a stranger to ourselves. We don't know the gift there, we don't know the uniqueness of ourselves, because we have lost our stories. We have become so busy about building up false images of ourselves to please others, to make others happy with us, to make them accept us, that we have lost touch with the real person we are gifted to be. We have chosen sin as a way of life, because sin is distortion. We now can't gently accept appropriate recognition and approval. No, we need it, we hunger for it, we set up situations for it. We have lost our sense of self in a radical way (i.e., at its roots). Yet the mystery of our redemption lies in the fact that we can regain our stories, that we can return to center, that we can live out of the fullness of who we are gifted to be. We cannot earn our justification; but we have been gifted with the possibility of reconciliation with ourselves, and therefore with God and our neighbor.

INTEGRATION

(Choose appropriate exercise/discussion questions):

1. Reread the Corinthians text. What does it mean to be an "ambassador" of reconciliation in light of our discussion today?

2. Draw images of "being off-centered." What colors express this experience? What are the feelings associated with this experience? Now draw images of reconciliation. What are the colors, feelings involved?

REFLECTION CONTINUES

Today you were marked with ashes; you were recognized by the community as one who had chosen an inauthentic way of life (sin) but who has chosen to embrace the cross, to choose life. The marking of ashes is a reminder, a call to repent and believe the good news of the Gospel. It is the marking of those who gather around reconciliation. Can you wear this badge of recognition?

INTEGRATION

(Choose appropriate exercise/discussion questions)

1. What did you experience as you were marked with ashes today?

2. How is this public wearing of ashes different than the condemnation of "public show"?

CLOSING PRAYER

Reread Gospel text slowly.

After silent reflection, all stand.

Leader: As we have been signed today with ashes
as a reminder of our call to repentance,
let us sign ourselves as a reminder of our
    identity.
Let us place our right hands on our fore-
    heads (pause);
and we remember the Creator God, the
    Giver of Life,
the One who formed us, knows us, loves
    us (long pause).
And let us place our right hands on our
    hearts (pause);
and we remember the Redeemer God, the
    Reconciler,
the One who offers freedom and peace to
    our hearts (long pause).
And let us place our right hand on our left
    shoulders (pause);
and we remember the Sanctifier God, the
    Empowerer,
the One who inspires creativity, healing
    and wholeness (long pause).
And we place our hand on our right shoul-
    ders (pause);
and we continue to remember the Sancti-
    fier,
the One who offers us reason and faith
    (long pause).
And we bring our hands together (pause);
We remember our identity as men and
    women marked by the Sign of the
    Cross,
and together we can assent with an Amen.

All: Amen.

*Doctrinal and Pastoral Issues: Sin, Repentance, Justifi-
cation, Lent*

Thomas H. Morris

First Sunday in Lent

Genesis 2:7–9; 3:1–7
Romans 5:12–19
Matthew 4:1–11

OPENING PRAYER

Song

"I Long for You, O Lord" (Dameans *Lord of Light* album, NALR) or similar song

Leader: Good and gracious God,
we long for you, we hunger for your presence.
Help us recognize our deep need for you as we recognize our sin and the need for repentance.

All: Recite in unison the responsorial psalm from today's liturgy: Psalm 51:3–4, 5–6, 12–13, 14, 17

REFLECTION

(Material for leader to develop)

Choices. We all make choices. Some choices are easy to make—where to go for dinner, what to wear, what time to plan to awaken, what movie to see. Life is filled with choices—and it is these choices which add color and texture and vibrancy to life. Choices help keep life exciting and dynamic. They keep us from becoming stale and boring. Human choices add the rich quality of reflection to them. Animals make choices based on instinct, drives, urges for survival, protection. Human choices are human precisely because men and women can step back from their choices, reflect on them, become informed about them, and make responsible decisions.

INTEGRATION

(Choose appropriate exercise/discussion questions)

1. What were some important choices you had to make this week? Describe the process you went through to come to the choice you made.

2. Why do some people find it hard to make decisions, to choose? Do you find making choices difficult? Why or why not?

REFLECTION CONTINUES

Not all choices made by men and women are human choices. Sometimes our choices reflect decisions based solely on drives, impulses, urges. Of themselves, these drives and urges are not necessarily wrong. But choices based solely on them are robbed of the reflection process that incorporates responsibility. So someone may over-indulge, go on a binge, or use another person to fulfill his or her desires. Such irresponsible choices are not reflective of full human living. They are off-centered choices. They reflect disorder and chaos. They fail to reflect the beauty of men and women who were created with the capacity for responsible choice-making.

INTEGRATION

(Choose appropriate exercise/discussion questions)

1. What do you think are some characteristics of responsible "choice-making"?

2. What are some everyday examples of choices based on urge, impulse, drives which are not responsible (e.g., choices made to satisfy urge for power, money, control, sex, honor)?

REFLECTION CONTINUES

Today's Gospel has to do with choices. Jesus is driven by the Spirit into the desert to pray. The desert is the place of renewal and refinement. The desert is the place of aridity and beauty at the same time. People are stripped naked in the desert and must face the truth of who they are: both gifts and limits. While in the desert, Jesus is faced with his own person and the interior struggles he must live with. These struggles become personified in the person of the tempter. The tempter calls Jesus to irresponsible choices, inauthentic living. The tempter beckons Jesus to choose a new center for his life instead of God: power (bread into stones), influence and control (throw self off temple), and exalted recognition bought at the price of false worship (all these kingdoms can be yours). Jesus lives in fidelity to who he is: gifted for responsible choices. He refuses the "easy way out," the way which leads away from fuller human life.

INTEGRATION

(Choose appropriate exercise/discussion questions)

1. How was the tempter calling Jesus to make false claims on power, influence and control, and exalted recognition through false worship?

2. Are these same choices made today?

3. Why is the desert necessary for full human living? Where can we find a desert today in our crowded cities, etc.?

REFLECTION CONTINUES

But why do we make such irresponsible choices? Why do we choose selfishness instead of relationship? Why do we seek building our own powerful (and isolated) kingdoms at the cost of everyone else? The first reading gives us a clue. We heard the beautiful account of God breathing into Adam's nostril the "breath of life" and thus Adam became a living being. Adam was animated and enlivened by the very life of God, and therefore Adam could share in the gift of God's way of life: compassion, justice, generosity, caring. At the center of each person is this very breath of God which gives each of us life. We are created in God's image and likeness and share in God's way of life. Yet in this same account we also hear how Adam and Eve fail to trust the Giver of gifts. They begin to seek for their own gain (distrust) rather than model the way of life that the Giver has breathed into them: the way of relationships and responsibility. They fail to trust and are disobedient.

INTEGRATION

(Choose appropriate exercise/discussion questions)

1. How is lack of trust tied in with irresponsible choices?

2. Name a time in your life when you have failed to trust the "breath of God" as gift of life.

3. What are the roots of this mistrust (e.g., fear, anxiety, past hurts, betrayal, abandonment)?

REFLECTION CONTINUES

The choices are still with us. But we have the possibility of freedom for responsible choices. We can step back and look at the implications. We need not be enslaved. We can make a difference in our choices. "Because the love of God has been poured out in our hearts . . . " (Rom 5:5). We can live from the center: the breath of God known as love.

INTEGRATION

(Choose appropriate exercise/discussion questions)

1. How must I change to be more faithful to the person I am?

2. What new choices can I begin to make?

CLOSING PRAYER

Have Gospel text enthroned with candle lit; all gather around in a circle, either standing or sitting.

Reader: Be attentive to the word of God according to the tradition of Matthew:
(read Gospel text of day: Matthew 4:1–11)

Leader: (after silent reflection)
We hear in our lives the tempter: Turn these breads into stones!
Lord, teach us how to respond. (silent reflection)
We hear in our lives: Throw yourself down and his angels will rescue you.
Lord, teach us to respond. (silent reflection)
We hear in our lives: All kingdoms can be yours if you worship me!
Lord, teach us to respond. (silent reflection)

Closing Refrain

Refrain from "I Long for You, O Lord" (Dameans)

Doctrinal and Pastoral Issues: Creation, Original Sin, Justification, Jesus' Self-Knowledge, Humanity of Jesus, Choice and Responsibility

Thomas H. Morris

Second Sunday in Lent

Genesis 12:1–4
2 Timothy 1:8–10
Matthew 17:1–9

OPENING PRAYER

Song

"Yahweh, the Faithful One" (St. Louis Jesuits, *Glory and Praise*, Volume 1) or similar song

Leader: Good and gracious God,
you promise us a future and give us a
blessing for today.
You gift us with life, and with all good
things.
Most especially, you gift us with Jesus
who shows us how to live life in full and
authentic ways.
As we break open this Word of Life today,
may we come to know Jesus more deeply
and thereby live lives which are changed,
transformed, renewed.
We make this prayer in the name of Jesus
the Lord,
through the power of your Spirit.

All: Amen.

REFLECTION

(Material for leader to develop)

We all want and need security, especially in our very active and fast-paced world. People are always moving, friends leaving, jobs becoming vacant, new opportunities emerging. Security gives us a sense of being settled, being rooted. And our security is not limited to the physical. We seek security in our relationships, in our family life, in our prayer, in our church, even in our God.

INTEGRATION

(Choose appropriate exercise/discussion questions)

1. Why is security important to you? What are some ways you seek security?

2. Name some of the various kinds of security. What do they all have in common?

REFLECTION CONTINUES

Security can become distorted, "too much of a good thing." Sometimes our security inhibits our growth and development, keeping us from seeing the beyond. Our security can become our personal drug, our way of coping with life. In extreme cases, security can become our god. We stop really living life and live for being safe.

INTEGRATION

(Choose appropriate exercise/discussion questions)

1. In the recent past describe one way you have chosen security over risk-taking. Why did you do that?

2. How can "being secure" lead to "being sterile"? Reflect on this as a group and see the possible relationship between security (extreme) and sterility.

REFLECTION CONTINUES

One acceptable distortion of security is the "holding-on" syndrome. "What a good thing we have here. Let's bottle it, can it, tie it down, contain it, hold on to it and keep it alive forever!" We see hints of this in today's Gospel text. Peter, James and John have an extraordinary experience: they experience Jesus in all of his glory, i.e., Jesus is transfigured (literally: changed in form or appearance). In this text our concern is Peter's response: "Let us erect three booths here! How wonderful that this is happening. Let's capture it and hold on to it!"

INTEGRATION

(Choose appropriate exercise/discussion questions)

1. To what do you cling at this time in your life so as not to lose it (e.g., a special evening, a relationship, a career)?

2. Clench your fists for a few moments. What do you

feel? How do they look? Imagine a plant or a small animal inside those clenched fists. Could such a creature live? Could you accept more life? Could you give to others with closed hands?

3. How does holding on rob someone/something of its life, its vitality, its capacity to grow? Discuss implications of holding on.

REFLECTION CONTINUES

How can we let go? How can we be freed so that we might be aware of the many transfigurations that happen both in our own lives and in the lives around us? Abraham in our first reading helps us understand the way of life for one who chooses to "let go." Abraham is called by God to leave all his securities: his homeland, his heritage, the familiar and safe in order to enter into a deeper relationship with God, i.e., to trust that God will not lead him astray. In response to such a posture of trust, God promises Abraham a new future with blessings both then and now. Abraham knew that it was only in taking risks, in jumping into the arms of God that he would be able to truly develop into full personhood. Abraham knew that he could not hold tight to anything, but must walk with hands open to receive anew the gift of God's love.

INTEGRATION

(Choose appropriate exercise/discussion questions)

1. What do I need to let go of in my life (e.g., career, prestige, respectability, the "right" group to belong to, etc.)?

2. What insight does Abraham's life offer you into the "letting go" process: the gradual development of loving relationship which leads to an eventual abandonment in trust?

REFLECTION CONTINUES

Where does this trust come from? How can we live in this trust? The letter to Timothy reminds us that it is not of our own doing. The more we work at trying to free ourselves by our own power, the more frustrated we will become. Rather, at the heart of being free, of letting go, is grace. When we respond to the invitations of grace, we learn interiorly the gift of relationship with God, and thus come to recognize our empowerment and capacity to trust. Perhaps it comes gradually; we

learn to trust family, friends, colleagues. When we can live in trust with God, we can truly be prayerful people. We can begin to "let go" and not seek the securities which cling and bind. Our security becomes the cross of Jesus Christ.

INTEGRATION

(Choose appropriate exercise/discussion questions)

1. Reflect on the experience of grace. How is grace experienced? What are some of the "stirrings" and indications of God's invitation to love which are part of ordinary life?

2. Discuss the notion of trust. What is the relationship between trust and the establishment and nurturance of an interior life of prayer?

REFLECTION CONTINUES

Let's return to Peter and the disciples with Jesus on the mountain. They have experienced Jesus as transfigured. Jesus was experienced as he truly was: there was an aura of vulnerability, transparency, honesty. Something wonderful is experienced. The transfiguration of Jesus becomes a moment of promise for a future with God, with a blessing for then and now. The call which roots the promise is heard in the voice: "This is my beloved Son. Listen to him." The call to trust is not to become wrapped up. The call to trust is to respond with our lives to the invitation of Jesus to the Gospel life. Then change can happen. True transfigurations are occurring wherever men and women have risked giving up their binding securities and chosen to live life again: the alcoholic reaching out, the teenager refusing to be defined by peers, the housewife refusing the stereotypes of culture, the man or woman of faith letting go of an immature notion of God. Don't lose the moment of the transfigurations because you're holding on to previous ones. Risk together. Live for the blessings given now and for the promised future. Let go of the securities that keep you bound.

INTEGRATION

Reread the Gospel text. What does transfiguration mean to you? What are some of the "ordinary" transfigurations which are happening around us? Do you have any personal encounters of this nature which you can share?

CLOSING PRAYER

Prayerfully read the responsorial psalm of the day
(Psalm 33:4–5, 18–19, 20, 22) using the sung antiphon
"Remember Your Love" (Dameans, from album *Remember Your Love*, NALR) between strophes.

Doctrinal and Pastoral Issues: Transfiguration, Old Testament Theology of Election, Grace, Trust

Thomas H. Morris

Third Sunday in Lent

Exodus 17:3–7
Romans 5:1–2, 5–8
John 4:5–42

OPENING PRAYER

Prayerfully recite the responsorial psalm of the day (Psalm 95:1–2, 6–9) with the sung antiphon from "Remember Your Love" (Dameans, *Remember Your Love* album, NALR) between each strophe. After psalm has been prayed:

Leader: Good and gracious God,
we acclaim you as the true God who created us
and offers us new life in Christ Jesus.
We pray that as we gather to break open your word
we may be more fully formed into the image
of your Anointed One, Jesus the Lord.
We make this prayer in trust and confidence
in the name of Jesus our Brother
through the power of your Spirit.

All: Amen.

REFLECTION

(Material for leader to develop)
We all know the experience of being thirsty. Maybe it was after a long marathon run, or a bicycle race. Perhaps it was after a long hike or a grueling afternoon on the sports field. Or maybe it came after hours of cleaning the house, washing the car, or baking out in the sun. However and whenever, we've all had the experience of thirst—the dryness of mouth, the sense of restlessness and feeling of dehydration. Thirst is a common experience.

INTEGRATION

(Choose appropriate exercise/discussion questions)

1. Describe an experience of "feeling thirsty." Was your thirst quenched by water?

2. Why is water important for life? Have available a bowl of clear, cool water. During the discussion invite the catechumens to dip their hands or face in the water, or to cup some and drink. Discuss the experience together.

REFLECTION CONTINUES

There are other kinds of thirst than our physiological thirst for water. Perhaps we can use the metaphor "desire" to describe these thirsts. We have a desire for knowledge, for truth, for certitude, for justice, for freedom, for relationships, for life. It seems that a basic human function is the drive to live life beyond the present situation. This desire is a yearning for fuller life, more meaning. We thirst to drink the waters of life in all of its various forms.

INTEGRATION

(Choose appropriate exercise/discussion questions)

1. In small groups, list the various "thirsts" we have as human persons. Share how these "thirsts" lead us away from living human lives (e.g., thirst for revenge, thirst for greed, etc.).

2. What are some of the "signs" that we thirst to live beyond our present situation (e.g., striving even in a apparently hopeless situation, dedication to a certain cause such as civil rights)?

REFLECTION CONTINUES

Our desires can become disordered. By this we mean that we can become so "caught up" in this thirst that we can fail to see the ordinary moments when that thirst is being gently quenched. Our first reading gives us some clue of this. Here Israel has been thirsting for freedom, for liberation from captivity. God has led Israel into freedom through the painful stripping process of the desert. And now Israel thirsts to satisfy herself only. She grumbles and complains about the lack of water. Israel has failed to trust the God who has saved her, the God who has led her to freedom. She has failed to trust God's providence and her thirst has become distorted.

She demands instant gratification, instant quenching of her thirst. She puts God to the test and threatens violence to Moses.

INTEGRATION

(Choose appropriate exercise/discussion questions)

1. Name the implications of becoming so caught up in our thirst.

2. Discuss the relationship between the thirst for human living and trust in God's providence. How can "thirst" become a god?

REFLECTION CONTINUES

The Gospel text offers us a different insight into thirst. In the beautiful reading of Jesus encountering the Samaritan woman, we hear Jesus' words: "But whoever drinks the water I give him will never be thirsty again." The woman, like Israel, fails to understand and asks for this water now so she will not have to return to the well. She is focused on quenching her bodily thirst. Jesus is speaking, however, of an interior thirst for life, for meaning. Jesus is speaking of the fundamental thirsts we have discussed so far. And while we will continue to seek fulfillment in these thirsts, there is a foundational stream of living waters which can satisfy, which can quench our thirst so that we will not make selfish self-fulfillment our goal, but rather self-realization in service of others.

INTEGRATION

List on newsprint or on the blackboard the basic concrete thirsts for living we have discussed so far. Create a parallel list of "fulfillments" of these desires. How are these "fulfillments" adjectives describing the experience of God?

REFLECTION CONTINUES

Jesus' invitation is to live out of a new center, a new life-spring. The key text from Romans helps us understand what this life-spring is: "The love of God has been poured out in our hearts through the Holy Spirit who has been given to us." The source of our life is truly God-within-us. It is when our thirsts flow from this source of life that we can be ordered toward self-realization which brings one into charity and service of others. Our thirst for meaning, for truth, for value can be fulfilled through the interior strength given to us by our God. We must drink from the well of our life and relationship with God.

INTEGRATION

(Choose appropriate exercise/discussion questions)

1. How well do we know our "own well"? Name the qualities in our depths which we can acknowledge and tap into as a source of life and energy.

2. Give each catechumen crayons and paper. Invite them to draw themselves, using the image of a well. What is this well made of? What is in the well? What do I need to see more clearly the life-giving waters in the well? Do I feel as though my well has dried up? Image these feelings, thoughts with the crayons and paper.

3. Have the catechumens draw or list their thirsts (if exercise with well was used, they can include the thirsts there) and write a personal prayer asking God to help them know their desire or thirst for God.

CLOSING PRAYER

Have the Scripture enthroned, with a candle lit. On the table next to the Scriptures have a clear bowl and a pitcher of cool water.

Reader: Reread the Gospel text (John 4:5–42). While the text is being read, slowly pour the water into the bowl. You may choose to abbreviate the text.

After silence, invite anyone who wishes to read his or her prayer for "desire of God." If no one wishes to do so, then spontaneously lead the group into prayer for our needs, focusing on the need for God.

Close the prayer with the song "Come to the Waters" (St. Louis Jesuits, *Glory and Praise* NALR) followed by an exchange of peace.

Doctrinal and Pastoral Issues: Exodus, Providence, Grace, Self-Awareness

Thomas H. Morris

Fourth Sunday in Lent

1 Samuel 16:1, 6–7, 10–13
Ephesians 5:8–14
John 9:1–41

OPENING PRAYER

Song

"Trust in the Lord" (St. Louis Jesuits, *Glory and Praise*, NALR) or similar song

Pray the responsorial psalm antiphonally. Between strophes, sing the refrain of "We Praise You" (Dameans, *Remember Your Love*, NALR) or similar praise antiphon.

REFLECTION

(Material for leader to develop)

Recovery comes with a cost. How odd, you may think. People would be glad to be healthy, to be restored. And many are. But perhaps the reason others choose non-health, to not be opened to healing love and power, is because they dread the cost of recovery. Recovery makes us responsible. Recovery demands of us that we witness to a new way of life. Recovery calls us to be people who are willing to risk.

INTEGRATION

(Choose appropriate exercise/discussion questions)

1. Name someone you know who is physically sick—who chooses sickness as a crutch to avoid responsibilities. List some common "excuses" people use to avoid responsibility.

2. Brainstorm some of the "risks" of recovery. Do you know someone who experienced a set-back (physical, emotional, spiritual) and chose to seek health through recovery? Describe their lifestyle after this period in their life.

REFLECTION CONTINUES

Our Scripture texts today talk about recovery in both obvious and subtle ways. They all speak of the responsibility given to those who respond to the call for life: David's anointing, the blind man who now sees and testifies to Jesus' work, the call to cast off darkness and be children of light. The image which speaks of this responsibility is the image of sight, of light, of right vision. Recovery is the restoration of vision. Perhaps our own vision has become distorted, askewed, marred or blurred. And perhaps it is that blurred vision that helps keep us irresponsible.

INTEGRATION

(Choose appropriate exercise/discussion questions)

1. List some examples around us—in our lives, in our world—of blurred vision (e.g., judging by race, creed, sex, status, culture or basic preference, appointments made solely on credentials, "preferred" ways of thinking, acceptable behavior, etc.).

2. Reflect on your own life. Where do you now experience darkness? Was there a time in your past you experienced darkness? Has there been light before? Is the light dimmed? What obstacles stand or stood blocking the light? What do you need to be "in the light"?

REFLECTION CONTINUES

Jesus came to bring healing, to herald a new kingdom of justice and compassion, a kingdom rooted in God's vision, God's light. Jesus' identification with God's work was manifested in his healing ministry. He brought light to those who suffered in darkness, be that physical, emotional, psychological or spiritual. Light has shone in our darkness.

INTEGRATION

Slowly and prayerfully review the story of the blind man in today's Gospel, but this time use the active imagination. (Note: Be sure to include appropriate periods of silence for reflection. Do not rush the meditation.)

Have all relax and become comfortable (not so comfortable that they fall asleep). The best posture is sitting (or kneeling) with the back erect so oxygen can freely flow through the body. Spend a few moments breathing deeply and quieting down, asking the Spirit to heighten our awareness of his presence with us and within us. Spend a few moments letting go of all concerns, anxieties and preoccupations. Acknowledge their presence and then give them permission to go.

After some quiet centering, begin to tell the story of the blind man again (except use the words blind person so all can identify):

Create the scene for them. Have them smell the roadside, inhale the flying dust, hear the crowds, the mumblings, the whisperings, the rush of people passing by. Experience the sense of movement as people try to be near Jesus, as well as the respect his presence commands.

After creating the scene, have all image themselves as blind people sitting along the roadside, not a part of the festivity, not able to see, and hence an outsider. Blind people were considered sinners, and therefore were probably the outcasts. They were most likely poor, either by social class or simply because they were robbed often. Invite all to sit there as the blind person and feel the sense of "left-out."

Invite all to identify for themselves the areas of their blindness: What has caused you to feel unacceptable, left out, poor? What is that terrible part of your life that keeps you from living with abundance? Get in touch with that experience or moment. It may be a past experience, a broken relationship, an infidelity, an abuse of gifts, unacceptance by another, whatever.

After some time getting in touch with their blindness, invite all to get back in touch with being on the roadside. "Hear the crowd approaching and Jesus' disciples talking about you—you! What does that feel like—to be singled out? Will they notice your blindness? Will they laugh at you, cast you aside? Hear the question: Whose fault was it? Who sinned? And hear Jesus' response for you. What is Jesus' response for you? Feel being touched by Jesus, inhale his presence, know he is there. You feel a paste-like mixture being placed on your eyes, smeared on them, rubbed in. What does that feel like? What do you feel?

And then a strange thing happens: Jesus speaks to you, softly, quietly so no one else can hear. "My friend, what is your blindness?" Feel the mud paste on your eyes, the breathing of Jesus near you. Feel the weight of your blindness, and respond. Tell Jesus in your own words what your blindness is. Then hear Jesus ask another question: "And do you want to recover from this blindness?" Respond with what you truly desire.

Jesus hears your answer. He places his hands on your eyes, holds them tightly, and utters a deep groan that almost seems to come from the bowels of the earth. He begins to pray: "Good and gracious God . . . " What is Jesus' prayer for you right now?

After this prayer, Jesus wipes the mud from your eyes, the mud formed to bring recovery. And you slowly begin to open your eyes. What do you see? What do you feel? Who is there for you?

At the end of this prayer, instruct all to quietly pray for the gift of recovery, and the courage to be responsible in recovery, knowing that the light has truly broken into our darkness. Invite all to write down their experience, and then invite those who wish to share their experience to do so with the group. At the end of the sharing, welcome each other into recovery with a sign of peace.

CLOSING PRAYER

The closing prayer can be incorporated into the experience above. After the sharing and before the exchange of peace, perhaps you may wish to invite spontaneous prayer of petition. Close with the refrain "We Praise You" (Dameans from *Remember Your Love*, NALR) or similar song of thanksgiving, followed by exchange of peace.

Doctrinal and Pastoral Issues: Old Testament Theology (Election, King), Healing, Personal and Social Sin, Social Responsibility

Thomas H. Morris

Fifth Sunday in Lent

Ezekiel 37:12–14
Romans 8:8–11
John 11:1–45

OPENING PRAYER

Opening song

"How Firm a Foundation" (Worship II) or other similar song

Leader: Good and gracious God,
day by day you gift us with new life.
As we gather to break open your word
may we come to a deepened awareness of
    your presence
which invites life.
We make this prayer in the name of Jesus,
who is both Brother and Redeemer,
through the power of your Spirit. Amen.

Communal recitation of Responsorial Psalm 129, with the refrain from "Remember Your Love" between each strophe.

REFLECTION

(Material for leader to develop)

Things get broken. Toys break, material wears thin, pottery gets smashed. And life can get broken. Relationships fail, dreams crumble, goals lose focus, marriages die, people betray each other, nations fight against nation, people compete against each other rather than with each other. At times nothing seems to last, nothing seems to be forever. Perhaps life is too fragile; perhaps our expectations are too high. But the hopes and dreams we place in people, in ourselves, in our country, in our church can wither and fade, leaving in their trail a sense of gloom and death. Life can seem broken at times.

INTEGRATION

(Choose appropriate exercise/discussion questions)

1. Give the catechumens paper and crayons. Ask them to spend some quiet time reflecting on their life, focusing on one event/time when life seemed shattered, when things seemed to die. Ask them to draw the experience. Invite them to share the drawing with another person.

2. Reflect on this past week's experiences. When did you personally experience a sense of death around you? When did you see it in others? As a group, draw up a list of "death-moments" experienced this week.

3. Private journal questions: What dreams, visions, goals seemed to have withered and faded for me? How was I affected by this? Where did this lead me?

REFLECTION CONTINUES

Such broken dreams and unkept promises speak of death. Death is a harsh and cruel reality. There is no escaping death. Death can strike at any moment and does not discriminate. In that sense, death is very humbling because we all stand on equal ground before the great mystery of death. Yet death also meets us in very "everyday" ways as we have discussed so far. Death is very present in our lives.

INTEGRATION

(Choose appropriate exercise/discussion questions)

1. Remember a time in your life when someone close to you died. What were your feelings? What did it teach you?

2. Discuss the mystery of death. Why does death make so many uncomfortable? How do we view our own death?

3. What are the qualities or characteristics of "death"? Why does "death" evoke feelings of hopelessness and even despair?

REFLECTION CONTINUES

Jesus is faced with the painful reality of death in today's Gospel. Lazarus, a dear friend, is dead. Jesus weeps because of the great loss and emptiness he experiences in the death of his friend, and he raises Lazarus to life. Jesus' focus is God and the work of God. All the signs and wonders Jesus works are meant to focus on the great abundance and generous compassion of Abba. Jesus restores life to that which appeared dead, hope where it seemed hopeless, a vision for tomorrow where grief seemed to be the only answer.

Lazarus returned from the dead. The breath of life flowed through his whole person. Yet we must be careful not to confuse this with the resurrection. Lazarus will die again. The corpse of Lazarus was resuscitated. The same man Lazarus walked again, was with his family and friends. While we can presume that his life was changed because of the experience, Lazarus was nonetheless the same man revived from the dead. Such is not the experience of resurrection. In the resurrection, Jesus was raised to glory and was transformed: he was no longer a body of this earth. We are talking about a different category of experience than "visual." The whole person of Jesus (his total humanity and therefore all his relationships) is transformed into God forever. The resurrection of Jesus is God's yes to Jesus, confirming and affirming Jesus' life and ministry. In the resurrection, that which is corruptible is transformed into incorruptible.

INTEGRATION

1. Describe areas in your life which have come back to life after being dead. How have you changed because of this experience?

2. What is the significance of Jesus' resurrection for us? How does it affect our way of life?

REFLECTION CONTINUES

Lazarus is raised from death as a sign of God's presence. We have a greater sign in the resurrection of Jesus. In Christ's resurrection, the possibility of new and transformed life is available for all of us. Though we may not share in the fullness of such transformed life, God has affirmed the self-sacrifing love and lifestyle of Jesus as reflective of full human living, living which can be transformative. Perhaps we lie in the tomb of our sin, or of our own blockage. Perhaps the very pulse of life has been drained from us because of lost loves and broken friendships. Maybe the zeal with which we began our work or study has dwindled. Perhaps we have allowed our dreams to wither and fade, leaving us dry and barren. Jesus calls out to us in a new way, a greater way than he did to Lazarus: "Come out!"

INTEGRATION

1. Reflect on what keeps you bound. What keeps you tied up and not free enough to allow God's healing love to enter into your life?

2. Recall times in your life when you experienced a transformation in your life or the life of someone else.

CLOSING PRAYER

Invite all to reflect on what keeps them "dead," what the wrappings are which keep life from pulsing through. Have each person draw these "bindings," labeling them appropriately.

Reread the Gospel text, placing greater emphasis on the Lazarus in the tomb. Dramatically proclaim the section "Lazarus, come out!" At this time repeat this text using the names of each person present. After silence, continue the reading with the next lines, ending with "Untie him and let him go free!" Lead the group in spontaneous prayer for their own unbinding and ultimate freedom in the risen One.

Doctrinal and Pastoral Issues: Death, Resurrection, Heresy, Christology, Healing, Paschal Mystery

Thomas H. Morris

Passion Sunday/Palm Sunday

Procession with Palms: Matthew 21:1–11
Isaiah 50:4–7
Philippians 2:6–11
Matthew 26:14–27:66

OPENING PRAYER

Song

"All Glory, Laud and Honor" (Worship II) or other similar song

Pray Psalm 22. Either (1) have one person do a dramatic reading, (2) pray the psalm antiphonally, or (3) pray the entire psalm in unison with a sung refrain at beginning and end.

REFLECTION

(Material for leader to develop)

Certain feelings and emotions run deep—so deep we can't seem to find their source. But we know when they are triggered. Often they are triggered by stories associated with those feelings. Our memory faithfully carries the fullness of the story (fact and emotion) to enable us to be captured and drawn again into the story, thus becoming active participants. Certain new stories also have this ability to draw us into the story. We know this especially from good story-tellers or from good drama. Familiar stories of meaning and new stories which call to our depths both have the ability to raise us to new levels of awareness and invite us into the very fiber of the story.

INTEGRATION

(Choose appropriate exercise/discussion questions)

1. What are significant stories for you (e.g. a certain Christmas at your grandmother's, or the death of a friend)? How do these stories stay alive?

2. The leader will share a significant personal story. After relating the story to the catechumens, the leader gives them an opportunity to process the story (what they felt, visualized, etc.) as well as the opportunity to share briefly some of their own stories.

3. Briefly summarize today's texts (passion text). Ask the catechumens to share the feelings, emotions, images, etc., they remember experiencing at the earlier proclamation of the text.

4. Why could the text be different today for them? How are they different now than when they last heard the text?

REFLECTION CONTINUES

As we enter into this sacred and holy week of our tradition, it is appropriate to focus for a few moments on Jesus' death. It seems that all of Jesus' life-praxis and preaching of the kingdom of God is brought together in these final moments of concern, fellowship, betrayal and finally death. We begin today with the great hosannas, the great cries of gladness and welcome. Jesus was such a powerful presence (both in word and action) that, as the Scriptures claim, the whole city was "stirred to its depths." Yet in a matter of days, Jesus is dead.

INTEGRATION

(Choose appropriate exercise/discussion questions)

1. Recall the values Jesus lives out in his life and ministry. List them and cite examples (e.g., compassion and forgiveness exhibited in table fellowship with sinners).

2. Have all catechumens write privately their response: Why was Jesus killed? What does this mean for you?

REFLECTION CONTINUES

Jesus made people uncomfortable because he lived and proclaimed an authentic humanity. He threatened those who lived the "status quo," the comfortable. Inauthentic human living had evolved into divisions, slavery (physical, emotional and psychological), the "saved" and the "damned," the safe. Jesus demanded liberation from all forms of oppression, and he rooted his claim in his experience of the liberating presence of Abba.

INTEGRATION

Have the catechumens reflect privately: In what areas of your life does Jesus leave you feeling uncomfortable? Choose one area and explore the following: What values does this area suggest? What values does Jesus challenge it with? What do I need in order to change?

REFLECTION CONTINUES

Jesus was faced with a choice. He could have reacted to those he made "uncomfortable" and his impending death, fought back, exerted his strength and made his claim stronger. He could have struck out at them (physically and emotionally) and continued the cycle of injustice and oppression. Or he could have backed-off, run away, moved his message to someplace else, retreated until the "heat" was off and therefore continued the cycle of injustice and oppression. Both of these choices would have failed to be congruent to Jesus' experience of self, especially as this self is formed by God's values. Jesus' third option was to actively remain in silent protest, to actively choose his posture of life, to actively choose to remain faithful to what he believed at the core of his person. This, though it would lead to death, would break the vicious cycle of injustice and oppression. He would refuse compromising God's values. The values of the kingdom were more important and essential than the value of self-preservation. Jesus is willing to die for who he is and what he lives by. Jesus is willing to die for the proclamation and inauguration of God's kingdom.

Jesus' death is an act of self-sacrifing love. We can't pretend that we don't know what happens next and wait until Easter. Jesus is raised by the Father! The Father confirms and affirms the way of life, the way of values Jesus lived by and preached. Jesus' resurrection is God's verdict of yes to self-sacrificing love. And everywhere and anywhere that people are engaged in true self-sacrificing love, more of God's kingdom is breaking into our world. God has declared God's allegiance with the poor and oppressed of humanity and creation. God chooses to empower for justice. This was Jesus' experience. Jesus died for this experience. Jesus now gives us life for this experience. We know that we may suffer now; we may even feel defeated. But there is the God-on-our-side who stands with us in the process of liberation and freedom. Jesus' death is a victory for the values of God. Can we stand under this banner?

INTEGRATION

Have the catechumens reflect privately: What is my oppression, my slavery or my bondage? Complete the sentence: Come, O Lord, and set me free from —

CLOSING PRAYER

Leader: Good and gracious God,
Jesus has given his life for us.
He has shown us the way to fuller life,
and gifts us with the Spirit so we may embrace this way of life.
As we enter into this most sacred week in our community,
may we listen more attentively to the stories
of our community as told in the Scriptures,
The stories of our family and friends as told in their eyes,
and the story of our own life as we come to know
our need for the healing freedom of the Lord Jesus.
Confident that we stand in the shadow of Jesus' cross,
we bring you our needs:
(spontaneous prayer-petitions)

Have a metal or ceramic bowl available and some blessed palm. After the spontaneous prayer, swing the palm, saying: "They greeted Jesus with shouts of joy, with hosannas and praise." Then slowly and reverently burn the palm in the bowl. As the palm burns, play the song "Ashes" (T. Conroy). When the song is completed, invite each catechumen to come forward and be marked again with the cross. As each is marked, say: "Receive and live the cross of Jesus, God's values in a broken world."

Dismissal in silence.

Doctrinal and Pastoral Issues: Christology, Soteriology, Storytelling, Symbol, Justice

Thomas H. Morris

EASTER

The New Creation

By Eugene A. LaVerdiere

The Easter Triduum is the highpoint of the liturgical year. It begins on Holy Thursday with a preparatory celebration of the whole paschal mystery, when we focus on Jesus' Last Supper, his farewell to history in word and deed and a gathering up of the Church into his death-resurrection. Its second day is Good Friday, when we dwell on John's account of the passion and focus on Jesus glorious return to the Father. It climaxes with the Easter Vigil, a celebration of the resurrection, an event which touched creation itself to the core and transformed all of history.

The Easter Triduum is a transitional period. It can be viewed as the conclusion of Lent, but it is also the introduction to the Easter season, with its seven Sundays of Easter, the feast of the Ascension and Pentecost Sunday. Most of the readings are taken from John's Gospel for this season, and fittingly so, since the resurrection of Jesus permeates the entire Gospel.

The Last Supper

On Holy Thursday, the Gospel reading for the Mass of the Lord's Supper is John 13:1–15. Passover was approaching, and the decisive hour had come when Jesus would demonstrate the total gift of his love and return to the Father. The forces of treachery had not really triumphed (vv 1–2). The body of the reading includes the washing of the feet (vv 3–12a) and part of a brief discourse by Jesus (vv 12b–15).

To appreciate the force of Jesus' action, we need to realize who participated, the disciples, an extremely varied gathering which still included Judas and Jesus the Lord. Kneeling before each disciple in turn and washing their feet, the Lord not only showed humility but destroyed any claims to human status and social prestige among the disciples. When the Lord himself kneels before the powerful and the humble of the world, they have to recognize their equality as persons before God. Peter's resistance when Jesus approaches him is an expression of pride, not of humility.

In the discourse, Jesus asked his disciples to do for one another and for others what he had just done for them. He thus showed the Church how to pursue its mission to the ends of the earth and gather all nations and peoples into one family of God,.

The Glorification of Jesus

On Good Friday, we read John's account of the passion, death and burial of Jesus (Jn 18:1—19:42), an account quite different from that of Matthew, which we heard on Passion Sunday. Matthew's telling of the events would have been incomplete without the resurrection account. Not so with John's, whose passion is the story of Jesus' glorious return to the Father. Unlike Matthew, John does not speak of the resurrection event. Like Mark and Luke, he presupposes it and focuses on the disciples' experience of the risen Lord.

Throughout the passion and to the very moment of his death, Jesus is in full command of the events. John gives no hint of Jesus' anguished prayer at Gethsemane. The arrest takes place in the garden, and Judas is there with the others, but there is no need for a betrayal sign. Jesus steps forward and presents himself (18:4–5). Before Pilate, Jesus makes a solemn statement on the nature of the kingdom and the purpose of his life (18:36–37). Before dying, he shows how his death and passage to God transforms our relationship to one another: "Woman, there is your Son . . . there is your mother" (19:26–27). Finally, when Jesus sees that everything has been fulfilled, he declares it so and gives us his spirit. He has drunk the cup the Father has given him to drink (see 18:11).

The Resurrection

At the Easter Vigil, the Gospel reading is Matthew 28:1–10, an account of the women's visit to the tomb (vv 1–7) and of Jesus' appearance to them (vv 8–10). In the other Gospels the women come to the tomb and find it empty. In Matthew they arrive on time for the resurrection and the opening of the tomb by an angel. However, this does not mean that Matthew thought the resurrection was directly observable. He does not describe it save through the extraordinary manifestations which accompanied it, the literary elements of theophany, such as we find in the Old Testament in the Sinai story. Further, it is not Jesus but an angel who first appears, dazzles the soldiers guarding the tomb, and speaks to the women. Only later, away from the tomb, does Jesus appear to the women, offer them peace and renew their commission. The Gospel and the mission which flows from it springs from the experience of the risen Lord.

The Visits to the Tomb

On Easter Sunday, the Gospel is either John 20:1–9, which tells of two visits to the tomb, or Matthew's account of the women's experience at the tomb (28:1–10), which we have already heard at the Easter Vigil (see above).

Mary Magdalene went to the tomb on the first day of the week, literally on day one of the week, an expression which recalls Genesis and its account of day one of creation. Like the other evangelists at this point in their Gospel, John is announcing a new creation, a new beginning for the human race in Christ the Lord. The creative word of God was about to burst into the world and destroy all darkness, but when Mary went to the tomb it was still dark (Jn 1:4–5). For her the empty tomb was a sign of death and hopelessness.

Hearing of her experience, Peter and the disciple whom Jesus loved also went to the tomb. Early in the tradition, this disciple may have been an historical figure, but by the end of the first century he represented every Christian. Together the two saw not only that Jesus' tomb was empty but that everything associated with Jesus' death, the wrappings, had been left behind. The early Church thus presented the empty tomb as a symbol of resurrection, Christian hope, and eternal life.

The Breaking of Bread

The evening Mass for Easter Sunday presents the story of two disciples leaving Jerusalem in discouragement and going to Emmaus (Lk 24:13–35). On the way they met the Lord but were unable to recognize him. They presented their view to him, a seeming stranger, of what had happened, and Jesus proceeded to expand their understanding of the Scriptures so that they might see in them a reflection of what they had experienced. With this, they invited Jesus, still a stranger to them, into their home. In the sharing of bread with Jesus the stranger, their eyes were opened in recognition, and they returned to Jerusalem to share the good news with the assembled community.

This reading is vital for understanding how to interpret the Scriptures in personal and pastoral situations. Sometimes they remain opaque because our approach to them is too limited and we fail to look at all the Scriptures. We are also taught that to recognize our risen Lord in the breaking of bread, we must be able to extend Christian hospitality to those who are strangers to us.

This same account is read on the Third Sunday of Easter.

The Gift of the Spirit

The first day of the week, the day of the new creation and the day on which the early Christians first experienced the risen Lord, is also the day on which the Lord breathed the Holy Spirit on the Christian community (Jn 20:19–23) and on which the early Christians continued to experience the risen Lord, share their faith and proclaim it in the weekly assembly (Jn 20:24–29). On the Second Sunday of Easter we thus learn much about the origins of Sunday as well as about the first Easter. We also learn that John's Gospel did not try to present all of Jesus' signs, but only as many as would enable us to have faith and life in his name (Jn 20:30–31).

We should note that Jesus came with the witness of his wounds to bring peace to disciples who were afraid of being wounded, and he sent them on their mission as he had been sent on his. As Lord, he could now breathe into them a Spirit of new life, his own, as God had breathed his life into Adam. Like him they were to be reconcilers, and this brought with it a serious responsibility. If they withheld Christ's peace, many would never be reconciled.

The appearance to Thomas and the disciples on the following first day of the week develops some of the same elements for Christians who were far removed from the first experiences of the risen Lord. With Thomas we are called to hear the voice of the risen Lord in the life and message of the Christians who preceded us in the Church and to experience his presence in our Christian assembly.

The Shepherd and the Sheepgate

For the Third Sunday of Easter, see above, "The Breaking of Bread." The Gospel reading is Luke 24:13–35, which we read on Easter Sunday evening. On the Fourth Sunday, it is drawn from Jesus' discourse on the shepherd and the sheepgate (Jn 10:1–10).

The image of the shepherd and the sheep who recognize his voice is plain in itself, but becomes even clearer when we know that many shepherds led their sheep into the same large fold for the night. Early in the morning, each sheep responded to the voice of its respective shepherd who then led his sheep out over the hillsides for pasturing.

The image of the sheepgate is not immediately clear. It becomes a very powerful statement, however, when we know that the gate of the sheepfold, when closed, is what protected the sheep from anyone or from any animal that would destroy them. Jesus says that he is that gate. He lies across the entrance of the fold, and anything which would threaten the flock first has to deal with him. In effect, Jesus says that he is prepared to lay down his life for his sheep (see Jn 10:14–18).

The Way, the Truth, and the Life

In John 14:1–10 (Fourth Sunday of Easter), Jesus opens his last great discourse. He is going away. The disciples are disturbed that they do not know where he is going and that they consequently cannot know the way. In response, Jesus says that he is the way and the truth and the life. His work among them, his mission and his signs, have shown them where he is going. His teaching, which spoke not for himself alone but for his Father, is the truth which will guide them. His life, the life shared with them in the gift of the Spirit in which they are recreated, sustains them on the way.

The Spirit of Truth

We continue with Jesus' last discourse (14:15–21) on the Sixth Sunday of Easter, as Jesus promises the disciples another Paraclete, the Spirit of truth which will maintain them strong until he returns. The life they now see in Jesus they too will enjoy upon his return, when they will fully live in him and he in them. They will live the eternal life which like a seed already has been planted in them. The condition for entering into the fullness of life, for enjoying Christ's love and his self-revelation to them, is that they obey the commandments he has given them. Above all they are to love one another (see 13:34–35).

The Ascension

Forty days after Easter, Ascension Thursday interrupts the flow of readings from John's Gospel with a passage from Matthew, the great commission which concludes the Gospel (Mt 28:16–20). The setting is the mountain to which Jesus had called the disciples. As elsewhere in Matthew it is more fruitful to think of the mountain as the symbolic site of divine revelation than to seek its precise geographical location. In the fullness of his authority, Jesus commissions the eleven disciples—Judas is no longer with them—to baptize and to teach. It is to this passage that we owe the Trinitarian formula used in our baptismal liturgy today. After the commission, Jesus assures the disciples of his solidarity and undying fidelity. He will be with them always. This covenant-inspired statement is an invitation for them also to be with him always.

Parting Prayer

Jesus' long farewell discourse in John's Gospel ends with a prayer (17:1–26). Today's reading (the Seventh Sunday of Easter) includes the prayer's introduction, in which Jesus' concern is about the fulfillment of the mission given him by the Father (17:1–8) and the beginning of his prayer for the disciples (17:9–11a).

The hour has come, that critical moment alluded to so frequently in the course of the Gospel. The hour of Jesus, the time of his glorification, is one of the principal motifs of John's Gospel. Jesus' glory coincides altogether with that of the Father. It comes when he has fulfilled his mission and prepared the disciples to carry it on once he has returned to the Father.

Jesus' prayerful concern is especially for his disciples. His own glorification is inseparable from their life and mission. It is in them that Jesus, the risen Lord, is glorified.

That Nothing Be Lost

We are accustomed to viewing Pentecost through the eyes of St. Luke and the episode he presented in the Acts of the Apostles (Acts 2:1–13). We are also coming to see it through the eyes of St. John and the appearance of Jesus in which he breathes the Holy Spirit upon the apostles (Jn 20:19–23). In Cycle A of the liturgy, we see it through another passage in John (7:37–39).

The Spirit flows from Jesus, the one who has been glorified, as living water from which all who believe in Jesus can drink. The waters of Pentecost, which recall the water from the well at Samaria, are the waters of baptism. There is no Christian baptism apart from the gift of the Spirit, and the gift of the Spirit is inseparable from the presence of the risen Lord. Jesus, through the Holy Spirit and the baptismal waters, reaches out beyond his historical life that none of those he had taught and none of those who would draw near to him later would ever be lost. He truly accomplished the task assigned to him by the Father.

Introduction to the Easter Season

Each session for the Easter Season follows these steps:

  Opening Prayer
  Reflections
  Response
  Closing Prayer

In each session the reflection section contains up to seven suggestions for the catechist to use.

These sessions contain many creative ideas for prayer, all in keeping with the Easter season. The author incorporates the use of music, prayers, rituals, symbols and film into the opening and closing prayers. Catechists and prayer leaders will find these materials well organized, but should naturally feel free to adapt them as circumstances require.

There is also a wealth of material to choose from in the reflection section. Catechumens are invited to share their faith by reflecting on their experience of the liturgy and the symbols of Easter, and by probing the meaning of the Scriptures. Reflection on the characters in the Gospel stories and use of the Church's magisterium (e.g., documents of Vatican II) further enrich the process.

In the response section, an action or activity is proposed as a way of integrating the message of the Gospel and the season. Further readings are also provided for the catechist, as well as the catechumen or sponsor. Doctrinal and pastoral issues are also enumerated for each Sunday.

Easter Sunday

Acts 10:34, 37–43
Colossians 3:1–14 or 1 Corinthians 5:6–8
John 20:1–9

OPENING PRAYER

Make a special effort to decorate the room where the session will be held. Use the Easter symbols, especially a Christ candle and a bowl of water. These will be used during the session.

Play the Hallelujah Chorus from Handel's Messiah as the group gathers, or sing "Morning Has Broken."

Then lower the volume of the music and invite the group to reflect quietly before the Christ candle, water and other symbols. After a few minutes, invite participants to share a word or phrase that the symbols conjure up for them. Examples might be: light, washing, sun, fresh, life to the full, Christ, etc.

All pray: Peter and John,
Racing to the tomb
Not understanding the resurrection,
Believing in an empty tomb,
Be with us in our race to the tomb.
Pray for us!
All you women at the tomb,
Holding your oils and spices,
Symbols of your love for the Lord,
Women in love,
Pray for us!
(*Seasons of Your Heart*, Macrina Wieder-
kehr, O.S.B., Silver Burdett, 1979, p.
159.)

REFLECTIONS

(Catechists should choose from among the following according to the needs of the group and the time available.)

1. A table could be arranged with various symbols of Easter used in the home, as well as in church, i.e., Easter candle, water, eggs, butterflies, lamb cake, lilies, Easter bread.

   Note that the symbols bring together many meanings. Invite participants to discuss the many meanings of some of these symbols: for example, the water represents the exodus experience of passing through the Reed Sea, as well as washing and cleansing. In going down into the water of baptism, one goes down into the tomb with Christ and then rises with him to live with him.

2. If you attended the Easter Vigil, share some of your feelings as you prayed with those celebrating sacramental initiation.

   Ask participants to share: What symbols stood out for you in the celebration? Light? Oil? Fire? Symbols bring together many meanings. What did these symbols bring together and help you celebrate as you participated in the Vigil?

3. Review the Gospel story for today and ask yourself: If I put myself in today's Gospel reading, who would I be?

   (a) Mary Magdalene at the tomb early in the morning?
   (b) Mary running to tell Peter?
   (c) Simon Peter running to the tomb?
   (d) "the other disciple" looking in the tomb waiting for Peter?
   (e) inside the tomb seeing and believing?
   (f) one of the disciples not mentioned, still sleeping?

   Mark your selection and discuss your reasons for your choice. Make use of a journal to jot down your reflections if that helps you focus on the exercise.

4. The gospels of today and next Sunday are taken from Chapter 20 of John's Gospel. The emphasis of this chapter is belief in the risen Lord.

   Have a discussion with catechumens, sponsors, catechists, and spouses, sharing from their perspective:

   What does it mean to believe in the risen Lord?
   How is this belief present in the lives of believers today?

5. Much is written today about stages of development, or "passages in life." Each stage presents its own challenges, questions, turmoils, and doubts. We call the progression from one stage to another a development. This pattern of growth or development includes physical as well as psychological, emotional, spiritual changes. The separations or points where

one moves into another stage may be called transition points, or "passages." In religious terms we can call these experiences "passover points" since they lead a person from death to an experience of resurrection into new life.

Reflect on times in your own life when you recognize a pattern of "passing over"—that is, letting go of one stage in life or an experience in order to rise to new growth. You may want to write this reflection in your journal. Examples: separating from the family to make one's own place in the world; accepting one's growing children.

Reflect and share:
In what ways are these experiences part of living out the Easter mystery?

6. In the reading from the Acts of the Apostles, Peter announces that salvation is for all people. "In every nation he who fears God and does what is right is acceptable to him."

Vatican II reiterates this theme in the *Constitution on the Church* (especially in Chapter 2, "On the People of God").

"All men and women are called to be part of this Catholic unity of the people of God which, in promoting universal peace, presages it. And there belong to or are related to it, in various ways, the Catholic faithful, all who believe in Christ, and indeed the whole of mankind, for all men are called by the grace of God to salvation." (#13)

One definition of the word "catholic" is universal. Discuss: In what sense then are the readings from Acts and Vatican II "catholic"?

If catholic means universal, discuss why you are choosing or continue to choose the "Catholic" expression of faith.

RESPONSE

Consider and discuss how you will keep the joy of the Easter mystery alive in your life during the Easter season of fifty days.

Consider how the refrain Alleluia might be your prayer.

Alleluia is a Hebrew word used often during Eastertime. It is a proclamation of victory and salvation. Alleluia exclaims Praise! Joy! in the face of God's constant loving presence. In the new life of resurrection, Alleluia sums up the Christian's prayer. In the cry Alleluia! resurrection is experienced, not explained.

During the Easter season, let the Alleluia resound from within you.

CLOSING PRAYER

(Invite the catechumens and others to gather around the bowl of water.)

Invite the participants to come to the water and make the sign of the cross after dipping their hands in the water.

Song

"Sing A New Song" (St. Louis Jesuits, *Glory and Praise*, Volume I NALR) or another Easter song.

Further Readings

A Book of Family Prayer, Gabe Huck (The Seabury Press, 1979)
Believing in Jesus, Leonard Foley (St. Anthony Messenger Press, 1981) Chapter 7
Documents of Vatican II, Constitution on the Church, Chapter 2, *Decree on Ecumenism*
Hope for the Flowers, Trina Paulus (Paulist Press, 1972)
More Radiant Than Noonday, Loretta Girzaitis (Twenty-Third Publications, 1981)
Of Fast and Festival, Barbara O'Dea (Paulist Press, 1982)

Doctrinal and Pastoral Issues: Easter, Resurrection, Catholicity, Christian Initiation

Ellen Bush

Second Sunday of Easter

Acts 2:42–47
1 Peter 1:3–9
John 20:19–31

OPENING PRAYER

Day after day, O Lord of my life, shall I stand
  before thee face to face?
With folded hands, O Lord of all worlds, shall
  I stand before thee face to face?

Under thy great sky in solitude and silence,
With humble heart, shall I stand before thee
  face to face?

In this laborious world of thine, tumultuous
  with toil and with struggle,
Among hurrying crowds shall I stand before
  thee face to face?

And, when my work is done in this world, O
  King of kings,
Alone and speechless shall I stand before thee
  face to face? (*Gitanjali*, Rabindranath Ta-
  gore, The Macmillan Co., N.Y., 1971,
  #76, p. 91.)

and

Meditation Series, Ikonographics, Louisville
  Kentucky: Two-minute film spots "Faith"
  and/or "Peace"

REFLECTIONS

(Select as many from the following as appropriate according to the needs of the group.)

1. Reflect on the following, mark a selection, and share
   responses.

   If I were to imagine myself in the Gospel I would
   be:

   (a) one of the disciples locked in and afraid
   (b) rejoicing at seeing the Lord
   (c) Thomas, not present in the room
   (d) a disciple trying to convince Thomas the Lord
       has appeared
   (e) Thomas doubting
   (f) Thomas seeing the Lord

2. Share an experience when you heard news that was
   too good to be believed.

3. Discuss: Why was Thomas unwilling to accept the
   disciples' story of the resurrection? Was his attitude
   unreasonable?

   How does it compare with the reaction of the other
   disciples when the women told them of finding Jesus' empty tomb? (Lk 24:1–10)

4. Thomas is struggling with faith. Invite catechumens,
   sponsors, spouses to answer from their own perspective and experience: Are there aspects of "faith" or
   "the faith" that you wish you could "see" to believe?

5. Both the second reading and the Gospel speak of
   faith. Often this term is associated with the Catholic
   faith. Discuss the difference between belief in the
   sense of "beliefs" and "faith" in the sense of today's
   Scripture readings.

   The following may be of interest for your discussion:

   Faith is personal knowledge of God. Christian faith
   is personal knowledge of God in Christ. Faith is not
   primarily belief in truths (propositions) which have
   been revealed to us by God through the Bible and
   the Church; rather it is the way we come to the
   knowledge of God as God. The object of faith, in
   other words, is not a doctrine or a sacred text, but
   God, our Creator, Judge, and Savior.

   Faith always exists in some theological form. As a result of the process of articulating faith experience,
   formulations, called beliefs, can be made. There are
   many Christian beliefs, which take many forms.
   Some are widely shared and officially approved,
   while others are held by only select groups. The
   whole Church continues to evaluate its beliefs in
   light of ongoing experience.

   "The Faith" (composite of beliefs) should not be confused with the broader meaning of faith which include both one's relationship with God and its
   expression. (Based on *Catholicism*, Richard Mc-
   Brien, Winston Press, 1983, pp. 24–28)

6. "Mysteriously Jesus comes to the disciples in the
   upper room. They had failed him and must have
   wondered what he would say when he saw them. Jesus arrives in an unusual way and wishes them only
   peace. In the midst of human failure and sin, Jesus

offers forgiveness and hope for a better future. Into this context John has placed the commission of the Church to forgive sins." (*The Gospel of John*, John O'Grady, Pueblo Publishing Co., p. 90.) Discuss the following questions:

When do you feel peace?
Have you experienced the peace of Christ?
Are these times different from each other?
How does this context of penance and forgiveness affect your understanding of forgiveness?
Peace is God's gift through Jesus in the midst of failure and sin.
How can the Church mediate it?
Does the power to forgive belong to the entire Church or only to Church leaders?
Do you think that weak, sinful people should be given the power to forgive sin?
What is the Christian's commitment to peace?

7. Discuss the characteristics of the early Christian community described in the reading from Acts. Are these aspects of the Christian life-sharing, prayer, etc., evident in the Christian community you are joining?

In what ways are you participating in the "communal life, the breaking of the bread and the prayer" of the Christian community?

RESPONSE

List the obstacles to your "total adherence to God" and write your own prayer of faith in the risen Lord.

or

Share your thoughts on how you live out your Christian commitment to peace.

or

Make a point to talk with your sponsor about the "communal life, the breaking of the bread and prayer." What is his/her participation in these aspects of the Christian life? How can you and your sponsor share these more deeply?

CLOSING PRAYER

Song

"All My Days" (St. Louis Jesuits)

Prayer

Thomas
honest apostle

so able to acknowledge your unbelief
blessed, finally, through *seeing*
Bless us in our unseeing (John 20:24–29)
Pray for us!

And Jesus
asking us to trust the Father (Matthew 6:25)
calling us to full gospel living (Matthew 5:1–12)
washing our feet in service and love (John 13)
promising not to leave us orphans (John 14:16–18)
Help us to receive the Spirit that you've sent (Acts 2:1–4)
Pray for us!
(*Seasons of Your Heart*, Macrina Wiederkehr, O.S.B., pp. 159–160, Silver Burdett, 1979.)

Further Readings

A New Look at the Sacraments, William J. Bausch, Twenty-Third Publications, 1977 Chapters 11–13.
Catholicism, Richard McBrien, Winston Press, 1980, Chapter 2.
Sign of Reconciliation and Conversion, Monica Hellwig, Michael Glazier, Inc., 1982.
Stories of Faith, John Shea, Thomas More Press, 1980.
The Challenge of Peace: God's Promise and Our Response, A Pastoral Letter on War and Peace, USCC, 1983.

Doctrinal and Pastoral Issues: Faith, Beliefs, Creed, Doubt, Peace U.S. Bishops' Peace Pastoral

Ellen Bush

Third Sunday of Easter

Acts 2:14, 22–28
1 Peter 1:17–21
Luke 24:13–35

OPENING PRAYER

Song

Refrain: Will We See Him in the Breaking of the Bread?

Will we see Him in the breaking of the bread?
Will we recognize His body and His blood?
Will He fill our hearts with His presence as we share His life among us?
Will we see Him in the breaking of the bread?

(Mention that this meditation is based on the story of the disciples walking along the road.)

Meditation

Leader reads slowly, inviting participants to relax and listen reflectively.

> This is the after-resurrection walk! "Did not our hearts burn within us as he talked to us on the road?"

> Is this the Stranger whose coming we prepared for, by taking off our shoes and standing reverently on silent, holy ground? Is this the Stranger we stood on tiptoe for, with anxious, waiting hearts? Is this the Stranger who healed our brokenness, the One who washed our feet and carried a cross? Is this the Stranger we raced to the tomb to find? Do we race around like that to find each other?

> (pause for reflection)

> Who is a stranger, except someone whose heart we haven't met? And, until you've met a heart, it can hardly bless you, can it?

> The truth is that we've been blessed beyond telling by a Stranger who walked into our lives and showed us His heart, who wept our tears, lived our life, and died our death.

> It sounds simple and poetic, except that we've been asked to do the same; for this is the

> Stranger who, according to Paul, left within our hearts the same power He carried in His own. (Eph. 1:18–20)

> (pause for reflection)

> Trusting the stranger means we take off our shoes to prepare for the coming of each new person who walks into our lives. It means that we stand on tiptoe to wait for the coming of each person into the fullness of life. It means that we are willing to wash the feet of all these strangers and to let them wash ours. It means that we race to the tomb within them to celebrate the tomb's emptiness, which is life.

> Finally, it's a promise to walk with them on that journey of all journeys, the journey within. (*Seasons of Your Heart: Prayers and Reflections*, Macrina Wiederkehr, O.S.B., Silver Burdett Co., 1979, p. 136.)

Sing Refrain

REFLECTIONS

(Please choose from among the following according to local needs.)

1. Before sharing the following story, invite the participants to answer the question the rabbi asks:

   When might the night end and the day begin?

   Leader tells the following story:

   > The rabbi addressed his students with the question, "When might the night end and the day begin?" One of the rabbi's students offered the reply: "When you can see a tree in the distance and tell it is an apple tree or a pear tree." The rabbi answered, "No." Another student responded: "When you can see an animal in the distance and tell if it is a sheep or a dog." Again the rabbi said, "No." "Well," his students protested, "When *can* you tell that the night has ended and the day has begun?" And, the rabbi responded, "When you can look on the face of any man or woman and see that he is your brother, that she is your sister—because if you cannot, then

no matter what time it is, it is still night!"

Invite the group to compare their answers to the rabbi's question with that of the rabbi and his students.

In light of the rabbi's answer, discuss:

> When do you think the Resurrection became a reality in the lives of the disciples?
> When they saw the empty tomb?
> When their hearts were burning?
> When they invited the Stranger to eat with them?

After the participants have been given time to offer their opinions, suggest that the Resurrection does not equal the empty tomb. Instead, the Resurrection takes meaning in the lives of Jesus' disciples, when they were able to recognize Him in the face of the "stranger". Like the message of the story the rabbi told his students, it is when we can see the face of Jesus in the "least of our brothers and sisters," that the Resurrection becomes a reality and not merely a historical event for us. (Adapted from *Jesus: The Model Teacher, The Life-Experience Approach to Catechesis, Leader's Guide*, Thomas A. Brown, Wm. H. Sadlier, Inc., 1978, p. 11.)

Ask participants to state this idea in their own words.

2. Invite someone to read the following introduction:

> Each of us, like the disciples going to Emmaus, has a story to tell of discovering the Lord's presence in our lives. Let us share some of that story through discussion of the following:
> When are our eyes opened so that we recognize the Lord walking with us?
> When are our hearts burning as he speaks to us? (Personal prayer times? Listening to the word proclaimed in the liturgy?)
> What keeps us from recognizing the Lord in all the events of our daily lives?

3. Part of the story of discovering the Lord's presence in our lives centers around our attitudes and relationships with others. Share these thoughts and discuss the following questions:

> Strangers do not always have to be recognized in order for them to bless us. But, they do need to be trusted.

> The disciples did not recognize the Stranger on the road to Emmaus as Jesus until He broke the bread and vanished from their sight. However, their trusting the Stranger that He

was must have begun way back on the road when He first started to explain the Scripture to them; and, they invited Him to stay with them. This is to remind you that the Stranger you long to recognize as Christ must have to be trusted in some other form before this deeper recognition can take place. (*Seasons of Your Heart: Prayers and Reflections*, Macrina Wiederkehr, O.S.B., Silver Burdett Co., 1979, p. 137.)

> Do we ever trust or recognize the strangers who need encouragement, help, support, food, or clothing?

> Who have been the strangers along the way for us who have offered help, encouragement to us in any way?

> Did we recognize them as Someone else?

> In what ways is the mutual sharing of material, emotional, or spiritual goods an experience of "breaking bread"?

4. Discuss the following statement in light of the film "A Clown Is Born" (Mass Media, Baltimore, Maryland) or the following paragraphs.

> Sacraments do not make an absent God present, but celebrate the presence of God in creation and community in such a way that they are transformed.

Over the centuries people have attempted to describe their experience of Christ's presence, especially in the Eucharist. In periods of history when more static language was used, especially to describe sacraments, the focus was on the presence of Christ in the bread and wine. Since the start of the liturgical renewal, there has been a restoration of a more wholistic approach to sacramental theology. The presence of Christ in the liturgy flows out of the experience of his presence in the life of the community and in all of creation. The whole world is sacramental, or can be, in the eyes of a believer. Just as everything can be prayer, so everything can be a channel of grace, that is, a means of meeting Jesus.

"A much broader notion of Jesus' presence has also helped Catholics to understand the Eucharist. At one time, many Catholics saw Jesus as only present in this sacrament. Some past devotional materials pictured Jesus as lonely, waiting in the tabernacle for someone to keep him company. Now, however, Jesus is seen more as the dynamic savior who is present throughout the world, in his church, in the Word, in the sacraments, and in people's hearts. The significance of the eucharist is that it sensitizes us to the universal presence of the Lord. To commune with Jesus in the Eucharist is to be brought closer to the mystery of his presence in everyday life. There is a link between our discovering Jesus in this food and drink and our finding him in family members, friends, strangers, and the poor." (*Rediscovering the Sacraments, Approaches to the Sacred*, Brennan Hill, W.H. Sadlier, Inc., 1982, p. 63.)

During the liturgy (Mass) we experience the presence of Christ in many ways. The Constitution on the Sacred Liturgy of Vatican II speaks about some of these presences of Christ:

> To accomplish so great a work (salvation) Christ is always present in his Church, especially in her liturgical celebration. He is present in the Sacrifice of the Mass, not only in the person of the minister, "the same now offering, through the ministry of priests, who formerly offered himself on the cross," but especially in the eucharistic species. By his power he is present in the sacraments so that when anybody baptizes, it is really Christ himself who baptizes. He is present in his word since it is he himself who speaks when the holy scriptures are read in the Church. Lastly, he is present when the Church prays and sings, for he has promised: "Where two or three are gathered in my name there I am in the midst of them" (#7).

5. The theme of journey and pilgrimage recurs throughout the spiritual tradition of the Eastern and Western churches, as well as in literature. One of the images for the Church in the documents of Vatican II is that of the people of God, who are pilgrims while on earth.

The story of the search for the Grail is often understood as the western version of the spirituality journey. It might also be the story of each one of us and our own longing for wholeness.

Reflect and share on the following questions. Invite participants to apply them to their catechemenate journey, their spiritual journey, or their life journey, according to their needs.

What do you seek from this journey?
What has brought us to this quest?
What is your experience of the journey so far?
What shall we take with us on our quest?

RESPONSE

Try to examine your life at the end of each day. To do

this: Think back over the day and reflect on times you did recognize the Christ walking with you along the road of your day. Thank him for this gift of risen presence.

Think of the opportunities you passed by when you did not recognize him in the faces of your brothers and sisters. Thank him for all the faces and strangers you have met that day. Ask that these faces bless you as you close your day.

CLOSING PRAYER

Have a cup filled with wine or juice (a large water goblet would serve well) ready to share at the end of the prayer.

Leader: We go forth in the light of God's blessing; In the name of the Father, and of the Son, and of the Holy Spirit.

Reader: Then the disciples recounted what had happened on the road and how they had come to know him in the breaking of the bread. While they were still speaking about all this, he himself stood in their midst and said to them, "Peace be with you." (Lk 24:35–36)

Leader: Invites prayers of intercession

All: Disciples of Jesus,
hearts filled with pain on the road to Emmaus,
trusting that Stranger who walked beside you,
and, finally, recognizing him
in the breaking of the bread,
we, too, are on an Emmaus journey.
Pray for us!

Leader passes around the cup for all to share.

FURTHER READINGS/RESOURCES

The Book of Sacramental Basics, Tad Guzie, Paulist Press, 1980.
Documents of Vatican II.
The Eucharist and the Hungers of the World, Monica Hellwig, Paulist Press, 1976.
Hinds' Feet on High Places, Hannah Hurnard, Tyndale House Publishers, Inc., 1976.
Rediscovering the Sacraments: Approaches to the Sacred, Brennan Hill, W.H. Sadlier, Inc., 1982.
Solitude to Sacrament, Katherine Dyckman, S.N.J.M.

and L. Patrick Carroll, S.J., The Liturgical Press, 1982.

The Way to Christianity: In Search of Spiritual Growth, Richard Chilson, C.S.P., Winston Press, 1979. See especially the Introduction.

Doctrinal and Pastoral Issues: Eucharist, Journeying, Self-Examination, Critical Reflection, Liturgical Renewal

Ellen Bush

Fourth Sunday of Easter

Acts 2:14, 36–41
1 Peter 2:20–25
John 10:1–10

OPENING PRAYER

All pray together Psalm 23 (or use a sung version of your choice).

After a period of reflection (perhaps with background music) invite the catechumens to share:

How do you experience Jesus as the good shepherd? Which verse of Psalm 23 best describes your experience?

(Option: Show filmstrip "My Shepherd Is the Lord", Episode 16, *Little People's Scripture Stories*, Roa Films, 1979, along with praying Psalm 23.)

REFLECTIONS

(Please select from among the following the reflections that would be most helpful for your group.)

1. The image of Jesus as the good shepherd is more familiar than the first image in today's Gospel, that of Jesus at the gate to the sheepfold.

   Jesus is the way, the gateway to the Father.

   His allegory told in verses 1–5 simply describes a familiar scene to his listeners, that of the sheepfold where many sheep-herders take their sheep for the night. It was easier for the flocks to be kept safe from wild animals as well as thieves when they were inside stonewalled corrals. In the morning the sheep-herders came back to the gatekeeper to claim their sheep. The sheep would recognize their own master's voice and rejoin him for another day of grazing.

   The scene is so familiar to Jesus' listeners they miss the allegory. In the remainder of today's reading, Jesus draws out the meaning point by point.

   He begins with: I AM the sheepgate. To be safe from thieves you must go through me. You will go in and out and find pasture.

Discuss:

Are doors important? What does a door mean? Why would Jesus compare himself to a door?

Do you think Jesus would require any kind of "password" to go in and out when he is the gate? If so, what would it be? (What about something related to recognizing him in the faces of our brothers and sisters?)

2. Jesus describes the personal relationship between the sheep-herder and his sheep in noting that the sheep-herder calls his own by name.

Discuss:

Is it important to know people's names?

What does it imply when you know someone's name?

Does Jesus know your name? What does this imply?

Is intimacy important for faith?

Are there times we experience the voice of God as that of a stranger? Could it be that at these times we have forgotten who we are?

3. Who are the thieves and marauders in our lives?

4. Leader reads:

Jesus concludes today's selection with: I have come that they may have life and have to the full. A brief exploration of the relationship between "life in all its fullness" and the human emotion of happiness is appropriate.

People seek happiness and find it at times; but it is not complete. Different people seek happiness in different ways—in security, contentment, in abundance of material goods. Others seek happiness in escape from constant change and demands of human living. Even in the achievement of a lifetime goal, the victory of an athlete, the union of two persons in love and marriage, the birth of a son or daughter— all these are the occasions of intense happiness. Yet in each instance the happy person soon discovers that there is more to life than what has already been experienced.

Some people respond to this situation by saying:

Well, true happiness will come in heaven and we have to suffer here on earth.

The fourth evangelist offers another view. Happiness can be found here and now. Authentic happiness comes from our union with Jesus. In knowing Him, loving Him, in offering our lives to Him in service of others. Heaven will continue in greater intensity what has begun here on earth. (Adapted from *A Commentary on the Gospel of John*, Robert E. Obach and Albert Kirk, Paulist Press, 1981, pp. 147–148.)

Ask participants to discuss:

In light of this reading, how would you describe "life in all its fullness"?

5. Invite participants to discuss the following questions:

What leaders do you respect and follow? Why?
Is it possible for political leaders to follow the ideal of Jesus' leadership?
Who takes the place of the good shepherd in the Church today?
Can anyone take his place? Are there different kinds of shepherds in a parish?

The reading below may be of interest in the discussion.

As Jesus explained the meaning of his story (allegory) the audience could see the references to the prophetic words of Ezechiel. God had spoken to the prophet about how He would care for his sheep (Israel), not like the shepherds (kings, rulers) of the day. Corrupt leadership had led Israel into exile. God promised to lead them out.

Jesus refers to the words of Ezechiel as an indictment of the religious leadership of his own day. Such leadership is symbolized by the hired hand or worse, the thief. Their interest in the sheep is only self-interest.

As Jesus reveals his leadership, He is casting his light on all leadership. When He who is the Light of the World makes known the nature of a true shepherd, all shepherds are exposed to judgement. Jesus is the perfect leader; in Him lives the ideal of all shepherds of God's flock. He is the gate because He is the right approach to the sheep; his is the only true way of tending the flock. (*A Commentary on the Gospel of John*, Robert E. Obach and Albert Kirk, Paulist Press, 1981, pp. 140–141.)

6. Not everyone in our society experiences pastures or a table spread with food.

Discuss the following statement from the U.S. bishops' pastoral letter on the economy:

Though in the Gospels and in the New Testament as a whole, the offer of salvation is extended to all peoples, Jesus takes the side of those most in need, physically and spiritually. The example of Jesus poses a number of challenges to the contemporary Church. It imposes a prophetic mandate to speak for those who have no one to speak for them, to be a defender of the defenseless, who in biblical terms are the poor. It also demands a compassionate vision which enables the Church to see things from the side of the poor and powerless, and to assess lifestyle, policies, and social institution in terms of their impact on the poor. It summons the Church also to be an instrument in assisting people to experience the liberating power of God in their own lives, so that they may respond to the Gospel in freedom and dignity.

Finally, and most radically, it calls for an emptying of self, both individually and corporately, that allows the Church to experience the power of God in the midst of poverty and powerlessness. (*Pastoral Letter on Catholic Social Teaching and the U.S. Economy*, NCCB, USCC, 1985.)

Do you see any signs of the Church or its members living out this challenge?

How do you see yourself called to follow Jesus in a "preferential option for the poor"?

RESPONSE

Jesus is the lamb of the new covenant as well
as the good shepherd.
By his wounds we are healed.

We were delivered by Christ's blood beyond all price: the blood of a spotless unblemished lamb. Jesus was led like a lamb to the slaughter as an offering for sin. Christ is the paschal lamb who has conquered death.

The litany "Lamb of God" is prayed at the liturgy while the bread is being broken for Communion.

Find a way this week to share your bread with someone in need and pray the litany "Lamb of God."

Lamb of God, you take away the sins of the
world, have mercy on us.
Lamb of God, you take away the sins of the
world, have mercy on us.
Lamb of God, you take away the sins of the
world, grant us peace.

CLOSING PRAYER

Song

"Like a Shepherd" (St. Louis Jesuits, *Glory and Praise*, NALR)

FURTHER READINGS

A Commentary on the Gospel of John, Robert E. Obach and Albert Kirk, Paulist Press, 1981.

More Radiant Than Noonday, Loretta Girzaitis, Twenty-Third Publications, 1981.

Pastoral Letter on Catholic Social Teaching and the U.S. Economy, NCCB, USCC, 1985.

Servant Leadership, Robert Greenleaf, Paulist Press, 1980.

Solitude to Sacrament, Katherine Dyckman, S.N.J.M. and L. Patrick Carroll, S.J., The Liturgical Press, 1979.

Growth Through Meditation and *Journal Writing: A Jungian Perspective on Christian Spirituality*, Maria L. Santa-Maria, Paulist Press, 1983.

Doctrinal and Pastoral Issues: Pastoral Leadership, Economic Justice, Good Shepherd

Ellen Bush

Fifth Sunday of Easter

Acts 6:1–7
1 Peter 2:4–9
John 14:1–12

OPENING PRAYER

Read the Gospel (Jn 14:1–12) slowly three times. Pause after each reading for reflection. Explain that there will be an invitation for sharing after each reading, indicating what kind of sharing will take place.

After first reading invite sharing of words from the text that stand out for participants.

After second reading invite participants to share phrases or insights.

After third reading invite shared prayer.

REFLECTION

1. Invite participants to reflect privately, and then share on the following. (Perhaps they would benefit from writing reflections in a journal.)

   How is Jesus the Way *for you?* the Truth *for you?* the Life *for you?*

2. The prayer collection of our Jewish ancestors included references to "ways" and "paths." Discuss and pray the following texts from the psalms.

   > Yahweh, lead me in the path of your right-
   >   eousness,
   > for there are men lying in wait for me;
   > make your way plain to me. (Ps 5:8)

   > God, examine me and know my heart,
   > probe me and know my thoughts;
   > make sure I do not follow pernicious ways,
   > and guide me in the way that is everlasting.
   >   (Ps 139:23–24)

3. Jesus' exchange with Thomas and Philip in this text includes some statements of Christology. This means the Johannine text has Jesus speaking about his identity and role as understood by the Johannine community. Philip expected a dramatic revelation of Jesus' identity. Even in this Gospel, which emphasizes the divine Jesus always with the Father, doing what the Father wishes, Jesus reveals God in the human way to Philip.

   Discuss Philip and his role in the story. Do you feel like him sometimes? Share examples. Remember that he is a sign that we are all continuing on our journey of faith. The Easter celebration has been a new beginning.

4. In the Gospel, Jesus encourages his disciples to avoid being troubled and anxious. Despite our Lord's teaching, how many of us are continually worried and upset over all kinds of things?

   Discuss this statement: The disciple of Jesus should be marked by a certain kind of freedom from tension and anxiety.

   In what way is this realistic? Isn't it naive in a world of nuclear build-up and economic instability?

5. Discuss: " 'As Jesus does the works of the Father, so those who believe in Jesus will do these things also.' (14:12) Indeed, the believer will do even greater things, because Jesus is going to the Father. The idea of our doing greater things might puzzle us. Jesus has healed the crippled, given sight to the blind, raised up the dead, and revealed the Father. How can believers do greater things than these? The key to understanding can be found in 5:20: 'For the Father loves the Son and shows him all that He himself is doing. He will show him even greater things to do than this, and you will all be amazed.' Until his return to the Father, Jesus' works are only signs of his power to give eternal life. The streams of life-giving water (the Spirit) cannot be poured out until Jesus is raised to glory (7:39). When he returns to the Father, Jesus will do greater things through those who believe, through the preaching and sacraments of his Church." (*A Commentary on the Gospel of John*, Robert E. Obach and Albert Kirk, Paulist Press, pp. 193–194.)

   How are the "even greater things" which Jesus promised happening in your parish? in your town or city?

RESPONSE

Reflect on what "greater things" the Lord is calling me

to do this week. Record in journal and/or share.

CLOSING PRAYER

Share the following: See if the text reminds you of the Gospel reading.

Myself?

I sat there in awe as the old monk answered our questions. Though I'm usually shy, I felt so comfortable in his presence that I found myself raising my hand. "Father, could you tell us something about yourself?

He leaned back. "Myself?" he mused. There was a long pause.

"my name . . .
used to be . . .
Me.
                    But now . . . it's you." (*Tales from a Magic Monastery*, Crossroad, 1981.)

Further Readings

The Gospel of John, John O'Grady, Pueblo Publishing Co., 1982.
A Commentary on the Gospel of John, Robert E. Obach and Albert Kirk, Paulist Press, 1979.
To Know and Follow Jesus, Tom Hart, Paulist Press, 1984.
Jesus Is Lord: Basic Christology for Adults, Thomas Zanzig, St. Mary's Press, 1982.
Christology at the Crossroads, Jon Sobrino, Orbis Books.
A Spirituality Named Compassion and the Healing of the Global Village, Humpty Dumpty and Us, Matthew Fox, Winston Press, 1979.

Doctrinal and Pastoral Issues: Jesus—The Way, Truth, Life; Christology; Discipleship

Ellen Bush

Sixth Sunday of Easter

Acts 8:5–8, 14–17
1 Peter 3:15–18
John 14:15–21

OPENING PRAYER

What Does God's Spirit Do Within Me?

The Holy Spirit in me
Will make me want to sing,
To be whole,
To be good,
To be pure of heart,
To be full of strength and life,
To bear wrongs patiently.

The Spirit in me will make me want to dance,
To help out others,
To be thankful,
To be sorry for my sins,
To be happy and forgiven,
To be full of light and peace,
Calm and steady.

Each morning, facing the sun,
I will thank our Father for the gift of this day,
Hoping to live in harmony with Him,
With the earth, with every living being.
(*Finding a Way Home, Indian and Catholic Spiritual Paths*, Patrick J. Twohy, 1983, Leo Aspenleiter and The University Press, Spokane, p. 85.)

(If possible, show the film, "The Spirit of God"—Teleketics, with the prayer, Franciscan Communications, Los Angeles, California)

REFLECTIONS

(Please choose from the following according to the needs of the group. Allow sufficient time for the closing meditation.)

1. Jesus repeatedly insists on the connection between love and fidelity to his commandment(s). "The one who obeys the commandments he has from me is the one who loves me" (Jn 14:21). Jesus is referring to a whole lifestyle. Loving God and living according to his way cannot be separated.

What commandment(s) is he referring to?

What must a follower obey?

Can you tell the difference in your life between obedience out of obligation and obedience motivated by love?

What happens if one lives only by obligation and not by love?

2. At Jesus' request the Father will give "another healer" (14:16) to stay with the disciples. As "another" helper, the Spirit will continue the work of Jesus. While Jesus is our Paraclete with the Father, the Holy Spirit becomes the Helper on earth. He has not left us orphans!

Invite participants to share ways in which the Holy Spirit has been another helper in their lives.

3. Invite some Catholics who pray in a charismatic way to share their spirituality with the group.

4. In the second reading we are told, "Always have your answer ready for the people who have asked you the reason for the hope that you all have. But, give it with courtesy and with a clear conscience, so that those who slander you when you are living a good life in Christ may be proved wrong in the accusations they bring."

Reflect and share about the things that give hope.

Does hope mean hanging on until better days? Discuss this definition in light of the following paragraphs:

Traditionally, the virtue of hope was reviewed in an individualistic manner, i.e., *my* hope for *my* salvation. In recent years the virtue of hope has assumed a different meaning. It is that virtue by which we take responsibility for the future, not simply our individual future, but the future of the world.

Hope is oriented toward the Kingdom of God, not as heaven alone, but as the renewal and re-creation of the whole world. God is not above us, but ahead of us, summoning us to co-create the future. (*Catholicism*, Richard McBrien, Winston Press, 1980, p. 973.)

The joy and hope and anguish of the men of our time, especially of those who are poor or afflicted in any way, are the joy and hope, the grief and anguish of the followers of Christ as well. Nothing that is genuinely human fails to find an echo in their hearts. For theirs is a community composed of men who, united in Christ and guided by the Holy Spirit, press onward toward the kingdom of the Father and are bearers of a message of salvation intended for all people. That is why Christians cherish a feeling of deep solidarity with the human race and its history. (*Pastoral Constitution on the Church in the Modern World,* #1.)

Hope does not diminish the importance of our duties in this life, but rather gives them special urgency. (*Catholicism,* Richard McBrien, p. 975.)

5. In the second reading Peter makes it sound as if Christians can expect to be misunderstood.

What aspects of a Christian lifestyle today are most likely to bring misunderstanding?

Are we willing to risk misunderstandings?

Invite participants to share experiences of being misunderstood for their decision of becoming a catechumen or candidate.

RESPONSE/CLOSING PRAYER

(Leader will lead an imaging meditation. Invite participants to get in a comfortable position and ready to relax. You might wish to play soft music during the prayer. This is a prayer form using the imagination to enter into the experience of prayer. We will join the disciples in their experience of the promise of the Spirit.)

Leader: (Slowly and reflectively)

In your imagination go to an airport or place where you have said goodbye to a loved one. You feel left behind. You either want the other person to stay with you or you want to go with him/her, but you cannot.

You linger as the last glimpse of your loved one disappears from sight.

Think of the disciples as Jesus spoke to them at the Last Supper about leaving them to go back to his Father. They either wanted to go with him or not have him leave. What would they do without him?

Listen to Jesus promise: "I will not leave you orphaned; I will come back to you. I will ask the Father to give you another

Helper to be with you always."

Let these words speak to you, too. Pray for the strength from Jesus' Helper you need to live by love, not by obligation.

Pray, too, for the strength you need to help create the future you hope for.

Thank the Lord for the gift of the Holy Spirit.

When you are ready, come back to us here in this room.

(When everyone is finished with the meditative prayer, invite the group to close with the following prayer from the rite of confirmation:)

All: All powerful God, Father of our Lord Jesus Christ
By water and the Holy Spirit
You free your sons and daughters from sin
And give them new life.
Send your Holy Spirit upon us
To be our Helper and Guide.
Give us your spirit of wisdom and understanding,
The spirit of right judgment and courage,
The spirit of knowledge and reverence.
Fill us with the spirit of wonder and awe in your presence.
We ask this through Christ our Lord, Amen.

Further Readings

A New Look at the Sacraments, William J. Bausch, Twenty-Third Publications, 1983.
Believing in Jesus, Leonard Foley, O.F.M., St. Anthony Messenger Press, 1981. See Chapter 10.
Catholicism, Richard McBrien, Winston Press, 1980. See especially Chapter 26.
The Prophetic Imagination, Walter Bruggemann, Fortress Press, 1978.
Rediscovering the Sacraments, Brennan Hill, William H. Sadlier, Inc., 1982.
The Mustard Seed Conspiracy, Tom Sine, Word Books, 1981.

Doctrinal and Pastoral Issues: Commandment of Love, Prayer, Christian Lifestyles, Hope

Ellen Bush

Ascension Thursday

(Thursday after Sixth Sunday of Easter)

Acts 1:1–11
Ephesians 1:17–23
Matthew 28:16–20

OPENING PRAYER

Leader: May the God of our Lord Jesus Christ, the Father of glory, grant you a spirit of wisdom and insight to know God clearly (Eph 1:17).

All: Amen.

Song

"Dying You Destroyed Our Death" (Erich Sylvester, Vol. 1)

All: May God enlighten your innermost vision that you may know the great hope to which God has called you, the wealth of God's glorious heritage to be distributed among the measure of the church and immeasurable scope of God's power in us who believe. Amen. Alleluia. (Eph 1:18)

REFLECTIONS

(Catechists should choose from among the following according to the needs of the group and time available. After each reflection, allow for quiet time and suggest sharing in small groups.)

1. Two persons will reread the Gospel slowly—one the words of the narrator (Mt 28:16–18a), the other the words of Jesus (Mt 28:18b–20). As the Gospel is read, ask each participant to imagine that he or she is one of eleven disciples on a mountain in Galilee in a stance of homage to the Lord Jesus.

   The catechists can offer these questions for reflection:

   What is Jesus asking you to do?
   What are your feelings as you listen to the word of Jesus?
   What is the good news for you as you listen to the Gospel?

   After reflection, share and discuss.

2. In the Gospel, Jesus gives the disciples authority and sends them on a mission. The mission of the Church reflects and continues the mission of Jesus. As declared in the Vatican II documents, the mission is threefold: to preach, teach and serve.

   What is the meaning of the mission for me in my own life?
   How do I share in this mission?
   How do I carry out this mission?

3. From the Gospel, Jesus speaks these words to us: "Baptize them in the name of the Father, of the Son and the Holy Spirit." (From the first reading) "Wait rather for the fulfillment of my Father's promise, of which you have heard me speak. John baptized with water, but within a few days you will be baptized with the Holy Spirit." "You will receive power when the Holy Spirit comes down on you; then you are to be my witnesses, yes, even to the ends of the earth."

   God calls each of us. How is God calling me? Who is the Holy Spirit? How does the Spirit enter my life and empower my life? Have you ever experienced the presence of God's Spirit? Where and how did the experience take place in my life?

4. The ascension as an extension of the resurrection offers hope. Jesus makes this promise, "Know that I am with you always until the ends of the earth" (Mt 28:20).

   Have you ever been alone and experienced the presence of another? What was this experience? How do I experience the hope of Jesus' resurrection? Do I really trust in God's presence and care for me, others and the world? How do I witness Christian hope in my daily life?

RESPONSE

Consider and discuss:

What are the gifts the Spirit brings? How do I use these gifts for serving others with whom I live? What is your experience of the Holy Spirit?

Come, Holy Spirit, come!

CLOSING PRAYER

All: Come, Holy Spirit, and fill our hearts and enkindle in us the feeling of love. Send forth your Spirit and we shall be re-created. We shall renew the face of the earth. Amen. Alleluia.

Song

"On Eagles' Wings" (Michael Joncas, *Glory & Praise* Vol. 2, NALR)

Suggested Readings

The Cost of Discipleship, Dietrich Bonhoeffer, New York, Macmillan & Co., 1969.

The Documents of Vatican II, Austin Flannery (ed.), (specifically the Dogmatic Constitution on the Church), Grand Rapids, William B. Eerdmans Publishing Co., 1984.

A Future To Hope In, Andrew M. Greeley, New York, Doubleday, 1970.

Doctrinal and Pastoral Issues: Call of God, Mission of the Church, Discipleship, Christian Hope, Role of the Holy Spirit

Joseph P. Sinwell

Seventh Sunday of Easter

Acts 1:12–14
1 Peter 4:13–16
John 17:1–11

OPENING PRAYER

Leader: Today we will pray in a way that can be called the prayer of quiet or centering. In this prayer way, we use a word or phrase for centering ourselves, to focus on the presence of God.

The psalm for this week offers some possible words and/or phrases. We will pray over the psalm to select our centering words, and then pray with the words we choose.

(Invite participants to pray with the psalm in whatever way you choose. They might read the text privately or someone could read it very slowly—Psalm 27). Invite them to choose a word or phrase they would like to pray with, e.g., The Lord is my salvation; have pity on me; dwell in the house of the Lord.

Invite them to repeat the phrase over and over quietly in their hearts.

Fr. Basil Pennington, author of *Centering Prayer*, gives four simple rules to follow in this prayer way:

(1) Relax; at the beginning, take a few minutes to quiet down and then move in faith to God;
(2) After resting a bit in the quiet, take a single text that expresses your feelings and begin to let it repeat itself within;
(3) When in the course of the prayer we become aware of anything else, gently return to the prayer word(s);
(4) At the end of the prayer take several minutes to come out, and mentally pray the Our Father. (*Finding Grace at the Center*, Abbott Thomas Keating, O.C.S.O., M. Basil Pennington, O.C.S.O., Thomas E. Clarke, S.J., St. Bede Publications, 1978, pp. 10–21)

Lead the prayer experience, allowing enough time for participants to relax, get into the prayer and come out of it slowly.

REFLECTIONS

1. The reading from the Acts of the Apostles speaks of the disciples gathered with Mary in the upper room. "Together they devoted themselves to constant prayer."

   Catechists should choose from among the following suggested reflections on prayer according to the needs of the group.

   Have a discussion on the experience of the centering prayer just experienced. Was it enjoyable? Difficult? Have you ever prayed this way before?

   Invite participants to write their definition of prayer in their journal and share with the group.

   Invite participants to write their reflections on the statement: "It is impossible not to pray," and share their reflections with the group.

2. In today's Gospel, Jesus prays to his Father: "Father, the hour has come! Give glory to your Son that your Son may give glory to you."

   In John's Gospel the hour of suffering is the hour of glory for Jesus. In his being lifted on the cross, he is raised up to live with his Father.

   The more we become involved with the Lord, suffering and glory will be indistinguishable in our lives, too.

   The reading from Peter exhorts us to rejoice insofar as we share Christ's sufferings.

   After brief reflection discuss: What helps us to recognize suffering as a sign of glory?

3. "Glory" is prayed about in various prayers in the liturgy.

   Discuss the meaning of "glory" in the following prayer texts and be aware of these meanings when you participate in the liturgy.

   The Gloria is an ancient hymn in which the Church, assembled in the Spirit, praises and prays to the Father and the Lamb. It is prayed during the eucharistic liturgy on Sunday.

   Glory to God in the highest, and peace to his people on earth.

Lord God, heavenly King, almighty God and
Father.
We worship you, we give you thanks, we
praise you for your glory.
Lord Jesus Christ, only Son of the Father,
Lord God, Lamb of God,
You take away the sin of the world, have
mercy on us;
you are seated at the right hand of the
Father, receive our prayer.
For you alone are the Holy One, you alone
are the Lord,
you alone are the most High, Jesus
Christ,
with the Holy Spirit, in the glory of God
the Father. Amen.

After the Lord's Prayer, we pray:

Deliver us, O Lord, from all anxiety as we
wait in joyful hope for the coming of our Savior, Jesus Christ.

For the kingdom, the power, and the glory
are yours, now and forever.

4. Discuss what you think is meant by "the kingdom,
the power and the glory."

Discuss whether or not you agree with the following
statement:

The Church is a sign of the glory of the kingdom. She is a sign that God's kingdom will be
made out of the ordinariness of human flesh.
She is a sign that the kingdom will be built out
of our world, by common people with feeble
talents who work and succeed only by the
power of God. (*An Introduction to the Faith
of Catholics*, Richard Chilson, Paulist Press,
1972, p. 102)

Pray the Doxology: Glory to the Father, and to the
Son, and to the Holy Spirit, both now and forever.
Amen.

5. Discuss what you think Jesus means when he speaks
of *knowing* the only God and Jesus Christ whom he
sent. Is it possible to *know* God? List two ways if
you answer Yes. (Remember that "knowing" in Hebrew thought expresses an intimate, loving union.)

6. Jesus goes on to say that *eternal life* is knowing God
in the one he sent, Jesus Christ.

Eternal life is salvation. Jesus brings salvation. Each
person must decide to accept it or fall into judgment, here and now.

Usually we think of judgment and eternal life taking
place in the future. They are the "last things." In

John's Gospel, however, the future takes place in
the present.

The traditional "last things"—death, judgment,
heaven, hell—fall into an area of study called eschatology. In John, eschatology is already realized. In
one sense there are no last things, for they have already been realized.

Does the idea of "realized eschatology" make any
difference in how you live your daily life?
If eternal life is now, is there an afterlife?

7. As the Church approaches Pentecost, how do you
pray for the outpouring of the Holy Spirit?

RESPONSE

Try to pray the centering prayer way at least once during the week. Let a "love word" surface from your
thoughts of God during the day.

CLOSING PRAYER

(Have several readers take paragraphs)

The Light Within Us

"You are the light of the world" (Mt 5:13)

Let us dare to say
That in the midst of awful stillness,
In the midst of anguish, darkness, emptiness,
There dwells complete, mysterious Light.

This is the Light
That forms our minds and hearts.
This is the Light
That falls on the words
Of our mouth
Making them alive and shining.

This Light is ready to emerge, break forth,
Even through the most broken
Minds, hearts, and bodies.

Light wishing to be born,
To be as it is,
Wonderful, Peaceful, Alive.

This light within us and within all things
Needs to enkindled
By our feeble acts of love,
Our emptiness, our reaching out.

Yet It is always there,
Greater than the force of a thousand suns,
Ready to shine through our eyes,

Tired with weeping,
And lighten up the whole world.

OR

Show filmstrip "With Open Hands" (Alpha Corporation)

Further Readings

An Introduction to the Faith of Catholics, Richard
    Chilson, Paulist Press, 1972.
A Book of Family Prayer, Gabe Huck, The Seabury
    Press, 1979.
A Commentary on the Gospel of John, Robert E. Obach
    and Albert Kirk, Paulist Press, 1981.
Finding Grace at the Center, Abbott Thomas Keating,
    O.C.S.O., M. Basil Pennington, O.C.S.O.,
    Thomas E. Clarke, S.J., St. Bede Publications,
    1978.
The Gospel of John, John O'Grady, Pueblo Publishing
    Co., Inc., 1982.
Solitude to Sacrament, Katherine Dyckman, S.N.J.M.
    and L. Patrick Carroll, S.J., The Liturgical Press,
    1982.
*A Spirituality Named Compassion and the Healing of
    the Global Village, Humpty Dumpty and Us*, Mat-
    thew Fox, Winston Press, 1979.
Stories of God: An Unauthorized Biography, John
    Shea, The Thomas More Press, 1978.
With Open Hands, Henri J.M. Mouwen, Ave Maria
    Press, 1975.

*Doctrinal and Pastoral Issues: Prayer, Liturgy, Eccle-
siology, Eschatology, Reign of God*

Ellen Bush

Pentecost Sunday

Acts 2:1–11
1 Corinthians 12:3–7, 12–13
John 20:19–23

OPENING PRAYER

Song

"Spirit of the Living God"

REFLECTIONS

(Please choose from the suggested "Reflections" according to local needs. Allow time for the closing prayer. Candles are needed for each participant if the meditation is used.)

1. The Pentecost event we celebrate today took place on what was a feast of Pentecost at the time of the disciples. It was a pilgrimage feast for the Jewish people in Jerusalem to thank God for the gathering of the harvest and celebrate the covenant. Like all Jewish festivals, Pentecost was not merely a commemoration of the Sinai event; rather it celebrated the continuous presence and activity of God in the lives and history of his people.

   Now, a new thing happens. On this covenant feast a powerful wind from heaven was heard throughout the house where the followers of Jesus were assembled. In Hebrew the same word "ruah" signified "wind" and "breath." That word appears in another important passage. In the Book of Genesis when God first created the human race, he "breathed" into Adam "the breath of life" (Gen 2:7). That was the first creation. What we have in the Pentecost narrative is the bold affirmation that here the Spirit of God had breathed life into a new creation. The wind of Pentecost created a new people of God. It is the culmination of the covenant begun at the death-resurrection of Jesus. At Pentecost the Church celebrates both that initial event and the coming of the Spirit on each generation of believers. (Adapted from *Of Fast and Festival: Celebrating Lent and Easter*, Barbara O'Dea, D.W., Paulist Press, 1982, pp. 62–63.)

   Review Exodus 24:12–18 with the participants and invite them to compare the story with that of Pentecost told in Acts 2:1–11.

   Sometimes this feast is called the "birthday of the Church." In light of this reading, discuss why this is appropriate.

   Discuss: In what way do we believe that the Lord breathes life in us?

2. In the forming of a covenant relationship with God both the action of giving and receiving were important. The Lord revealed to Moses in thunder and lightning and gave him tablets of the law; but, that was not enough. There was a need for response. Moses, face radiant with blinding light, descended the mountain, and presented the law to the people. Having listened to the words, they responded with one voice, "All that the Lord has said, we will do." In Jewish tradition both actions were significant: the giving of the law by God and the receiving of the gift by the people. These two acts of offering and acceptance constituted the covenant. (Ibid, #1, p. 61.)

   The Spirit is Christ's inestimable gift to the Church. In the Gospel Jesus invites his disciples: Receive the Holy Spirit. Gift given, gift received. Two factors of the covenant.

   Reflect and discuss how you are a part of a covenant relationship with God.

   What is our responsibility to make this gift of the Spirit still received and lived out in the Church?

3. In the story of the Pentecost event, we are told that the apostles went out and "began to express themselves in foreign tongues and make bold proclamations as the Spirit prompted them."

   From the New Testament evidence it seems that there were two types of tongues: the one, an ability to speak in a foreign language; the other, to speak ecstatically. The latter would consist in charismatic acclamations in response to the Spirit's operation in the soul. The Pentecost phenomenon perhaps included both types. The disciples speak in languages understood by pilgrims and travelers, from many different nations. Here one speaks in one tongue, there someone replies in another. It need not have been that a single individual spoke and was understood at the same time by persons of various tongues. That some were giving expression to unintelligible ecstatic experience would seem to have prompted the mocking comment, "They are full of new wine." (*The New Testament Reading Guide—The Acts of the Apostles*, Neal M. Flanagan, O.S.M., The Liturgical Press, 1964, pp. 27–28.)

Discuss experiences or attitudes you have about "speaking in tongues." What is your understanding of this passage?

In what ways do we have a commission like the apostles to go out and speak to others of the Lord?

4. Paul is also talking about the Holy Spirit and the spread of the Church to all nations and languages. But mostly he is intent on telling us all to use whatever talents and gifts God has given us within the body of Christ that are for the good of all. There are different ministries, but the same Lord.

How do you see your talents as part of that gift of the Spirit given to each person for a good purpose?

The Spirit was sent by Jesus to unite his followers into a community of people, the Church, whose task is to continue the work of Jesus. List three ways that you, as an individual, can unite with the Church in continuing Jesus' work.

5. Discuss this statement: "The gift of the Holy Spirit is not a gift to be kept to oneself."

6. Luke, the author of Acts, is making a definite point in referring to the folks from many countries being able to understand the message about Jesus. His point is that the Spirit of God is a gift for all people. At that time there was a certain feeling among some that followers of Christ would have to be Jews first. Luke is emphasizing the universal good news.

" . . . the wind was heard *all* through the house."

"*All* were filled with the Holy Spirit."

"Devout Jews of *every* nation were staying in Jerusalem."

Describe how this gift of the Spirit should influence our attitudes toward persons who are different or who live in different countries.

7. The apostles did not know what they were waiting for after Jesus told them to wait until they were clothed with power from on high. After the Holy Spirit came at Pentecost, they were filled with confidence to spread the good news of Jesus. Describe in your own words a time you were confused and unsure and then discovered the confidence to grow and act in a new way.

RESPONSE

Reflect and write in your journal:

> The gift I have received from the Spirit which I am most grateful for is . . .

Reflect and write in your journal about how you will live out this gift this week.

CLOSING PRAYER—FIRE MEDITATION

Before moving into the closing meditation on fire, invite participants to reflect and share some of the following ways fire is part of our lives.

What are some of the different forms fire can take: campfire, fire on hearth, sun, lightning, summer heat, electricity, fireworks

other . . . . . .

What are your usual contacts with fire? cooking, sunbathing, candlelight, lightning, cigarettes

other . . . . . .

What are the properties of fire? heat, radiance, light, consuming, movement, action

other . . . . . .

When do you feel or act in fire ways that are helpful? warming others, filled with enthusiasm, letting light shine

other . . . . . .

What is it like to have too much fire? flaring up, boiling over, raging, having an acid tongue, burned-up

other . . . . . .

What is it like to have too little fire? burned out, low in spirits, lack of energy, gray, no spark

other . . . . . .

Fire Meditation

Each person will need a lighted candle for the meditation and a comfortable place to sit undisturbed.

1. Invite participants to be seated. Tables will be helpful as the flame of each person's candle needs to be at eye level. Place candles about a yard from each person, the flame at eye level a little below the eyes.

2. Invite participants to focus with simple attention on the flame. Encourage them to let all noises, sights in the room, and thoughts about the day slip away as they concentrate on the flame.

   Let them know that their eyes will naturally close. The flame will then be on the back of their eyelids. Invite them to continue to focus on this internal flame. Don't think about it, just experience it. Let it be. When it gets faint, open the eyes again and repeat the process of focusing and letting the eyes close.

3. Say: Let the flame draw you to your center. Picture the flame there, in your center. Let it live in you. Feel its warmth. Let it illuminate our whole being and then radiate out.

4. As a transition back to the room and being with others, invite participants to repeat or hum a favorite refrain. (*The Woman Sealed in the Tower*, Betsy Caprio, Paulist Press, 1982, pp. 79–81.)

Further Readings

Growth Through Meditation and Journal Writing: A Jungian Perspective on Christian Spirituality, Maria L. Santa-Maria, Paulist Press, 1983.

Of Fast and Festival—Celebrating Lent and Easter, Barbara O'Dea, Paulist Press, 1982.

Original Blessing, Matthew Fox, Bear and Co., 1983.

The Treehaus Catechetical Filmstrip Library of Basic Christian Teachings, Vol. 3, "The Holy Spirit Gift of Life." Set of four filmstrips with guides.

The Way to Christianity: In Search of Spiritual Growth, Richard Chilson, Winston Press, 1979.

The Woman Sealed in the Tower, Betsy Caprio, Paulist Press, 1982.

Doctrinal and Pastoral Issues: Holy Spirit, Charisms, Gifts and Fruits, Symbols

Ellen Bush

Trinity Sunday

(Sunday After Pentecost)

Exodus 34:4b–6, 8–9
2 Corinthians 13:11–13
John 3:16–18

OPENING PRAYER

Leader: Glory be to the Father, to the Son and to the Holy Spirit,

All: As it was in the beginning is now and ever shall be, world without end. Amen.

Song

"What You Hear in the Dark" (Daniel Shutte, S.J., *Glory & Praise*, Vol. 2, NALR)

> God, we praise you.
> One God three persons,
> be near to people
> formed in your image,
> close to the world.
> Your love brings life. Amen
> (From the morning prayer of the Liturgy of
>   the Hours for Trinity Sunday.)

REFLECTIONS

(Catechists will select from the following as appropriate to the needs of the group. After each reflection, allow for quiet time and suggest sharing in small groups.)

1. "The Lord is a merciful and gracious God, slow to anger and rich in kindness and fidelity."

   Reflect and share how you have experienced the graciousness of God the Creator, the mercy of God the Son and the fidelity of the Holy Spirit in your life.

2. Remember someone who loved and loves you and important times with that person. What are the qualities of that person's love for you? How did and does this person enhance your faith life and growth? After silent reflection ask participants to share their reflections as an experience of God the Trinity giving life.

3. Read and reflect on John 3:16. Consider these questions: What experience in your life helps this passage come alive? What happened? Who was present? What meaning does the experience have now in light of the above Scripture passage.

4. The Trinity is an expression of God as community and unity. Reflect on the second reading (2 Cor 13:11–13). The words of this letter encourage conversion, support, peace and hospitality as a way of building community. List the strengths and weaknesses of these qualities in your Christian family and/or community. How can I encourage the strengths and heal the weaknesses?

5. The world is God's creation. "God did not send his Son to condemn the world." After reflection, ask participants to discuss the following: How do I redeem/save creation? How do I respond to social sin and evil, e.g., materialism, consumerism, abuse of power, etc.?

RESPONSE

Consider and discuss the following:

How can I make fresh in my life and world the love of God who is the loving parent, who is a compassionate friend, and who is a faithful caring spirit?

What do I need to change? Remember that God cared for you with an everlasting, unconditional, merciful love.

CLOSING PRAYER

All pray together:

> Father, Son and Holy Spirit,
> we praise you and give you glory.
> We bless you for calling us to be your holy
>   people.
> Remain in our hearts and guide us in your
>   love and service.
> Help us to let our light shine before others,
> and lead us to the way of faith.
> Holy Trinity of love,

we praise you now and forever. Amen.
(From *A Book of Blessings*, Canadian Conference of Catholic Bishops, 1981)

Song

"Doxology" (Bob Dufford, S.J., *Glory & Praise*, Vol. 1)

Suggested Readings

Catholicism, Richard McBrien, Winston Press, 1981.
Becoming Catholic, J. Killgallon, M. O'Shaugnessey,
    G. Weber, ACTA Foundation, 1980.
Rich in Mercy, John Paul II, United States Catholic
    Conference, 1981.

*Doctrinal and Pastoral Issues: Trinity, Love of God and
Others, Building Christian Community, Social Responsibility*

Joseph P. Sinwell

Feast of Corpus Christi

(Second Sunday After Pentecost)

Deuteronomy 8:2–3, 14b–16a
1 Corinthians 10:16–17
John 6:51–58

OPENING PRAYER

(Read aloud thoughtfully. Pause after the invitation and again before the closing.)

Leader: Let us pray:
God, you offered food to the Israelites in the desert. Now through your Son, you offer the bread of everlasting life to us. Open our hearts to receive your Spirit. May we become one in mind and heart. Help us to heal the divisions that separate us. Guide our reflection and sharing. We ask this in the name of Jesus, the bread of life.

All: Amen.

Suggested Song

"One Bread, One Body" (John Foley, S.J., *Glory & Praise*, Vol. 2, NALR)

REFLECTIONS

(From the following, the catechist chooses the one(s) most appropriate to the local needs and, after each reflection, allows quiet time and encourages discussion in small groups.)

1. The Eucharist is a symbol and sacrament of unity. We are called to celebrate in the breaking of Jesus' body and blood at the table of the Lord. Talk about the Eucharist. Tell a story of a family or community meal or celebration where you experienced unity with others. Listen to each other's stories. How do the stories differ? What are key similarities and differences? How do these relate to your understanding and belief in the Eucharist?

2. When we come together to celebrate the Eucharist, we witness to being members of the body of Christ. We are brothers and sisters in the Lord, sharing in God's life.

When you have worshiped at the Eucharist, what has been your experience of Jesus and community? Reread the Gospel. The Gospel emphasizes Jesus' giving of his body and blood as life-giving. How do you enliven in your daily life and the life of others? How have you failed in the last week to give life to others, e.g., through support, care, listening, presence, etc.? Write in your journal one thing that you want to remember about the Eucharist and one way concerning how you can improve being a life-giver.

3. We are the body of Christ, the Church of Christ. Read 1 Corinthians 10:16–17 slowly. How do you experience the diversity of the body of Christ? Name and list the ways in which members of the body of Christ are united and divided from one another? (Allow the entire group to share their lists.) How do you encourage or cause these divisions in your own life? Name one attitude or behavior you need to change to begin to heal these divisions.

CLOSING PRAYER

Choose and place a cup (metal, pottery or glass) in a prominent place. Explain its significance: The blessing cup is a tradition we can use. The cup can become a sign of unity—oneness in prayer, blessing and concern.

Leader: Father, we ask your blessing on us all as we dedicate this cup together, in the name of the Father, and of the Son, and of the Holy Spirit.

Read Scripture

1 Corinthians 10:16a

Is not the cup of blessing we bless a sharing in the blood of Christ?

Petitions

(Leader's part can be shared by different participants)

Leader: May this cup symbolize our care for each other, Lord, we pray.

Response: Bless us, Lord.

Leader: May it represent a shared love which

grows by your grace each day, Lord, we
pray. RESPONSE.

Leader: May it be a sign of the trust that we have
in you and in each other, Lord, we pray.
RESPONSE.

Leader: May we willingly share our hopes, dreams
and fears, our joys and disappointments
around this cup of blessing, Lord, we pray.
RESPONSE.

Collect

Leader:

Holy be this cup which we raise in blessing. May we grow in a sense of mutual love
sharing in this one cup.

Sharing of the Blessing Cup

(The cup is passed around the entire group)
Pray together the Our Father or sing "Earthen Vessels"
(John Foley, S.J., *Glory and Praise*, Vol. 1, NALR.)
(Adapted from *The Blessing Cup* by Rock Traunikar, St.
Anthony's Messenger Press, 1979)

Suggested Readings

Sacraments and Sacramentality, Bernard Cooke,
     Twenty-Third Publications, 1983, Mystic, Conn.
Eucharist from Kingdom Come Series, George Mc-
     Cauley, Argus Communications, Texas, 1978.
*The Church: Communion, Sacrament and Communica-
tion*, Robert Kress, N.Y., Paulist Press, 1985.
The Promise of Paradox, Parker J. Palmer, Notre
     Dame, Ave Maria Press, 1980.

*Doctrinal and Pastoral Issues: Eucharist, Body of
Christ, Ecclesiology, Personal and Social Sin, Conversion, Community*

Joseph P. Sinwell

ORDINARY TIME

Jesus and His Teaching

Part I: The Law

By Eugene A. LaVerdiere

In this first series of Sundays in Ordinary Time, most of the Gospel readings are taken from Matthew's Sermon on the Mount (Mt 5—7), a brilliant synthesis of the law of Christ, from its introduction, the Beatitudes (5:1–12) to its conclusion on the need to put the Christian way of life into practice (7:24–27).

For the First Sunday, see the last Sunday of the Christmas season, the Baptism of the Lord, with which it coincides. The Second Sunday, in which John witnesses to Jesus as the Lamb of God and God's Chosen One, the Suffering Servant of the Lord, evokes the climax of Jesus' life and mission, the passion-resurrection, as he begins his public life (Jn 1:29–34). The Third Sunday's Gospel calls and gathers the early disciples (Mt 4:12–23), who will then gather around Jesus on the mount of Christian revelation to hear him set out his vision, mission, law and way of life (Fourth to Ninth Sundays).

The Lamb of God

Every Gospel witnesses to the fact that John the Baptist was the last and most important figure preparing the way for Jesus and his mission. This is reflected in the lectionary, not only on the Second and Third Sundays of Advent (Mt 3:1–12; 11:2–11) but also on the First Sunday in Ordinary Time, which celebrates the baptism of the Lord (Mt 3:13–17). On the Second Sunday in Ordinary Time, John again has a prominent role as one who publicly witnessed to Jesus (Jn 1:29–34).

John's presentation is very different from that of the Synoptic Gospels. First, in John 1:29–34 (see also 1:19–28), the Baptist's hesitation about the identity of Jesus is alluded to as something of the past, in contrast with Matthew 11:2–11 and Luke 7:18–28, where he sends messengers to inquire whether Jesus is the one who is to come. Second, John's Gospel never mentions that Jesus was actually baptized by John. Rather, it emphasizes John's role as a witness that Jesus is the Lamb of God and God's chosen one, both of which probably refer to the Suffering Servant of the Lord (see Is 42:1) who was led like a lamb to the slaughter as an offering for sin (see Is 53:7, 10).

Call of the First Disciples

Nazareth is the town where Jesus had been brought up (see Lk 4:16). Capernaum is where he lived as an adult, and it is along the shore of the Sea of Galilee that he began to preach and that he called his first disciples (Mt 4:12–23). Such is the theme for the Third Sunday in Ordinary Time.

After John had been handed over, Jesus took up his mission, proclaiming the very message which had led to John's arrest: "Reform your lives! The reign of God is at hand" (4:17; see 3:2). Knowing what had happened to John, Jesus recognized the risk he was taking. One day he too would be arrested and handed over.

The disciples were called from the midst of their work to be Jesus' associates in his life and mission. Their lives would never be the same. From the very beginning, Matthew mentions that Simon is now called Peter (4:18; see 10:2 and 16:13–19). For Luke, Peter's role is to lead the Church and strengthen his brothers and sisters, especially in moments of crisis. For Matthew it is to be the rock foundation of the Church. Following Jesus brought a whole new set of relationships which transcended family ties and a total commitment to the reign of God Jesus was announcing. The disciples could no longer be ordinary fishermen.

The Beatitudes

The Beatitudes (Mt 5:1–12) constitute the introduction for Jesus' Sermon on the Mount, in which Matthew gathered many sayings of Jesus into a great synthesis of Christian living. The Sermon on the Mount is the law of Christian discipleship. The mountain which Jesus ascends to interpret the old law and present the Christian way of life is not so much geographical as theological, the place where revelation is given, as had been the case at Sinai.

The Beatitudes (Fourth Sunday in Ordinary Time) present Jesus' challenging vision in a form characteristic of wisdom literature: "Blessed are . . . for they shall." Note, however, that for the poor in spirit (5:3) and those who are persecuted for righteousness' sake (5:10), we read: "Blessed are . . . for theirs is," since the reign of God has already broken into the world in the life and teaching of Jesus. The reason that the poor in spirit, those who mourn, etc., are blessed is not that they are poor in spirit or because they mourn, but because they have been granted the kingdom of God and they shall be comforted. The good news is proclaimed to the poor. The form of the last Beatitude is very different. In it, Jesus speaks directly to the persecuted community of Matthew. The other Beatitudes must have formed a rhetorical whole framed by "Theirs is the kingdom of God" (5:3, 10) before its addition.

A Prophetic Challenge

The Sermon on the Mount began by presenting the human reversals characteristic of the reign of God, the Beatitudes, as they are commonly called (Fourth Sunday). After this vision statement, it continues with a short mission statement (5:13–16), Jesus' prophetic challenge to those he had called (Fifth Sunday in Ordinary Time).

Jesus addressed his disciples directly, using two images to describe who they are, the salt of the earth and the light of the world. The disciples' mission is as vital as salt is to life and light is for sight. Like Jesus (see 4:16), the disciples must let their light shine that others might see the goodness in their mission activity—not, however, for the disciples' glory but that all might praise their heavenly Father. In Matthew 6:1–18, this last point is further developed and applied to religious acts in general and to giving alms, praying and fasting in particular.

The Fulfillment of the Law

In the Gospel for the Sixth Sunday in Ordinary Time, we continue our reading of Jesus' Sermon on the Mount (5:17–37). After the vision and mission statements of 5:1–12 and 5:13–16, attention turns to the interpretation of the law and the prophets for the followers of Jesus.

First, a number of general principles affirm that the righteousness, or justice, of Jesus' disciples must surpass that of the scribes and Pharisees (5:17–20). In 5:21–48, we are then shown how this is to be realized. Jesus presents six areas, four of which are taken up in today's reading, in which the Christian commandment goes beyond what the disciples were accustomed to hearing in the synagogues from the Pharisees and the scribes. In these antithetical statements, which treat of murder, adultery, divorce, oaths, retaliation and hatred of one's enemies, Jesus shows how the law and the prophets are fulfilled, not abolished, by his teaching. Fulfillment of the law, in this context, is not limited to the mere observance of the law. Rather, it refers to ful-

fillment in the way we speak of prophecy being fulfilled. The law and the prophets are fulfilled and perfected in the new revelation brought by Jesus, and unless the disciples live by this new revelation, they will not enter the kingdom of heaven.

Loving One's Enemies

The Gospel for the Seventh Sunday in Ordinary Time includes the last two antithetical statements concerning the fulfillment of the law (Mt 5:38–48). In Jesus' new law, the old law of retaliation, "An eye for an eye, a tooth for a tooth" (Ex 21:24; Lv 24:20; Dt 19:21), is completely revoked. Its purpose, which had been to prevent endless feuding and loss of life, is now positively fulfilled in the spirit of Christian generosity, which extends to the needy as well as to anyone who strikes a Christian.

This fifth antithesis is closely related to the sixth and last concerning love. The commandment to love one's neighbor is clearly biblical (Lv 19:18), but the commandment to hate one's enemy is not. Matthew attributed it to the interpretation heard in the synagogue. It is this interpretation that Jesus revokes. Our heavenly Father loves everyone, the good and the bad, the just and the unjust. His children must do the same. Christians must love everyone including their enemy. Otherwise their righteousness would not even be greater than that of the pagans.

Undivided Commitment

The Fourth to the Seventh Sundays in Ordinary Time gave us a continuous reading of Matthew 5 in its entirety. We then pass over Matthew 6:1–23, part of which is read on Ash Wednesday (6:1–6, 16–18) and take up Matthew 6:24–35 (Eighth Sunday), in which Jesus speaks of the need for an undivided commitment and service: "You cannot serve God and money." The disciples have too little faith. They are anxious and they worry about their earthly needs, and this distracts them from their commitment to God and the kingdom. If they sought the reign of God, their other needs would be met. For his own children, our Father has a provident love which goes far beyond his ordinary providence.

Putting the Word into Practice

The readings from the Sermon on the Mount end with a statement on Christian prophecy and the Sermon's general conclusion. Jesus has given his disciples a charter for Christian living, a new law of righteousness. The theme on this Ninth Sunday is that it is not enough to hear and proclaim Jesus' word. His disciples must put it into practice.

It is not enough to acclaim Jesus as Lord, to prophesy, to cast out demons and to work miracles. Ecstatic prayer and doing extraordinary things are nothing unless the disciples also do the will of Jesus' Father as he has just revealed it. Those who do not will never enter the kingdom of God (7:21–23).

Nor is it enough to hear Jesus' word. Again it must be put into practice. The parable ends with a parable about two men, one wise (he puts Jesus' words into practice), the other foolish (he does not), both of whom built a house, one on the rock, the other on sand. The house built on the rock withstood the storm, the other did not (7:24–27). When Jesus ended the discourse, all recognized that he did not teach like the scribes. He taught with authority. In his voice, they heard the ring of God's word.

Introduction to Sundays 2–12 in Ordinary Time

Each catechetical session in this section contains the following parts:

> Looking at Life
> Sharing Your Life
> Knowing Our Faith
> Making the Faith Our Own
> Living Our Faith
> Prayer

Additionally, the *basic message* of the Sunday readings is summarized in a few words. This focuses the session and assists the catechist in planning.

As an aid to prayer, the responsorial psalm of the day is noted at the end of each session. The catechist may wish to expand the prayer time by inviting the catechumens to pray spontaneously, and by summarizing the session with a prayer drawn from additional sources. After the prayer concludes, allow some time for informal discussion and socializing.

The method followed in these sessions moves from experience to tradition to application. In Looking at Life and Sharing Your Life the catechumens are invited to reflect and share on an aspect of their lives that relates to the basic message. In Knowing Our Faith, the group listens again to a reading of the Gospel. Discussion starters are offered to lead the group into a deeper understanding of the Gospel and to appropriate it in Making the Faith Our Own. Living Our Faith suggests directions and possibilities for putting this dimension of faith into practice. Finally, the Doctrinal and Pastoral Issues most relevant to the readings are highlighted.

2nd Sunday in Ordinary Time

Isaiah 49:3,5–6
1 Corinthians 1:1–3
John 1:29–34

BASIC MESSAGE: The Value of Witnessing

LOOKING AT LIFE

The catechist calls the catechumens and sponsors together and invites them to sit in a circle. He or she greets them and begins the session. Recall a witnessing situation. It may be a witness to an accident, a signing of a document, a witness in a court of law, or for a marriage annulment.

Allow time for individual reflection and small group sharing on these questions:

What did you say or do at that time?
About whom were you giving witness?
To whom were you giving witness?
Were you contested in your witnessing?

SHARING YOUR LIFE

Allow for discussion and continued reflection on these questions:

Why were you called to be a witness?
Why did you give that witness?
Why would you be a witness for any situation?
What was the cost of your witnessing?
What is the value of a good witness?
What are the characteristics of a good witness?
Why would you witness on behalf of Jesus?
Why was John the Baptist a good witness?

KNOWING OUR FAITH

Read, reflect and dialogue about John 1:29–34.

Catechist chooses from following topics areas suited to local needs.

Point out and discuss with candidates

– John not recognizing Jesus at first.

– John recognizing Jesus through the power of the Holy Spirit.
– John recognizing Jesus as the one who takes away the sins of the world.
– The symbolism of the dove symbolizing the Holy Spirit descending upon Jesus.
– The "chosen one of God" is the one in whom the Holy Spirit dwells.
– That Jesus is the one who baptizes with the Holy Spirit.
– That Jesus witnesses to the Father through the Holy Spirit. At this point the catechist could develop some aspect of the doctrine of the Trinity.
– Why John was a good witness. At this point the catechist could develop some of the witnesses to Jesus throughout the centuries. These are the martyrs and saints. Examples you could use are St. Stephen, St. Paul, St. Lawrence, St. Augustine, St. Francis, St. Thomas More, St. Elizabeth of Hungary or St. Elizabeth Ann Seton.
– Discuss the cost of discipleship.

MAKING THE FAITH OUR OWN

John the Baptist, other martyrs and saints throughout the ages were witnesses to Jesus "the chosen one of God."

What was the cost of their witnessing?
What were the consequences of their witnessing:

– to themselves?
– to others?
– to the Church throughout history?

How does your witnessing to Jesus compare to that of John and the martyrs and saints you have reflected upon?
What does this tell you about death and resurrection?

LIVING OUR FAITH

Would you like to become a better witness of Jesus, "the chosen one of God"?
What will this witnessing look like?
What will be the cost of this witnessing?

When will you begin this witnessing?
Who will support you in this witnessing?

PRAYER

Responsorial Psalm

Ps 40
R/. Here I am, Lord! I come to do your will.

*Doctrinal and Pastoral Issues: Christian Witness, Holy
Spirit, Trinity, Discipleship*

Michael Koch

3rd Sunday in Ordinary Time

Isaiah 8:23–9:3
1 Corinthians 1:10–13, 17
Matthew 4:12–23

BASIC MESSAGE: Life After a Tragedy

LOOKING AT LIFE

The catechist calls the catechumens and sponsors together and invites them to sit in a circle. He or she greets them and begins the session. Begin by telling or asking a participant to tell what he or she did after a tragedy. Examples could be:

– A family member got killed in a car accident.
– A spouse unexpectedly walked out of a marriage.
– A fifteen year old daughter got pregnant.
– Your best friend is diagnosed as having terminal cancer.
– You lost your job because you did not cooperate with corruption.
– You were financially swindled by a business partner.

What was your first reaction?
When and where were you when you got the news?
Who was the first to comfort you?
What did you decide to do after the tragedy?
Were you able to pick up the pieces and continue on?

SHARING YOUR LIFE

Why did you react to the tragedy as you did?
Why did you decide to pick up the pieces and go on rather than give up?
Why can a tragedy be a turning point in life?
How do you think Jesus felt after he got the news that his friend and relative John had been arrested, imprisoned and beheaded after speaking the truth?

KNOWING OUR FAITH

Read, reflect and dialogue about Matthew 4:12–23.

Catechist selects topics from following areas suited to local needs to point out and discuss with participants:

– The reason for John's arrest, imprisonment and beheading.
– The witnessing of John for the truth.
– The meaning of this turning point in the life of Jesus, moving from his home town of Nazareth and settling in Capernaum.
– The fulfillment of the prophecy from Isaiah 8:23—9:1 in the first reading.
– The return of Israel to God begins in pagan-infiltrated Galilee with Jesus' message, "Repent, for the kingdom of heaven is close at hand."
– The first to respond to Jesus' preaching are Peter and Andrew, James and John, who become his first disciples and participate in Jesus' mission.
– The cost of discipleship.
– The proclamation of the good news followed by cures.
– A new light shines in Israel.
– Read, reflect and dialogue about 1 Corinthians 1:10–13, 17.

Point out and discuss:

– The tragedy of the divisions among the Corinthian Christians.
– That following a disciple of Christ too exclusively, rather than Christ, can bring division into the Christian community.
– That a person is baptized into Christ and not into a human leader.

MAKING THE FAITH OUR OWN

The tragedy of John's death, was a turning point for Jesus. He consolidated all his efforts to be about "the Father's business."

– How was your tragedy a turning point?
– Did you imitate Christ?
– How was your tragedy an opportunity to draw closer to Christ and live a more profound Christian life?

Partisanship brought tragedy to the Corinthian Christian community. Paul boldly spoke up and preached reconciliation.

– How were you able to forgive and be at peace with the person or events which caused the tragedy in your life?
– Do you feel closer to Jesus now? to Paul?
– What does this tragedy tell you about death and resurrection?

LIVING YOUR FAITH

What valuable things did you learn from your tragedy?
How can you use your tragedy for your own good?
Would you like to share what you learned from your
    tragedy?
With whom are you going to share this new reality?
When are you going to share this new insight into life?

PRAYER

Responsorial Psalm

Ps 27
R/. The Lord is my light and my help.

*Doctrinal and Pastoral Issues: Death and Dying, Suf-
fering, Forgiveness, Cost of Discipleship*

Michael Koch

4th Sunday in Ordinary Time

Zephaniah 2:3, 3:12–13
1 Corinthians 1:26–31
Matthew 5:1–12

BASIC MESSAGE: *The Beatitudes—a blueprint for Christian living*

LOOKING AT LIFE

The catechist calls the catechumens and sponsors together and invites them to sit in a circle. He or she greets them and begins the session. Invite the participants to enumerate some secular values and preoccupations.

Examples are:

– Climbing the economic ladder.
– You have to be tough in this world to succeed.
– If you don't get the other guy first, he'll get you.
– Every man for himself.
– Fight for your rights.
– Charge as much as the market can bear.
– If you don't look after yourself first, no one else will.

Catechist points out some advertisements and commercials where these attitudes are predominant.

SHARING YOUR LIFE

(Provide time for quiet reflection and sharing)

Why do so many people believe and hold to some or all of the above attitudes?
Why are they poor attitudes?
What would life be like if everyone held the above attitudes and lived them out?
Have you ever been tempted to buy into these attitudes?
Why did you pursue these attitudes?
Why did you decide to relinquish these attitudes?
Why must there be better attitudes than the above?
Why would Jesus refuse to hold such attitudes?

KNOWING OUR FAITH

Catechist selects appropriate topic from those listed below.

Read, reflect and dialogue about Matthew 5:1–12.

– That this is the beginning of St. Matthew's Sermon on the Mount.
– When Matthew wrote, "Jesus went up the hill," he was trying to show that Jesus is the new Moses who is giving a new teaching, a new law. "There he sat down . . ." When a Jewish rabbi was teaching officially he sat down. This indicates that this is Jesus' official teaching.
– That the Sermon on the Mount is not a single sermon, but Matthew's compendium of Jesus' teaching.
– That Jesus is the Beatitudes par excellence.
– That the Sermon on the Mount is Jesus' ordination address to the Twelve.
– That the Beatitudes are not addressed to all the people indiscriminately, but to the disciples, to those who have left all to follow Jesus (those who have become catechumens).
– That each Beatitude has two parts. The first part describes the humiliation of the present; the second, the glory to come.
– That the followers of Jesus recognize their poverty, their creatureliness, their dependence upon God.

MAKING THE FAITH OUR OWN

The Beatitudes are profound Christian teaching.
How do the attitudes and values you hold compare with the attitudes and values given in the Beatitudes?
Do you believe the Beatitudes make a good program for spirituality?
Do you believe Jesus lived the Beatitudes?
How do you feel toward Jesus after studying the Beatitudes?

LIVING OUR FAITH

Are your attitudes and values in need of revision?
Would you like to model your life on the Beatitudes?
What will be the cost of this conversion?
When will you begin?
How much time will you allocate for prayer so that the Lord may achieve this conversion and growth in you?
Whom will you call upon for support?

PRAYER

Responsorial Psalm

Ps 146
R/. How happy are the poor in spirit; theirs is the kingdom of heaven.

or some other prayer.

*Doctrinal and Pastoral Issues: Beatitudes, Vision of
God's Kingdom, Conversion*

Michael Koch

5th Sunday in Ordinary Time

Isaiah 58:7–10
1 Corinthians 2:1–5
Matthew 5:13–16

BASIC MESSAGE: *Our Christian Vocation*

LOOKING AT LIFE

The catechist calls the catechumens and sponsors together and invites them to sit in a circle. He or she greets them and begins the session. Begin by discussing the taste of a meal to which no salt has been added.

How did you feel about that meal?

Discuss the value of salt as a substance which:

– enhances the taste of food.
– can be used as a preservative.
– in ancient times was used as payment, hence salary.
– in ancient times was used to seal covenants of friendship.

Discuss your experiences during an electrical power failure:

– What could you do or not do in the dark?
– How did you manage to get around in the dark?
– How did you help others get around in the dark?
– How could you find someone in the dark?
– What evils could happen in the dark?

SHARING YOUR LIFE

Why would you not tolerate food without salt?
Why should you make some effort to see to it that electrical power and light are restored after a breakdown?
Why do you think Jesus referred to his disciples as:

– "you are the salt of the earth"?
– "you are the light of the world"?

KNOWING OUR FAITH

Read, reflect and dialogue about Matthew 5:13–16.

Catechist chooses appropriate issues for reflection.
Some samples are:

– That this passage is the continuation of the Sermon on the Mount.
– The significance of the statements being in the present tense "you are . . . " and not in the future tense, "you will be . . . "
– Compare Jesus' statements, "I am the light of the world," and "You are the light of the world." Note the identity of Jesus with his disciples.
– Our Christian vocation, which flows from, "In the same way your light must shine in the sight of men, so that, seeing your good works, they may give the praise to your Father in heaven."
– How the symbols of salt and light help us to identify our Christian vocation.
  Like salt, those in union with Christ can help give better taste and joy to life; they can help preserve Christian values.
  Like light, those in union with Christ can help others to see where they are going; they can be beacons pointing to Christ.
– "Seeing your good works" in relationship to the first reading from Isaiah 58:7–10.
– Doing what Isaiah 58:7–10 says is being the salt of the earth and the light of the world.
  Promoting *social justice* is a very important part of our Christian vocation. At this point the catechist could familiarize the catechumens with the Church's social teaching. The catechist could expose the catechumens to the papal social encyclicals and documents from Pope Leo XIII to Pope John Paul II. The catechumens should also be introduced to the social teachings of the American and Canadian bishops.

MAKING THE FAITH OUR OWN

We are good followers of Christ if we are the salt of the earth and the light of the world. We are salt and light when we do the "good works" described by Isaiah 58:7–10.

What quality of salt and light would you rate yourself?
What have you done to make Isaiah 58:7–10 a reality?
How familiar are you with the Church's social teaching?
What contribution have you made to social justice?

LIVING OUR FAITH

Would you like to be better Christian salt and light?

Would you like to help make Isaiah 58:7–10 a reality?

Would you like to read and study some of the papal social encyclicals?

When are you going to start this study?

Where can you implement this teaching?

Who will support you in this effort?

Where are you in need of conversion?

How do you feel toward Jesus at the end of this session?

PRAYER

Responsorial Psalm

Ps 112
R/. The good man is a light in the darkness for the upright.

You may wish to have some spontaneous prayer to conclude.

Doctrinal and Pastoral Issues: Call of God/Christian Vocation, Social Encyclicals, Social Responsibility, Symbols of Salt and Light

Michael Koch

6th Sunday in Ordinary Time

Sirach 15:15–20
1 Corinthians 2:6–10
Matthew 5:17–37

BASIC MESSAGE: *The Moral Behavior of the Christian*

LOOKING AT LIFE

The catechist calls the catechumens and sponsors together and invites them to sit in a circle. He or she greets them and begins the session. The catechist could begin by asking for an enumeration of different philosophies people use to determine their moral behavior. Examples are materialism, secularism, hedonism, stoic, Hinduism, Islamism, Christianity, consumerism, communism, etc. Also give concrete examples of the above philosophies.

SHARING YOUR LIFE

Why do various people choose these philosophies as a way of ordering and living one's life?

Why do many people choose "the self" around which everything must revolve?

Why have you chosen not to follow these ways of life?

Why do you have difficulty in purifying yourself of these ways of behaving?

Why was Jesus not satisfied with any of the above?

KNOWING OUR FAITH

Read, reflect and dialogue about Matthew 5:17–37.

Catechist points out and discusses one or more of following areas:

– There are five antitheses, as they are called. They are teachings on murder, adultery, oaths, revenge and loving your enemy.

– The first three are in today's Gospel. The last two are found in next week's Gospel.

– "Do not imagine that I have come to abolish the law or the prophets." Matthew quotes this against the Gnostics who held that everything should be destroyed and restart from scratch. Jesus shows the continuity of the past, present and future.

– Jesus broke the oral or scribal law many times (for which he was hated by the scribes and Pharisees) but he never deviated from the Ten Commandments and other principles.

– Jesus taught that the underlying attitudes toward the law should be *reverence* and *respect*—reverence for God, reverence for his name, reverence for God's day, respect for parents, respect for life, respect for personality, respect for property, respect for truth, respect for another's good name, and respect for oneself. This reverence and respect flows from mercy not sacrifice, from love not legalism.

– "You have learned how it was said to our ancestors. . . . But I say this to you. . . . " This shows that Jesus spoke with great authority. Jesus boldly reinterpreted the old law and makes a new law for his kingdom.

– A desire is generated in the heart; it is formulated, conceptualized and judged good or evil by the mind. The ego encourages, tolerates or aborts it. The swollen desire, with the approval or the overriding of the ego, may then go on to be verbalized and finally acted out.

Discuss Jesus' understanding of human nature and that in his kingdom external behavior regulated by law was not good enough. In his kingdom inner motives (which only God can see) must also be included for total integrity.

– In the old law murder was evil. In the new law selfish anger and destruction of another's reputation is also evil. Verses 23 and 24 show that peace between brothers and sisters must be dealt with before a sacrifice is acceptable to God. Verse 25 shows that trouble should be sorted out and not allowed to pile up to make worse troubles for the future.

– In the old law adultery was evil. In the new law a lustful look and divorce are also evil.

– In the old law breaking an oath was evil. In the new law any swearing is also to be avoided. Respect for the truth should be so profound that even a *yes* or *no* means being serious.

– Discuss how moral decisions are made.

MAKING THE FAITH OUR OWN

Moral behavior is an important element in Christian living.

How does your view on murder, adultery and oath-taking compare with Jesus' teaching?

Is there an area in which you need greater clarification?

Is the Church's teaching today faithful to the teaching of Jesus?

Would you challenge the Church on its moral teaching?

LIVING OUR FAITH

How would you like to help make the moral teaching of Jesus more viable in the Church?

Do you have a problem with anger belittling others?

How do you feel toward Jesus at the end of this session?

Are you prepared to pay the cost of discipleship?

When are you going to get started?

Who will be your support?

PRAYER

Responsorial Psalm

Ps 119
R/. They are happy who follow God's law.

You may wish to have some spontaneous prayer to conclude.

Doctrinal and Pastoral Issues: Moral Decision Making, Law, Christian Morality

Michael Koch

7th Sunday in Ordinary Time

Leviticus 19:1–2, 17–18
1 Corinthians 3:16–23
Matthew 5:38–48

BASIC MESSAGE: *The Christian Attitude of Non-Violent Living*

LOOKING AT LIFE

The catechist calls the catechumens and sponsors together and invites them to sit in a circle. He or she greets them and begins the session. The catechist could bring up the question of violence. List places in the world where there is violence. Examples are: Northern Ireland, Lebanon, South Africa, Nicaragua. Include conflict relationships, such as management and labor, Israelis and Arabs, and the superpowers.

What is going on in these conflict situations?
What is to be gained by continuing these conflicts?
Who are the victims in these conflicts?
Do you have enemies you prefer to hate?
Have you been tempted to exercise revenge?
How do you feel towards the statement "Revenge is sweet"?

SHARING YOUR LIFE

Why are there places of conflict in the world?
Why do people tolerate so much suffering and property destruction?
Why is there such a deep desire to "get even" in the hearts of men and women?
Why is it so hard to trust a stranger?
Why is revenge futile?
Why did Jesus not accept the teachings "An eye for an eye and a tooth for a tooth" and "Love your neighbor and hate your enemy"?

KNOWING OUR FAITH

Read, reflect and dialogue about Matthew 5:38–48.

Catechist selects topic relevant to group's issues:

– The Gospel today is about the last two of the five antitheses.
– The "eye for an eye and tooth for a tooth" injunction in the Old Testament was not meant to sanction revenge but to restrict it. You might look at it in this way.

Prior to Moses the practice was two eyes for one eye and two teeth for one tooth, i.e., pay back with interest. Three eyes and three teeth are destroyed.

In Leviticus 24:19 we see an improvement. The teaching is one eye for one eye and one tooth for one tooth. Both parties are now equal. Two eyes and two teeth are destroyed.

Jesus teaches no eyes for an eye and no teeth for a tooth. Offer the wicked man no resistance. The outcome is the destruction of one eye and one tooth, but it is the eye and the tooth of the non-violent person. Following Jesus' teaching causes the least amount of violence. If the other person followed the teaching of Jesus there would be no loss of an eye or loss of a tooth. There would be peace. If we follow Jesus, the best we can expect is to lose my eye and my tooth, which is another way of saying a Christian can expect to be crucified. Revenge has no place in the kingdom of God.

– "You must love your neighbor and hate your enemy." For the Jews in the days of Jesus, loving your neighbor meant a fellow Israelite. It was not considered sinful to hate a Gentile.

Jesus points out that the love of God makes us all brothers and sisters. Jesus expands the understanding of neighbor to mean anyone. You could point out the story of the good Samaritan in Luke 10:29–37.

MAKING THE FAITH OUR OWN

Where do I stand vis-à-vis revenge and loving my enemy?
Reflect on the profoundness of Jesus' teaching.
Who are the models in our time that we can be inspired by and imitate?
Examples are Mahatma Gandhi, Martin Luther King, and Pope John Paul II forgiving Ali Agga.
Where are the opportunities in my life for exercising such Christian attitudes?

LIVING OUR FAITH

What do you think of Jesus and his teaching on revenge and loving your enemy?

Would you like to live more in the imitation of Jesus?

What areas of your life are in need of further conversion?

What will it cost to imitate Jesus more closely?

Are you ready to pay that price?

When are you going to get started?

PRAYER

Responsorial Psalm

Ps 103
R/. The Lord is compassion and love.

You may wish to conclude with some spontaneous prayer.

Doctrinal and Pastoral Issues: Social Justice, Non-Violence, Social Sin

Michael Koch

8th Sunday in Ordinary Time

Isaiah 49:14–15
1 Corinthians 4:1–5
Matthew 6:24–34

BASIC MESSAGE: *The Christian Attitude toward Material Possessions*

LOOKING AT LIFE

The catechist calls the catechumens and sponsors together and invites them to sit in a circle. He or she greets them and begins the session. Ask the participants to reflect for a moment on their material possessions.

Do you now have the material possessions that you need?

Would you like to own more material things?

How much time do you spend earning, spending and worrying about material possessions?

How worried are you about security in the future, especially in old age?

How do poor people handle future security?

Are you envious of the material possessions of others?

SHARING YOUR LIFE

(Allow for period of reflection and then discuss.)

Why do you want to own more material possessions?

Why are you envious of the material possessions of others?

Why do you worry about future security?

Why do you think owning much in the way of material things gives you status and worth?

Why do many people put more trust in material goods than in other people? in God?

Why do you think Jesus pointed out the folly of trying to "be the slave of both God and of money"?

KNOWING OUR FAITH

Read, reflect and dialogue about Matthew 6:24–34.

Point out and discuss:

– The characteristics of a slave in the days of Jesus.
  • the slave was not considered a person but a thing.
  • the slave had no rights of his own.
  • the slave had no time which was his own.
– Our relationship to God.
  • before God we have no rights.
  • God must be the undisputed master of our lives.
  • the Christian has no time off from being a Christian.
– Money, or, better, mammon, becomes perverted when a man puts his ultimate trust in material things. Then material things become, not his support, but his god.
– The relationship between ownership and stewardship.
– The three basic principles which undergird Jesus' teaching:
  • All things belong to God.
  • People are always more important than things.
  • Wealth is always a subordinate value.
– How a man, a company or a country acquires its possessions.
  • at the expense of honesty and honor.
  • at the expense of the weak.
  • at the expense of a higher value, e.g., human life, God.
  • at the expense of hard work, cooperation and ingenuity.
– How a man, a company or a country uses its possessions.
  • not use it at all, e.g., hoard it.
  • use it completely selfishly.
  • use it as power to destroy someone or something else.
  • use it to free self and others for higher values.
– The divine providence of God. Jesus teaches that a man must not worry about his future security. Jesus knows the basic human needs, food, drink and shelter. Jesus teaches that his Father who creates and treasures human life will also see to it that whatever is necessary to sustain it will also be available.
– That worrying about future security is a sign of mistrust and weak faith in God. Worrying is a sign that we do not believe God loves us.
– Our worrying contributes nothing to our ultimate outcome.
– That worrying destroys the joy of seeing the presence of God now.
– Read and enjoy the first reading, Isaiah 49:14–15.

MAKING THE FAITH OUR OWN

(Reflect and discuss)

How big is the gap between what Jesus teaches about material possessions and your position?

Do you really believe that trusting God is safer than trusting in material possessions?

Do you really believe Jesus when he says worrying about our future security adds nothing to our life?

Do you really believe Jesus when he teaches us to live one day at a time: "Tomorrow will take care of itself."

LIVING OUR FAITH

(Reflect and discuss)

Are you prepared to pray more and worry less?

Are you prepared to re-evaluate your spending to see if it is in line with the Gospel message today?

Can you feel at ease with whatever the future brings?

Determine the cost of your discipleship.

When are you going to begin a deeper conversion?

Who is going to help you in your conversion?

PRAYER

Responsorial Psalm

Ps 62
R/. In God alone is my soul at rest.

Doctrinal and Pastoral Issues: The Providence of God, Christian Stewardship, Christian/Gospel Poverty and Lifestyle

Michael Koch

9th Sunday in Ordinary Time

Deuteronomy 11:18, 26–28
Romans 3:21–25, 28
Matthew 7:21–27

BASIC MESSAGE: Christian Integrity—Listen and Act

LOOK AT LIFE

The catechist calls the catechumens and sponsors together and invites them to sit in a circle. He or she greets them and begins the session. The catechist may ask the participants to recall persons in their lives who listen poorly, talk a lot and do little. Then ask them to recall persons in their lives who listen attentively, talk little, and do much.

Which of the two type of persons do you trust more?
To which of the two persons are you more attracted?
Which type is a better witness of Christianity?
Which person has the greatest integrity?
Which person would you be willing to follow?

SHARING OUR LIFE

(After period of reflection, discuss in small groups)

Why are some persons poor listeners?
Why do some persons spend all their time talking?
Why do many people never do what they say?
Why do so many Christians talk about Christianity but never live it?
Why do so many persons lack Christian integrity?
Why do so many people admire Mother Teresa of Calcutta?
Why would Jesus say that mere talkers will not enter the kingdom of heaven?

KNOWING YOUR FAITH

Read, reflect and dialogue about Matthew 7:21–27.

Point out and discuss:

– Admission to enter the kingdom is reserved for those who do "the will of my Father."
– The Church in the days of Matthew was troubled by charismatic prophets and healers who promoted a fantastic, frothy type of Christianity. They were primarily concerned with emotionalism, exorcisms and working miracles (as understood in those days).
– The Church in the days of Matthew on the other hand was also troubled by strict Pharisaic Jewish orthodoxy which was consolidating itself after the fall of Jerusalem.
– Matthew, quoting Jesus, says that neither of these two brands of Christianity is acceptable.
– According to Matthew, true Christianity is found in the great sermon (Matthew 5, 6 & 7).
– The genuine Christian is the one "who listens to these words of mine and acts on them." This Christian has integrity. The words and actions of this Christian are congruous. This Christian can give effective witness. "These words of mine refer to the great sermon."
– The Christian "who listens to these words of mine and does not act on them" lacks integrity and is an ineffective witness for Jesus. Such a Christian says one thing and does something else.
– The imagery of the sensible man building his house on rock and the stupid man building his house on sand.
– Jesus is God's most profound revelation because of his perfect integrity. Jesus is God's greatest witness to humanity because his words always match his deeds. His life was congruous with his Father.
– Read and enjoy Deuteronomy 11:18, 26–28.

MAKING THE FAITH OUR OWN

(Reflection in silence, then discuss)

What is the quality of your Christian integrity?
Have you adequately *listened* to the word of God? Have you put on the mind of Christ?
Do you believe that your sincerity can only be proved by your practice?
Do you believe that your Christian witness is jeopardized when you talk a lot about Christianity but never live it?
Compare your integrity with the integrity of Christ and with that of some great saint.
Reflect on: Knowledge must become action.
　　　　　Theory must become practice.
　　　　　Theology must become life.

LIVING OUR FAITH

(Reflection in silence, then discuss)

What do you think of Jesus and his integrity?
Would you like to have Christian integrity like Jesus?
How are you going to make your actions correspond to
    your talk?
How are you going to make your heart correspond to
    the heart of Christ?
When will this conversion begin?
Who is going to support you in your efforts?

PRAYER

Responsorial Psalm

Ps 31
R/. Be a rock of refuge for me, O Lord.

*Doctrinal and Pastoral Issues: Christian Integrity,
Christian Discipleship, Ecclesial Conversion, Christian
Witness*

Michael Koch

10th Sunday in Ordinary Time

Hosea 6:3–6
Romans 4:18–25
Matthew 9:9–13

BASIC MESSAGE: *God's Universal Love; The Call Of The Sinner*

LOOKING AT LIFE

The catechist calls the catechumens and sponsors together and invites them to sit in a circle. He or she greets them and begins the session. Ask the participants to reflect on the various people they meet from day to day.

List the names of the people you like to be with.
List the names of the people you don't like to be with.
Have you ever had a meal with a transient or a poor person?
Discuss that meal.
Have you spent time with a person who is socially unacceptable—e.g., divorced, homosexual, convict, transient, etc.
What did your friends think when they found out you did this?

SHARING YOUR LIFE

(After a period of reflection, discuss in small groups)

Why do you enjoy being with people you like?
Why are you fearful and avoid people you don't like?
Why did you eat with a socially unacceptable person?
Why did you not eat with a socially unacceptable person?
Why did your friends compliment you, or criticize you?

KNOWING OUR FAITH

Read, reflect and dialogue about Matthew 9:9–13.

Point out and discuss:

– Matthew's situation as a tax collector.
  • Matthew was a Jew collecting taxes for Rome.
  • The people's hatred for tax collectors.
  • Matthew's loneliness and meaningless life.
  • Matthew's longing to belong, his need for acceptance and recognition.
  • Jesus, seeing the heart of Matthew, invites him: "Come, follow me."
– Matthew's conversion to leave all and follow Jesus.
– Eating with someone meant you accepted and protected the guest as friend.
– Jesus' reaching out and making welcome the downtrodden and sinners.
– The contempt of the Pharisees toward Jesus.
– Jesus' remark, "It is not the healthy who need the doctor, but the sick."
– Jesus' universal love when he said, "What I want is mercy, not sacrifice. And indeed I did not come to call the virtuous, but sinners."

MAKING THE FAITH OUR OWN

(Reflection followed by discussion)

Compare Jesus' universal love and your own attitude toward universal love.

How do you compare with Jesus?
With whom do you more closely identify—Jesus, Matthew, the Pharisees or the friends of Matthew?
Do you believe that accepting and loving a sinner opens the door for the conversion of the sinner?

LIVING OUR FAITH

(Reflect and follow with discussion)

Would you like to be more open to the downtrodden, the unfortunate, the handicapped?
Would you like to be more like Jesus?
What concrete thing do you plan on doing?
When are you going to do this?
Who will support you in this new attitude and behavior?

PRAYER

Responsorial Psalm

Ps 50

R/. I will show God's salvation to the upright.

Doctrinal and Pastoral Issues: Christian Love and Mercy, Christian Call, St. Matthew, Concern For the Poor and Neglected.

Michael Koch

11th Sunday in Ordinary Time

Exodus 19:2–6
Romans 5:6–11
Matthew 9:36–10:8

BASIC MESSAGE: *Christian Leadership*

LOOKING AT LIFE

The catechist calls the catechumens and sponsors together and invites them to sit in a circle. He or she greets them and begins the session. The catechist could ask the participants to name a variety of organizations and institutions. It could be church organizations, school groups, community clubs, or civil governments at various levels.

How would you rate the leadership?
How are decisions made in the group or institution?
How well does the leadership serve the membership?
How well does the membership support the leadership?

SHARING YOUR LIFE

Why does an organization require leadership?
Why does conflict arise between leadership and membership?
Why does a group or institution deteriorate when the leadership is weak?

KNOWING OUR FAITH

Read, reflect and dialogue about Matthew 9:36—10:8.

Catechist selects appropriate areas to point out and discuss:

– The compassion of Jesus. "When Jesus saw the crowds he felt sorry for them because they were harassed and dejected, like sheep without a shepherd."
– Compare the attitude of Jesus and the attitude of the Pharisees. The Pharisees saw the common people as chaff to be destroyed and burned up; Jesus saw them as harvest to be reaped and to be sowed. The Pharisees in their pride looked for the destruction of sinners. Jesus in love died for the salvation of sinners.

– Point out this truth as found in the second reading, Romans 5:6–8.
– Jesus' recognition that "the harvest is rich, but the laborers are few" required some kind of organization to continue his work.
– The calling of the original Twelve, their names, their variety of backgrounds, their faithfulness.
– The authority and power given them by Jesus.
– A large part of the work of the Twelve was healing and reconciliation.
– At this point the catechist could develop the development of the Church's leadership throughout the centuries. This could be an opportune time to teach about the structure of the Church's leadership of deacon, priest and bishop. The sacrament of holy orders could be taught. The ministry of the Pope in the Church could be explained.
– Another dimension which could be developed is the relationship of holy orders to the sacrament of reconciliation.
– Develop issue of the priesthood of the faithful and role of the laity.

MAKING THE FAITH OUR OWN

Jesus provided for the continuity of his mission by selecting and training the original Twelve.

How do you understand what the infallibility of the Pope means?
How do you believe the college of bishops carries out leadership in the Church today?
How are you called to be leader in the church?
What is the role of the laity?

LIVING OUR FAITH

How can you help make the ordained leadership in the Church more effective?
How would you like to participate in the Church's leadership by becoming involved in some type of lay ministry?
Do you pray for vocations?
When are you going to do something about all the above?

PRAYER

Responsorial Psalm

Ps 100
R/. We are his people, the sheep of his flock.

For Vocations to All Ministries

We may use this prayer to ask the Lord of the harvest
to invite more people to accept and carry out various
ministries and vocations which are open to Christians
today.

> Father in heaven,
> we praise you for calling us to be your people.
> Send more workers into your harvest
> to share your truth
> and to lead us all to salvation.
> Make your people strong
> with your word and your sacraments.
> We ask this grace
> in the name of Jesus our Lord.
> All answer Amen!
> Holy Mary . . .
> All answer Amen!
> *****
> Heavenly Father, Lord of the harvest,
> call many members of our community
> to be generous workers for your people
> and to gather in your harvest.
> Send them to share the good news of Jesus
> with all the people on earth.
> Father,
> we ask this prayer
> through Christ our Lord.
> All answer Amen!
> (From *A Book of Blessings* by the Canadian
>   Conference of Catholic Bishops)

*Doctrinal and Pastoral Issues: Sacrament of Orders,
Infallibility, Ecclesiology, Role of Laity, Christian Vocation*

Michael Koch

12th Sunday in Ordinary Time

Jeremiah 20:10–13
Romans 5:12–15
Matthew 10:26–33

BASIC MESSAGE: The Courage To Witness Christianity

LOOKING AT LIFE

The catechist calls the catechumens and sponsors together and invites them to sit in a circle. He or she greets them and begins the session. Ask those present to recall an event in their lives where they were called upon to witness their Christianity—e.g., the abortion question, military question, justice questions.

Were you bold, clear, forceful and respectful when you stated the Christian position?
Were you afraid of the challenge and did you try to change the topic of conversation?
Do you concretely live your Christianity?
Do you avoid situations where you might be called upon to witness Christianity?

SHARING YOUR LIFE

(After period of silent reflection discuss in small groups)
Why do you fearlessly proclaim the Christian message?
Why do you hesitate and why are you unable to give Christian witness?
• I don't know my faith well enough to articulate it intelligently.
• It gets me involved more than I want to.
• I am afraid of ridicule.
• I am afraid I might lose my job or my friends.
• I am afraid I might have to suffer or be persecuted.
• I am afraid God will let me down.
• I am afraid ultimate vindication will not happen.
Why are Church leaders sometimes afraid to speak Christian truth?
Why do you think Jesus had to assure the Twelve after he sent them on a mission not to be afraid?

KNOWING OUR FAITH

Read, reflect and dialogue about Matthew 10:26–33.

Point out and discuss:

– Jesus has just commissioned his twelve disciples to be his apostles. He said, "Remember, I am sending you out like sheep among wolves; so be cunning as serpents and yet as harmless as doves" (Mt 10:16).
– The reasons why the apostles were afraid.
– Three times Jesus says "Do not be afraid" in this pericope.
  • "Do not be afraid of men"—because the truth will ultimately triumph—because the message is not theirs; it is the message of Christ.
  • "Do not be afraid of those who kill the body." This refers to those who persecute Christians. "Fear *him* rather who can destroy both body and soul in hell." The context indicates that *him* refers to the Father. Infidelity to God is a greater tragedy than infidelity to the new.
  • "So there is no need to be afraid"—the witness has God's assurance and protection. If God cares for an insignificant sparrow, why not the witness, who is worth much more?
– The view that rejection, persecution and martyrdom are separable from the prophetic vision.
– The suffering of the witness is the supreme manifestation of the cross of Christ.
– Various ways we can deny Christ.
  • by our words
  • by our silence
  • by our actions
– The consequences of loyalty to Christ:
  • the faithful witness will be honored by Christ before his Father.
  • the unfaithful witness will be disowned by Christ before his Father.
– Read and enjoy Jeremiah 20:10–13.

MAKING THE FAITH OUR OWN

(Reflect and then discuss)
How big is the gap between Christ's call to be his witness and your fear of acting?
Do you believe the Father will give you the strength to be a witness for Christianity?
Do you believe that persecution and suffering is an inevitable part of witnessing for Christ?
Do you believe that God will care for and protect his witnesses?

Do you believe that Christ and Christian truth will ultimately triumph?

LIVING OUR FAITH

(Reflect and then discuss)
Are you satisfied by the way you are giving witness to your Christian faith?
What are you going to do about it?
What will be the cost of your discipleship?
In time? In energy? In boldness? In suffering?
Will you pray to the Lord for courage?
When are you going to be a more serious witness?
Where will you turn for support?

PRAYER

Responsorial Psalm

Ps 69
R/. In your great love, answer me, O God.

Doctrinal and Pastoral Issues: Christian Suffering, Martyrdom, Christian Hope, Gifts of the Holy Spirit, Courage and Fortitude

Michael Koch

Jesus and His Teaching

Part II: The Reign of God

By Eugene A. LaVerdiere

Between the Easter Season, which ends on Pentecost, and the resumption of Sundays in Ordinary Time, we celebrate Trinity Sunday, Corpus Christi and the Sacred Heart of Jesus. Every other feast in the liturgical year celebrates an event. These three feasts are unique in that they celebrate a mystery. Liturgically, this is somewhat awkward, but it does provide an opportunity to reflect on some very important aspects of Christian belief.

From the Tenth to the Thirty-Fourth Sunday in Ordinary Time, all the Gospel readings are taken from Matthew 9—25. In the first series of Sundays in Ordinary Time, we focused on Jesus and his teaching. Many of the readings came from the Sermon on the Mount (Mt 5—7), and we were able to gather them under the title "The Law of Christ." This second series also presents Jesus and his teaching, but its scope is much broader. The most appropriate title for these Sundays is the most basic theme of Matthew's Gospel itself, "The Reign of God."

God's Only Son

All of Christian life and belief is summed up in the mystery of Jesus, God's only Son. On Trinity Sunday, which is the Sunday after Pentecost, we focus on the only Son's relationship to the Trinity. It is through the Son that we know the Father and experience the gift of the Holy Spirit. John 3:16—18 speaks of the Son as an extraordinary manifestation of God's love. He came to serve the world, not to condemn it, and all who welcome him in faith receive eternal life through him.

On Corpus Christi, we reflect on the only Son's gift of himself as nourishment for the life of the world. The communication of the Father's love takes place in eucharistic sharing, which sums up every aspect of Jesus' life as nourishment (Jn 6:51—58). It is important to realize that those who receive Jesus as nourishment join him in offering their own lives as nourishment to others. The flesh and blood of Christ is given through the self-sacrifice of his followers.

On the feast of the Sacred Heart of Jesus, we celebrate the only Son's intimate knowledge and love of the Father and the way he introduces us into that loving knowledge. The love of Christ, a love which Christians must extend to one another and to all other members of God's family with gentleness and humility, transforms Jesus' yoke, the carrying of the cross, into an easy burden (Mt 11:25—30). The same Gospel text is read on the Fourteenth Sunday in Ordinary Time.

Called to Mission

The first disciples were called for the Christian mission (see the Third Sunday in Ordinary Time). On the Tenth Sunday, this theme is taken up in the story of Matthew's own call. Here we see how the call to discipleship reaches us in our daily preoccupations, whatever they may be, and how that call is renewed and celebrated at the table of the Lord. In every age there have been those who label others as sinners and insist on their exclusion from the Lord's company. As we see from the Gospel, all are sinners. Jesus calls those who recognize their sinfulness. The call to discipleship and mission is a reconciling call (Mt 9:9—13).

On the Eleventh Sunday, we reflect on the mission of the Twelve (Mt 9:36—10:8), among whom we find Matthew the tax collector. They are to go to the lost sheep of the house of Israel (10:2), who were without a shepherd (9:36), and announce the good news of the reign of God. Their mission is to extend the work of Jesus. On the Twelfth and Thirteenth Sundays, the Gospel readings are from Jesus' discourse to the Twelve. In the mission, they are not to be intimidated by anyone. They may be persecuted, but no one can destroy their soul (10:26—33). In all they do they must place their new life in Christ above all their natural relationships. When others welcome them, Jesus himself is being welcomed (10:37—42). The Gospel for the Fourteenth Sunday, whose theme is the gentle yoke of Jesus (11:25—30), is repeated from the Feast of the Sacred Heart of Jesus.

Parables of the Reign of God

Matthew's Gospel is famous for its great discourses. On previous Sundays, we have already reflected on two of these, the Sermon on the Mount (Mt 5–7) and the missionary discourse (Mt 10:1—11:1). From the Fifteenth to the Seventeenth Sundays we now read the third discourse with its parables concerning the reign of God.

On the Fifteenth Sunday, we begin with the parable of the sower, a statement concerning the purpose of the parables, and an interpretation of the parable of the sower (13:1–23). The parables of Jesus were intended to be clear, and they were clear, but they were also very challenging. The parable of the sower, for example, demands that Jesus' auditors recognize whether they are rocky ground, thorns, a footpath or good soil. This implied self-appraisal is what still makes the parables hard to understand.

On the Sixteenth Sunday, we have the parable of the good seed, wheat, and the weeds, two additional parables, the mustard seed and the yeast, and an explanation of the parable of the wheat and weeds for the disciples (13:24–43). These parables show how the reign of God grows and develops to full maturity. The good seed grows in the midst of the weeds until the harvest. The two short parables help us see that at first the reign is very tiny and hidden but that it will surely grow to be very large and will effectively transform all that is in touch with it. Such parables, like those read on the Seventeenth Sunday (13:44–52), which focus on the value of the reign, encouraged the Matthean community as it readjusted its expectations concerning the reign of God.

Forming the Church

The Church has an important role in the coming of the reign of God. From the Eighteenth to the Twenty-Fourth Sundays all the Gospel readings show how Jesus the Christ formed his Church in view of God's reign (13:54—18:35). We begin with a story which is popularly referred to as the multiplication of loaves, but for which a better title would be the miraculous sharing (14:13–21). The focus of the story is not so much on the bread and what happened to it as on the work and responsibility of the disciples who are not to disperse the crowd but to gather it in one sharing community.

On the following Sunday, Jesus is presented as walking over the water in the midst of a storm, while the disciples struggle in the boat (14:22–33). They need to learn that he is with them as Lord of creation ready to bring order into the midst of chaos and that as co-creators they are called to join him in that work.

The stormy crossing of the sea mirrored the Church's transition from a purely Jewish-Christian community to one which was open to Gentiles. In Jesus' extraordinary encounter with a Canaanite woman, a Gentile, the Gospel repeats the theme of Jesus' mission being to the lost sheep of the house of Israel (see Eleventh Sunday). In the same passage, however, Jesus foresees that the mission will one day open up to the Gentiles (15:21–28), something which was being realized in the life of the Matthean community.

On the Twenty-First and Twenty-Second Sundays, the Gospel raises the question of Jesus' identity and its implications for the life of the disciples and the Church. Jesus cannot be described merely as a new John the Baptist, Elijah or prophet. As Peter confesses, he is the Christ, the Messiah, the Son of the living God. It is on the basis of this confession that Peter is declared the rock foundation of the Church (16:13–20). The Rock, however, still had to learn and accept that as the Messiah or Christ, Jesus would also suffer and die and then be raised up on the third day. Any turning away from the passion-resurrection, for Peter and the Church as well as for Jesus, would be judging not by God's standards but by human and even satanical standards (16:21–28).

On the Twenty-Third and Twenty-Fourth Sundays, the Gospel readings are from Jesus' discourse on the life of the Church. Both readings emphasize the work of reconciliation. The first presents an approach to reconciliation within the Church (18:15–20). We should note where reconciliation begins, namely, with the person offended. In the early Church reconciliation penetrated every facet of the life of the Church. Jesus had come to remove divisions, to bring peace and to gather all peoples in one family of God. The Church is called to do the same by pursuing its mission in his name. The second reading (18:21–35) is about unlimited forgiveness. Forgiveness does not depend on the number of times someone has struck out against a Christian. A parable shows how the loving mercy of God is the norm for Christian forgiveness.

The Lord's Generosity

The parable of the workers in the vineyard (20:1–16) is the Gospel reading for the Twenty-Fifth Sunday. Its theme of God's boundless generosity—God is like the owner of the vineyard—is an excellent follow-up for the Twenty-Fourth Sunday's teaching about placing no limits on forgiveness. Like so many of Matthew's parables, the parable of the workers is a parable of the reign of God. We are invited to identify with the various workers as well as with the owner. As one of those who started work early in the day, we are made to deal with our resentfulness when the owner gives to the latest arrivals as much as he gave us. As one of those who did but one hour's work, we learn the meaning of gratitude.

From the Twenty-Sixth Sunday to the end of the liturgical year, the readings are taken from Jesus' teaching in the temple at Jerusalem. In a series of encounters, which begin with a challenge to Jesus' authority by the chief priests and the elders, we have intimations of the approaching passion of Jesus, even in the parables read from the Twenty-Sixth to the Twenty-Eighth Sundays.,

The parable of the two sons is the Gospel reading for the Twenty-Sixth Sunday (21:28–32). Jesus is speaking to those who had challenged his authority. They are wonderful with words but extremely slow with deeds. Like the son who first refused to work for his father but then changed his mind and did so, the tax collectors—remember Matthew the tax collector—and prostitutes will enter the reign of God ahead of them.

The parable of the tenants who killed the workers sent by the owner into the vineyard is the Gospel reading for the Twenty-Seventh Sunday (22:33–43). The tenants hoped to secure the vineyard for themselves. To this end, they even killed the owner's son. The owner consequently leases his vineyard to others. So will God offer the kingdom to another nation.

Spurned generosity is the theme for the Twenty-Eighth Sunday (22:1–14). The parable is about a wedding banquet to which those invited refuse to come until the banquet hall is finally filled with everyone encountered in the byroads. The one without the proper garment is one who has not put on Christ. He is present at the banquet, but his presence is one of betrayal rather than of solidarity.

Jesus and the Pharisees

Jesus' teaching in the temple continues with two encounters with the Pharisees (22:15–21; 22:34–40) and a warning to the crowds and the disciples about the Pharisees (23:1–12). These are the readings from the Twenty-Ninth, Thirtieth and Thirty-First Sundays.

The first of these deals with the paying of taxes to Caesar. The Pharisees had thought to trip him up by forcing Jesus to take a position either against Caesar and the government or against the Pharisees and their following. Jesus turned the tables on them by requesting a coin. Religious Jews did not carry images of Caesar, let alone bring them into the temple. Jesus had trapped the Pharisees in their own device.

The second Gospel reading raises the issue of the greatest commandment. In his response Jesus quotes the law accurately. He first states that the greatest commandment is that of the love of God, but then adds that a second commandment is just like it. Love of neighbor is inseparable from love of God.

The third of these readings about the Pharisees is a warning not to imitate them. Like the son who agreed to follow his father's orders but then did not do so (21:28–32), their words were bold but their deeds meager. Their lives were filled with outward display and self-exaltation. They loved the titles "Rabbi" or "Teacher" or "Father." Jesus' followers are to avoid all

such behavior. They are not to follow the Pharisees in their insistence on titles. Jesus the Messiah is their teacher; God is their Father. Jesus' point is not that these titles are bad in themselves but that they are not to be used in any way that would associate them with the Pharisees.

The Coming of the Son of Man

On the last three Sundays of the liturgical year, our readings are drawn from Jesus' great discourse on the fulfillment of creation and history and the coming of the Son of Man (Mt 24—25). First we have two parables, that of the ten virgins (25:1–13) and that of the silver pieces (25:14–30). The parable of the ten virgins (Thirty-Second Sunday) is one of Matthew's parables on the coming of the reign of God. Its emphasis, of course, is on the need for watchfulness, lest we be away when the Master comes. The parable of the silver pieces (Thirty-Third Sunday) expands the theme from simple watchfulness to that of enterprising labor on behalf of God's reign. When the Lord comes we are to have placed everything entrusted to us in the Lord's fruitful service.

On the last Sunday of the year, the Thirty-Fourth, which is also the Feast of Christ the King, the Gospel reading speaks to us of the return of the Son of Man in judgment (25:31–46). We should note that his judgment will be just and severe, but, even more important, we should note the criteria on which the Son of Man's judgment will be made. The norm is love of neighbor, nourishing the hungry, visiting the imprisoned and clothing the naked. Those who are faithful to this commandment will have nourished, visited and clothed the Son of Man, in whom all the hopes of humanity are found. The Son of Man is the ultimate human being, one who fulfills the human vocation to be the image and likeness of God.

Introduction to Sundays 13–22 in Ordinary Time

In this section, each catechetical session follows these steps:

Gathering Prayer
Reflection Questions
Thematic Presentations
Integration Questions
Closing Prayer

The section on thematic presentations contains one or two outlines on the scriptural themes for the catechist to use in his or her presentation.

The gathering and closing prayers for these Sundays employ a variety of resources including prayers by Thomas Merton and Anthony de Mello, and others from the sacramentary. As always music is recommended for listening to or, where possible, for singing. When more than one option for prayer is presented, the catechist should choose the option that he or she considers better for local needs.

The process for these sessions begins with reflecting on the Gospel through use of reflection questions. After a period of faith sharing, the catechist develops one of the themes expressed in the thematic presentations. This is followed by another discussion using the integration questions. The doctrinal and pastoral issues relevant to each Sunday have been noted at the end of each chapter.

13th Sunday in Ordinary Time

2 Kings 4:8–11, 14–16
Romans 6:3–4, 8–11
Matthew 10:37–42

GATHERING PRAYER

Father, let the light of your truth guide us to your kingdom through a world filled with lights contrary to your own.

Christian is the name and the Gospel we glory in.

May your love make us what you have called us to be, and your strength give us courage to do your will.

Amen.

Listen to the song "Life Up Your Heads" from the album *A Song Shall Rise* by Terry Talbot.

REFLECTION QUESTIONS

(Catechists will choose those which are appropriate to local needs)

1. Reflect on a time in your life when you were "turned off" or angered by the challenge of a higher ideal. What can you learn about yourself as you reflect on this situation? What can you learn about your relationship to Jesus?

2. What do you hear in the Scripture, "Whoever loses his life for my sake will gain it"?

3. Up to this point in your faith journey, have you had to "pay a price" to live out your faith? Reflect on that experience. What does the Gospel say about this experience?

THEMATIC PRESENTATION

Theme

"To Lose One's Life for Christ's Sake—The Call to Discipleship"

Outline

I. Matthew describes what the cost of discipleship

was during his time.
  A. Family ties were often strained, even broken, as the traditions of Judaism were challenged and abandoned.
  B. Jesus' teaching not only caused division between people but called individuals to examine and struggle inside themselves. He asks us to "lose our life in order to gain it."
  C. Christians affected the people with whom they came in contact. They were forced to confront people on issues in every area of life.

II. These same "costs of discipleship" still exist today. Look at each one in light of today's world and relate them to your personal story of faith.
  A. How has your faith caused strain, perhaps even division in your family? Share an experience of your own or of someone else that you know.
  B. Jesus' call to discipleship may cause turmoil within a person. The call to "lose oneself" for Christ's sake is a call to growth. How have you experienced this in your life? Is this a "one-time" call? Explain.
  C. As disciples, our lives should affect those around us. That means that we must take our faith to the "marketplace" of our world. How have you answered this call to discipleship? Have you ever had to stand up for your Christian values in the "social arena" of your life? Talk about that experience.

III. Give an example of a modern-day disciple. Tell about the price he or she has paid. What effect has this person had on you? on the world? What does Christ promise this kind of person?

INTEGRATION QUESTIONS

1. Reflect on the cost of discipleship, as outlined by Matthew. How have these affected your life? Use (II–A, B, C) of the outline for the three areas.

2. Can you identify some specific areas in your life in which you are being called to grow? Is this what Jesus meant as he calls you to "lose your life" for his sake? Spend some time reflecting on this call.

3. Jesus promises that one who "gives a cup of cold water to one of these lowly ones because he is a disci-

ple will not want for his reward." What is this reward of which he speaks? What are your feelings as your ponder this?

4. The values of a Christian permeate all areas of our life. How will my values affect the people around me this day? Is this the effect that Jesus would want?

CLOSING PRAYER

Leader

Jesus prays for us, his disciples. He knows that we will experience conflict within ourselves, and within the world in which we live. He prays a prayer full of hope for us, and expresses his love for us. He wants nothing less than to share with us the unity that he has with his Father.

Read John 17:23

Song

"The Prayer of St. Francis"

Doctrinal and Pastoral Issues. The Call of God, Discipleship, Sacrifice, Dying and Rising in the Paschal Mystery.

Khris H. Ford

14th Sunday in Ordinary Time

Zechariah 9:9–10
Romans 8:9, 11–13
Matthew 11:25–30

GATHERING PRAYER

Set the scene for prayer with a few moments of silence in a comfortable position. Ask that the problems of the day be offered up and that our minds and hearts will be focused on what the Lord wishes for us to bring away from this time together. After a few moments of silence play a recording of "Come Unto Me," *Glory and Praise* Vol. II, North American Liturgy Resources, 1980.

or

Say the following prayer:

Father, Lord of heaven and earth, I thank you because you have shown to the unlearned what you have hidden from the wise and learned. We pray that you will reveal yourself to us as we seek to know you in your word. Help us to respond to you in simplicity and purity of heart. We believe that your burden is easy and light. Grant that we may respond to your call to come, in Christ Jesus. Amen.

Then sing or listen to "Praise the Lord, My Soul," *Glory and Praise*, Vol. I, North American Liturgy Resources, 1977.

REFLECTION QUESTIONS

1. What kinds of burdens are you carrying? What burdens did you carry with you as we gathered together?

2. How have you put on the "yoke" of Christ?

3. Reflect on the words of our Lord, "Come to me." What does it mean to come to the Lord in faith?

4. Give one concrete example, in the recent past, that you have responded to the Lord in faith.

Allow time for the participants to reflect and/or write on the questions. Then ask them to share their answers in small groups (3 to 4).

THEMATIC PRESENTATIONS

Theme 1

Does becoming a Christian (Catholic) mean that life is always "easy and light"? What is this "yoke" of Christ?

Outline 1

I. When we try to live out of the strength of our own resources alone we become burdened. Describe how the following human weaknesses may cause us to be burdened in life:
   A. Pride—Our need to be recognized, to be winners, to "save face" causes life to be more of a burden to us.
   B. Loneliness—Failure to recognize life as a journey with God and his people can make life seem filled with darkness.
   C. Selfishness—Our desire to be in control of things and people and our unwillingness to share God's gifts often isolate us from God.

II. Christ promises to share our burdens and to refresh us spiritually if we follow in his way. Read the following scriptural references to this. Comment briefly on what they say to you.
   A. Mt 11:28–30
   B. Lk 5:1–11
   C. Jn 15:8–17

III. Following Christ's ways is to take on the "yoke" of Christ. We are called to be his disciples.
   A. The call to discipleship is scriptural:
      1. Jn 15:16–17
      2. Eph 1:3–22
      3. Jn 1:35–51
   B. Those same words call people today. Reflect on the lives of one or two modern-day disciples: Mother Teresa, Martin Luther King, etc.
   C. Give a brief reflection on your own call to discipleship. Tell how you have taken on the "yoke" of Christ.

IV. Christ shares our burdens through the support of the body of Christ, the Church.
   A. We pray for one another as a community.
   B. We offer support to one another in times of special need and in times of celebration.
   C. Give examples of how your own parish community shares the burdens of its members.

Theme 2

Accepting the Good News of Christ—The Gift of Faith

Outline 2

  I. What is faith?
    A. Faith is a response to Christ's call.
      1. Reflect on how we may experience the call to faith. Tell about your own experience.
    B. Faith is a belief in God and his teachings.
    C. Faith is a commitment to live by God's teachings.
    D. The gift of faith is Gift and is not earned, but freely given to us.

  II. Signs of genuine faith
    A. Gal 5:6
    B. Jas 2:14–18
    Read and reflect briefly on these scriptures.

  III. How faith comes to an adult
    A. Growing in faith is a mysterious and uniquely individual process. Point out examples of conversion in Scripture: Paul, Zacchaeus, etc.
    B. We cannot earn faith by ourselves. It is Gift.
    C. We can continuously strengthen our faith—ongoing conversion. Tell some ways in which this can be assured: prayer, Scripture study, etc.
    D. Give some personal reflections on how your faith has developed—your ongoing conversion story.

INTEGRATION QUESTIONS

1. What kind of burdens do you need help shouldering? How will you share these burdens with Christ?

2. How am I called to take on the "yoke" of Christ today—in my family, my community, my work environment?

3. How will accepting this invitation from Christ make my load lighter?

4. Faith is a commitment to live by God's teachings. Paul says that true faith results in works of love. In what ways does my life reflect this faith? In what ways does it not? How can I change this?

CLOSING PRAYER

Read the following meditation on Jesus' calls to the disciples to "come." Quiet instrumental music during the reading, and for a few moments following, makes this reading even more effective.

"The Offer"

I call to mind the times
when Jesus Christ said "Come!"
to people in the Gospel.
I imagine that I hear that word
addressed to me today
and I respond to it.

When two of John's disciples
asked Jesus where he lived,
he said, "Come and see."

I talk with him about the things that I have seen
since the day he first invited me
to be with him,
the things that he has shown me.

I then recall the words of Philip,
"Show us the Father—
that is all we want."
Is there anything I still desire him to show me?

To each of his disciples Jesus said,
"Come, follow me."
I ask myself what following him has done for me
over the years.

Another "Come":
Jesus says to fishermen by the lake,
"Come and I shall get you to catch human beings."
I think of the inspiration
I have sometimes brought to others.
I think of those whose goodness or whose talents
I have drawn out by my love.
I think of the times when I brought faith
where there was fear,
solace where there was pain,
love to replace indifference,
peace to temper violence.
I think of those who were absorbed in daily trifles
until, because of me,
they heard a call to something greater.
And I rest in the sound of his words,
"Come, and I shall get you to catch human beings."

"Come to me, all you who are tired and weary,
and I shall give you rest."
An invitation to find my rest in him!
What words spring to my lips
when I hear him say those words to me?

And finally, "Anyone who is thirsty
should come to me and drink."
How does one slake one's thirst
on Jesus Christ?

(Taken from *Wellsprings, A Book of Spiritual Exercises*, by Anthony DeMello, Doubleday, 1984)

Conclude your session with spontaneous prayer for help in the areas of our life identified as "burdens." The leader should begin with his or her prayer. In between each individual's prayer the group sings the refrain of "We Praise You," *Glory and Praise*, Vol. II, North American Liturgy Resources, 1980. This could be sung at the beginning of the prayer after a brief explanation of the procedure to be followed.

Doctrinal and Pastoral Issues: Faith, Conversion, Discipleship

Khris H. Ford

15th Sunday in Ordinary Time

Isaiah 55:10–11
Romans 8:18–23
Matthew 13:1–23

GATHERING PRAYER

Psalm 65 (Done as a responsorial reading)

Response: Part of the seed landed on good soil
and yielded grain many times over.
Let everyone heed what he hears!

or

Psalm 62 (Read together aloud)

In God alone is my soul at rest;
my help comes from him.
He alone is my rock, my stronghold,
my fortress: I stand firm.

How long will you all attack one man
to break him down,
as though he were a tottering wall,
or a tumbling fence?

Their plan is only to destroy:
they take pleasure in lies.
With their mouth they utter blessing
but in their heart they curse.

In God alone be at rest, my soul,
for my hope comes from him.
He alone is my rock, my strong hold,
my fortress: I stand firm.

In God is my safety and glory,
the rock of my strength.
Amen.

(Taken from *The Lord Is My Shepherd*, by
David E. Rosage, Servant Books,
1984)

REFLECTION QUESTIONS

1. Psalm 95:8 says, "Oh that today you would hear his
   voice, and harden not your hearts . . . " How have
   you heard God's voice today?

2. Read the Gospel passage carefully. Reflect on this
   question. What kind of soil was I today, and during
   this past week? Explain your answer.

3. Am I a person of hope? How do I reflect this?

4. Think of a situation/event in which there were nu-
   merous "roadblocks" along the path to some accom-
   plishment or destination. What were some of these
   "roadblocks" and what enabled you to continue to
   see beyond them?

THEMATIC PRESENTATIONS

Theme 1

Am I open to the word of God?
What kind of "soil" am I?

Outline 1

I. The parable speaks of deterrents to the seeds'
   growth. Discuss deterrents in our lives. Give ex-
   amples of how the following deterrents have been a
   part of your life, and of others.
   A. Busy-ness
   B. Lack of trust
   C. Pride
   D. False gods (power, money, other people)

II. "But what was sown of good soil is the man who
    hears the message and takes it in." How do we do
    this?
    A. Reading/praying/meditating on the Scriptures
    B. Confronting the Scriptures
    C. Accepting the challenge of the Scriptures

III. How God's word multiplies in those who are open.
     A. Give an example in Scripture of how this has
        happened.
     B. Give an example from your own life where this
        has taken place.

Theme 2

As Catholic Christians we are called to be a people of
hope.

Outline 2

I. This parable may be seen as a story of hope.
   A. In this parable we can trace Jesus' story of re-

jection and final triumph.

  B. We may also see this as a story of the growth of the kingdom.

  C. We may relate it to our life story with its pitfalls and roadblocks.

  D. Choose one of the above and retell the parable in this story form—growth in the Kingdom, your own story, or Jesus' story. Draw parallels from the original parable.

II. Scripture calls us to be a people of hope.
  A. 1 Tim 5:5, 6:17—hope in God
  B. Heb 6:18–20—hope in Christ
  C. Rom 4:18—Abraham is a model of hope
  D. Rom 5:2, Eph 1:18, Col 1:23—we are called to hope

III. As sowers of the seed we must have hope.
  A. Tell a story of how your "hope" touched another, or how you have been touched by the hope-filled spirit of someone else.

INTEGRATION QUESTIONS

1. Reread the Gospel (Mt 13:1–23). It is the story of God's love poured out for you, his word sown as the food for your hunger.

  On what kind of soil will his word fall?

  What are those forces that work against you as you attempt to open yourself to the word?

  Pray for the grace to be strong. Pray for openness to his word.

2. How will you read God's word differently this week?

  How will his word be food that is multiplied through you?

3. What kind of seeds have I been sowing lately?

  Have they been seeds of hope?

4. How can my life better reflect the hope that I have in the Lord?

5. Think of one person who needs the hope that you have in your life. Make a plan to share this. Write it down and then share what you will do with someone close to you. Pray about the seed that you will sow.

CLOSING PRAYER

Song

"Speak, Lord," *Glory and Praise*, Vol. II, North American Liturgy Resources, 1980.

Spontaneous Prayer with the Scriptures

Everyone should have a Bible and enough light to be able to read. Begin with a leader sharing an occasion when the Scriptures spoke to him or her in some special way. Read that particular Scripture. Then extend the invitation to the rest of the group to read a passage of Scripture that has special meaning for them. Ask that each reading be followed by a few moments of silence for "listening." When it seems that all who wish to read have had an opportunity, the leader ends with the following:

> Almighty God and Father,
> you have placed your word within our hearts,
> through the Gospel we have received.
> May your word within us grow
> that we may yield good fruit
> and be gathered into your kingdom.
> May we live by your word
> that others may reap what is sown by us,
> and so come to know you,
> and Jesus Christ, whom you have sent,
> who lives and reigns with you and the Holy Spirit,
> one God forever and ever. Amen.
> (Prayer taken from "Share the Word," July/ August 1984, The Paulist Fathers)

Song

"Only in God," *Glory and Praise*, Vol. II, North American Liturgy Resources, 1980.

Then the leader begins:

Psalm 23 may be thought of as the prayer of hope. Let us pray this psalm together.

(Have available typed copies of the psalm for each person to read.)

Doctrinal and Pastoral Issues: Hope, Openness, Parables, God's Word

Khris H. Ford

16th Sunday in Ordinary Time

Wisdom 12:13,16–19
Romans 8:26–27
Matthew 13:24–43

GATHERING PRAYER

Leader prays:
Almighty and ever-living God,
your Spirit makes us your children,
confident to call you Father.
Touch our hearts;
help them grow toward the life you have promised,
Touch our lives;
make them signs of your love for all men.
Above all, Father,
may we love you in all things
and above all things,
and reach the joy you have prepared for us
beyond all imagining.
We ask this in the name of Jesus, your Son.
Amen

or

O God, thy sea is so great
and my boat is so small.
Yet, like the mustard seed that grows
to support a sturdy bush,
you promise me growth
and support, also.
Help me to understand that,
though my boat is small,
with your help I can make a difference.
Through the Spirit I can be a light to the world.
Amen.

Follow the above prayer with the song:
"Abba, Father," *Glory and Praise*, Vol. I, North American Liturgy Resources, 1977.

REFLECTION QUESTIONS

1. Ask someone to read (slowly and deliberately) Matthew 13:24–43. Copies of the reading should be distributed to everyone, so that all may follow along as it is being read. Then, reread the readings. This time ask participants to underline/circle any words and/or phrases that stand out to them as they are listening to the reading.

   Next, ask everyone to look back over the words/phrases that they marked. Ask them to jot down notes, to the side, telling why they underlined it or any thoughts they may have about the words. They should indicate any general or over-all feelings that were elicited by the Scripture passages.

   Lastly, break up into groups of 3–5 persons. Discuss those things that were marked and the comments that people wrote about these passages. Discuss the question: What does this passage say to me about the end times?

2. Think of a situation that is a modern-day parallel to the parable of the mustard seed and the leaven. Share this with another person.

3. How has God been the leaven in your life this past week?

4. Think of someone who has been a positive influence in your life. What about that person has made him or her "leaven" in your life?

THEMATIC PRESENTATIONS

Theme 1

What does the Catholic Church teach about the end times? What does this say about how I am to live?

Outline 1

I. The end times will be times of completion, not of destruction.
   A. Vatican II, The Church in the Modern World, #39
   B. Phil 1:6
   C. Rom 8:38–39
   Read and share the content of the above three resources.

II. Christ will appear in judgment.
   A. Jn 5:25–30
   B. Mt 25:31–46
   Read and comment on the above references in light of the parable and judgment.

III. How must I live in order to foster the coming of the kingdom? Give your own personal answer to this, using the following "categories" as a guide.
   A. Be a person of hope.
   B. Be a just person (Mt. 25:31–46). Give an example of what this might mean in your everyday life.
   C. Be patient with sinners.
   D. Live out an understanding of the interdependence of the body of Christ; none of us will fully arrive until we all arrive.

IV. Give a personal statement of witness to your belief in the end times? Tell how you live your life differently than the unbeliever? How is your life a statement about your beliefs of the end times?

Theme 2

The Mustard Seed—The Acorn: Can I Really Make a Difference?

Outline 2

Our modern world sends us the message that only big things matter. The story of the mustard seed tells us that small things can make a difference.

I. Tell a personal story of how some small act made a difference to someone.

II. Talk about the symbol of yeast and how great things from small beginnings is demonstrated.
   A. The kingdom began with only twelve and has spread to billions in the course of history.
   B. This can be likened to the age-old adage: "Great oaks from tiny acorns grow."
   C. The seed can only reach its potential through the power of God.
      1. 1 Cor 3:6–7
      2. Wis 12:13, 16–19

III. We can "tap" into God's power through prayer.
   A. Rom 8:26–27
   B. 2 Cor 1:11
   C. Rom 15:13
   D. Relate a personal experience of having received power (strength) through prayer.

INTEGRATION QUESTIONS

1. The whole of our lives may be seen as "weeds among the wheat." As I prepare for the kingdom this week, what weeds in my attitudes and actions do I need to bundle up and burn? How will I do this?

2. Like yeast in the dough, God's power is within us and radiates outward. It is in this radiating that the good news is spread. What evidence do I see that confirms the reign of God in my world today?

3. As a Christian, do I radiate this message of hope? Am I leaven? How can I better fulfill this role of spreading the kingdom?

CLOSING PRAYER

Read aloud Matthew 13:43. Then spend a few moments in silent reflection. Read the following guided meditation:

Feel the warmth and radiance of the son's love. Imagine the warm feeling you've had as someone drew you close and held you.

(Pause for a few moments of silence.)

See, in your mind's eye, the Father beckoning you—his outstretched arms, his joy, his desire to have you join him forever.

(Pause for a few moments of silence.)

Play the song "Eye Has Not Seen," *Gather Us In*, by Michael Joneas.

Close by saying the Our Father together.

or

Sing: "Earthen Vessels," *Earthen Vessels*, St. Louis Jesuits, North American Liturgy Resources, 1975.

Doctrinal and Pastoral Issues: Last Judgment, Kingdom of God, Humility

Khris H. Ford

17th Sunday in Ordinary Time

1 Kings 3:5, 7–12
Romans 8:28–30
Matthew 13:44–52

GATHERING PRAYER

Listen to "Behold the Kingdom," *The Painter*, John Michael Talbot, Sparrow Records, 1980.

Read Matthew 13:44–52 aloud.

or

Leader says this prayer:

Father, your Scriptures ask us, "Have you understood all this?" We respond, "Lord, we understand. Help our misunderstanding." Amen.

Song

"Speak, Lord, I'm Listening," *Glory and Praise*, Vol. I, North American Liturgy Resources, 1977.

REFLECTION QUESTIONS

1. Ever since the time of David there had been talk of the kingdom. What is unique about the message of the kingdom that Jesus brings? What does this Gospel tell us about that?

2. How would you explain the kingdom of God to an unbeliever?

3. What does this parable tell you about the priorities in your life?

4. Take each of the parables in this week's Gospel and write a one sentence "lesson" for each one. (What is the point of each?)

THEMATIC PRESENTATIONS

Theme 1
What Is the Kingdom of God?

Outline 1

I. Read Mark 4:30–32. It is a restatement of Matthew 13:31–33—What is the kingdom of God like?

   A. Talk about the symbol of the bird nesting mentioned in the passages. It is also used in Daniel 4:12 and Ezekiel 17:22–23; 31:6. It represents the concept of a great empire embracing all peoples.

   B. God reigns over all, but to "belong" to the kingdom we must experience interior change.

     1. Matthew 13:44–45: We must uncover the "hidden treasure" and "find the pearl."

II. What is interior conversion?

   A. Talk about the Gospel. What did the man do when he uncovered the treasure, when he found the pearl? Why?

   B. Tell a personal story of "uncovering the treasure" in your own life. What happened as a result? In particular, share what sacrifices and changes you were called to make.

III. To belong to the kingdom we must submit and commit.

   A. When we submit we offer ourselves, and show our willingness to be guided by God.

   B. When we commit we give ourselves wholly to obedience to the commandment to "love one another" (Jn 13:34).

     1. We commit to follow in Christ's footsteps.

     2. The Beatitudes provide us with a description of what we should strive for (Mt 3:3–12).

IV. "Thy Kingdom Come"

   A. Those who belong to the kingdom on earth work to extend it to all people through prayer, study, and example.

   B. The kingdom is here and now. But it will only come to completion in heaven.

Theme 2

What does the Catholic Church teach on the understanding and interpretation of the Scriptures?

Outline 2

I. The books of the Bible were inspired by the Holy Spirit.

   A. The Bible is unlike any other book because of its divine inspiration.

   B. Because it is God's word to us it binds both the Church and each of us.

II. The Books of the Bible have human authors.
   A. God acted in and through human authors so that they made full use of their powers and abilities while writing what God wanted written.
      1. They wrote as other authors did, though guided by God's inspiration (Lk 1:1–4; 1 Cor 7:12)
      2. They employed the various literary styles of their time, and their individual writing styles.

III. What is the inspired meaning of Scripture?
   A. Books of the Bible teach the truth which God wanted them to teach "for the sake of our salvation" (Vatican II, Constitution on Divine Revelation).
      1. Not all truth is relevant to our salvation. Those that are not are not divinely inspired.
   B. The inspired meaning of Scripture is that which the human authors, directed by God's inspiration, wanted to convey to their readers for the sake of salvation.
   C. We can seek out this meaning by:
      1. Studying the literary styles of the authors, such as the parable. For example, the parable of the prodigal son tells us the truth of God's love and forgiveness. The point is not that there actually was a son forgiven by an actual father.
      2. Reading the Scriptures over and over increases our understanding.
      3. Using passages we understand to help us interpret more difficult passages is a great help in seeking out their meaning.
      4. Calling upon the Holy Spirit to assist us is essential for real growth in understanding.

IV. Give a personal testimony of the part Scripture plays in your life. How does the inspired word speak to you? How do you seek out the "truth" revealed in a particular passage?

INTEGRATION QUESTIONS

1. How was the kingdom of God most evident to you today? Was there a time this week when I resisted belonging to the kingdom? How can I respond differently this week?

2. Jesus asked the question: "Have you understood all this?" The parables have always been one of the most puzzling parts of Scripture. How could we answer a confident "yes" to Jesus' question? Perhaps we can answer this question better. Do you believe that which you do understand?

Are you prepared to act upon this understanding? What does this section of Scripture demand of me at this time.

3. What new understandings of Scripture as inspired writings have I gained? How will I use this new understanding?

CLOSING PRAYER

Read the following meditation:

"The Find"

Jesus says, "Here is a picture of the kingdom. It is like a treasure buried in a field. The man who found it went and, through joy, sold everything he had—and bought that field."

I have a treasure:
the thing I value most in life.
I relive the events
that led me to discover it.

I think of the history of my life
from the time I found this treasure . . .
what it has done for me
and meant to me.

I stand before this treasure
(God or Jesus Christ
or a conviction, value, or ideal
or a person, task, or mission)
and I say, "Of all the things I have
you are the dearest."
And I see what happens to me
when I pronounce that sentence.

I think how much I would gladly do
or give (even life itself, maybe)
in order to preserve this treasure.
If it is not that important,
I acknowledge this with sadness—
and I hope for a day when I shall find a treasure
for which through sheer joy I shall be ready to give up
    everything.

I am a treasure.
Someday, somewhere, someone discovered me.
I should have no awareness of my worth
if someone had not found it.
I recall and relive the details of the finding.

I am a multifaceted treasure.
There were many things concealed in me
that different people drew out
and revealed to me.

I joyfully review each one of these
and gratefully remember the persons who uncovered
    them.

Finally I stand before the Lord
and find, to my surprise,
that he considers me a treasure.
I see reflected in his eyes the many lovely facets
that only he could have observed in me
and I rest in the love he gives me.
(Taken from *Wellsprings*, by Anthony DeMello, Doubleday, 1984)

*Doctrinal and Pastoral Issues: Divine Inspiration, Rev-
elation*

Khris H. Ford

18th Sunday in Ordinary Time

Isaiah 55:1–3
Romans 8:35, 37–39
Matthew 14:13–21

GATHERING PRAYER

Read Psalm 145 as a responsorial reading.

Response: The hand of the Lord feeds us. He answers all our needs.

or

Listen to and/or sing: "Amazing Grace"

REFLECTION QUESTIONS

1. What does this story tell us about Jesus as a person? Use some adjectives that would describe him based on this story.

2. Based on this Gospel, how do you think Jesus would respond to the problem of world hunger?

3. What is your definition of grace?

4. When, this past week, did you experience God's grace?

5. Do you see your hunger for Eucharist, your thirst for baptism, as gift, as grace?

THEMATIC PRESENTATIONS

Theme 1

Is this a story of world hunger? What does Jesus teach us about this?

Outline 1

I. Discuss the following interpretation of this story:
   A. The generosity of the disciples with the five loaves and fish moved the people to share their own food.

II. How can I make this miracle of multiplication possible in my own life? In this way I can be a part of the solution to the problem of world hunger.
   A. Give thanks for the gift of the food you have.
      1. In the story Jesus first looked up to heaven and gave thanks.
      2. In giving thanks we acknowledge God as the source, but also recognize his interest in meeting our physical and spiritual needs.
      3. Mahatma Gandhi once said, "To the million who have to go without two meals a day, the only acceptable form in which God may appear is food."
      4. The pilgrims were an example of giving thanks for their little harvest and very rough first year. Yet look how that first Thanksgiving has multiplied its effect.
   B. The second thing that made the miracle possible was a willingness to share. Jesus said that we should not send the crowds away hungry but we should feed them out of our own resources.
      1. A willingness to share God's gifts to us frees us from worry. We know that God will not leave us hungry when we offer it all to him, to his people.
      2. God will make our resources sufficient to meet the needs. Relate the story of Moses when called to lead his people out of slavery.
      3. Relate a time in which you have trusted in God and he has used and even multiplied your resources to provide for some need.
   C. Third, God works the multiplication miracle through the hands of the disciples, through you and me.
      1. When we give others the gifts from God, we get caught up in the generosity. We see the needs of others, have a new understanding of them, and receive a feeling of satisfaction.
      2. It is not enough to just send a check. We need to be personally involved in the giving, if possible. In this way we build a sense of fellowship, as well as a love of God.
      3. Share a time in which you have received God's gifts through the hands of another.
   D. "The fragments remaining, when gathered up, filled up twelve baskets." God always gives us more than enough. (Is 55:7; Eph 3:20; Ps 23)

1. Because we have excess is no excuse for wasting it. We must "gather it up" and use it wisely.
2. Leftovers should be shared for the good of all of God's people.

E. Give an example of how these principles applied have helped a world or local problem—or how you feel they could.

Theme 2

What Is Grace? (focus on Is 55:1–3)

Outline 2

Today's first reading is an invitation to grace. What, then, is grace?

I. A definition of grace: a gift or favor which deepens our relationship with God.
   A. Grace is experiencing a deeper relationship with God in our daily life experiences.
   B. We may experience God's grace through our experiences with others in our life.
   C. We may experience grace in both the positive and the negative experiences of our life.
   D. Give some personal examples of grace-filled moments.

II. Grace is not something we earn. It is a gift, freely given to all who are open to it.
   A. Reread the Isaiah reading.
   B. Sanctifying grace—this means a gift that makes us holy. This refers to the graces we receive in and through the reception of the sacraments.

III. Grace builds on grace.
   A. Grace, or God's loving presence within us, can transform us.
      1. Give an example of how human love transforms situations. How much more can God's love within us accomplish?
   B. Grace causes us to do good works and therefore to grow further in grace.
      1. The Gospel for this week—the multiplication of the loaves and fish—is an example of this.
      2. Give an example in your own life.

INTEGRATION QUESTIONS

1. Read the following quote from Mother Teresa of Calcutta:

"I have no feet but your feet to carry me into the slums, the factories, and the offices of your cities. I have no hands but your hands to reach out to the helpless, the homeless, and the hopeless. I have no tongue but your tongue to tell my brothers and sisters why I came to live with them, and why I suffered and died for them. I have no help but your help to announce my Kingdom to the hungry and to invite them to the banquet prepared for them since the creation of the world."

Then, discuss the following two questions:
- How will I respond to Jesus' invitation to be his body here on earth?
- Can there be multiplication miracles in my life? How?

3. Make a list of grace-filled moments. Include both positive and negative experiences, big events and less significant ones. Hand this list out in the form of an "Inventory of Grace-Filled Moments". Ask all to check those events that have taken place in their life and then to go back and look back at the ones that they marked. Have I ever considered this as an event/experience of grace?

Choose one of these and write about it. Describe it fully and tell how God's grace filled you. How were you changed? Why do you think this particular grace-filled event occurred at that particular time?

4. Challenge the participant to be particularly aware of grace-filled moments in the coming week. Jot these down at the end of each day. Describe the event and your feelings surrounding it. Pay special attention to the concept of grace multiplying grace. Share one of these events with a small group the next time we gather together.

CLOSING PRAYER

Song

"All That We Have," *Glory and Praise*, Vol. II, North American Liturgy Resources, 1980.

Use one of Paul's greetings in his letters as a final sending-forth blessing (Phil 1:1–2 (3–8); Eph 1:1–8)

or

The leader may say this prayer:

Father, we thank you for your loving-presence within us. We praise you for those moments of grace we have experienced in the past. We ask that you would open our eyes, and make our senses more keenly aware of those special times of relationship with you. Help us to cultivate our hunger for Eucharist, our thirst for baptism, so that we might truly know these as grace-filled! Through Christ our Lord we pray. Amen

Sing or listen to "Come to the Water," *Glory and Praise*, Vol. II, North American Liturgy Resources, 1980.

Doctrinal and Pastoral Issues: Miracles, Grace, Social Responsibility, Hunger

Khris H. Ford

19th Sunday in Ordinary Time

1 Kings 19:9, 11–13
Romans 9:1–5
Matthew 14:22–33

OPENING PRAYER

Listen to the song "Miracle of Life," *Glory and Praise*, Vol. II, North American Liturgy Resources, 1980.

Leader does the following reading:

The freedom to accept miracles is necessary to be free to accept God's Son, Jesus. Graham Greene drove this point home in his play *The Potting Shed*, which tells the story of Henry Callifer, a famous philosopher who lectured around the world. Callifer was an agnostic who zealously and publicly rejected all miracles.

As he lay dying, all the family was called to his bedside except his son James, who was always excluded by his father. James was the sort of young man who could not live with or without a psychiatrist. As soon as the funeral was over, he was determined to discover why he was always treated as an outsider. He called on his uncle, an alcoholic priest, and pressed him to explain why he was never accepted as a son by his father. His uncle finally explained to him that, when he was a boy, he accidentally hanged himself in the potting shed while playing. When the gardener and the priest found him, his body was already cold and lifeless. But the gardener and the alcoholic priest knelt down and prayed in faith. Breath returned to the boy's body as surely as it had left. But since Callifer could not accept the possibility of miracles, therefore he could never accept the boy. The son and miracles were all tied up together.

If you cannot accept the miracles of Jesus and the possibility of miracles, then you will be unable to accept the miracle of the Incarnation.

OR

Lead the following prayer:

My Lord God,
I have no idea where I am going.
I do not know for certain where it will end.

Nor do I really know myself,
and the fact that I think
that I am following your will

does not mean that I am actually doing so.
But I believe that the desire to please you
does in fact please you.
I hope that I have that desire
in all that I am doing.
I hope that I will never do anything
apart from that desire.
And I know that if I do this
you will lead me by the right road
though I may know nothing about it.

Therefore will I trust you always
though I may seem to be lost
and in the shadow of death.
I will not fear, for you are ever with me,
and will never leave me to face my perils alone.
Amen.
(Taken from *Thoughts in Solitude* by Thomas Merton, 1956, 1958, Abbey of Our Lady of Gethsemane.)

Then sing "Blessed Be God Forever," *Glory and Praise* Vol. I, North American Liturgy Resources, 1977.

REFLECTION QUESTIONS

1. Write and share on the following questions: What are my feelings about the miracles of Jesus as told to us in Scripture?

   Do I believe in miracles for today?

2. What does the word faith mean to you?

3. Name three things that you accept and/or know to be true (not by faith).
   Ex. I know that the sun rose this morning.

   Name three things that you accept on faith.
   Ex. I believe that the sun will rise tomorrow.

   What is the difference between these two sets of statements?

4. Peter had the benefit of gazing into the eyes of Jesus, of touching his outstretched hands, as he walked toward him on the water. Though we don't have quite that same "concrete" contact, there are things that will help us as we journey toward Christ in Faith. What are some of these things? What do you find most helpful to you as you attempt to "keep your eyes" on Christ?

THEMATIC PRESENTATIONS

Theme 1

Do I believe that God could perform a miracle such as this one in my own life? Do I really believe in miracles for me?

Outline 1

I. The miracles of Jesus
   A. Scripture makes mention of some forty miracles of all kinds.
   B. Even anti-Christian pagans and first century Jewish historians conceded that Christ was a wonder-worker.
   C. Jesus' miracles show us that Jesus' life was solely dedicated to doing the will of the Father.

II. Jesus walking on the water
   A. Jesus responded to the fear of the disciples.
   B. Peter sees Jesus, gets out of the boat, and walks on the water. Peter's faith falters and he sinks. Jesus saves him.
      1. Parallel this to an experience of looking up to someone and attempting to model their faith behavior.
   C. Peter not only wanted to be like Jesus but he tried. He took the first steps toward him—literally.
      1. God challenges us to be like Peter, to take the first step toward him.
   D. Peter tried but failed when he took his eyes off Jesus and began to look at the waves and turbulence around him.
      1. Doubting and worry about a situation, rather than looking at the answer, often causes us to fail. Relate a personal example of this.

Theme 2

What is "faith"? What does it imply?

Outline 2

I. Define faith: trust in God
   A. This trust comes through receiving and accepting God's word.
   B. This trust of God implies commitment of heart and mind.
   C. This trust implies obedience to the commandments and the new laws of the Gospel.
   D. In order to be totally obedient and to commit one's whole self, there must be acknowledge-

ment of one's failings and repentance—conversion.

II. One of the implications of faith is discipleship.
   A. The call to discipleship is a call to the imitation of Christ. That is, it is a call to do the will of God.
   B. Jesus' miracles were an invitation for us to also be miracle workers.
      1. In order to be a miracle worker for Christ we must always keep our eyes on him. Draw the parallel between what happened to Peter when he got concerned with the rough sea and what happens to us when we get "sidetracked."
      2. We must put our full trust in Christ if we are to answer his call to discipleship—to be miracle workers. We must be willing to take a risk.
   C. Give some examples of modern-day disciples.
      1. Mother Teresa of Calcutta
      2. Gandhi
      3. Martin Luther King (and/or any others that you are familiar with)
   D. Give a personal example of a call to discipleship. Describe the risk involved, the temptation to not trust and to take your eyes off of Christ. Describe your response.

INTEGRATION QUESTIONS

1. Is there a dilemma or situation in my life that needs a "miracle"?

   What are the steps I must take to make this possible?

   Am I willing to take these steps?

2. Name three or four things that would be different in your life if you were not a person of faith. (You must assume that you are still living in our present society, with its laws and rules.)

3. In what particular area of your life do you feel you are being called to be more faithful? In other words, in what area do you most need to work on imitating Christ?

   What can you do this week to help you in moving toward Christ in this area?

CLOSING PRAYER

Read the following reflection:

Research on army parachutists
has revealed an interesting truth:
Fear is highest for the novice jumper
at the moment he receives the "ready" signal
inside the airplane.
The prospective jumper has already reached
what has been called the "point of no return."
He has no place to go but down.

Strangely, it is at this very moment
that his fear begins to decrease.
In fact,
his fear lessens steadily during the free fall,
which is actually the time of greatest danger.

The researchers conclude
that the maximum amount of fear
usually occurs when the novice jumper realizes
that he is about to commit himself irrevocably
to a dangerous action.
As soon as this commitment is made,
the fear immediately begins to decline.

Eugene C. Kennedy
(Taken from "You," 1974, The Thomas More Assn.)

Then sing or listen to the song "Be Not Afraid," *Glory and Praise*, Vol. I, North American Liturgy Resources, 1977.

Doctrinal and Pastoral Issues: Faith, Miracles, Faithfulness, Discipleship

Khris H. Ford

20th Sunday in Ordinary Time

Isaiah 56:1, 6–7
Romans 11:13–15, 29–32
Matthew 15:21–28

GATHERING PRAYER

O God, the Father of our Lord Jesus Christ, our only
Savior, the Prince of Peace, give us the courage to consider seriously the great dangers we are in by our many
unfortunate divisions. Deliver us from all hatred and
prejudice and whatever else may hinder us from union
and concord. There is but one body and one Spirit, and
one hope of our calling, one Lord, one faith, one baptism, one God and Father of us all. So may we all be of
one heart and one soul, united in the holy bonds of
truth and peace, of faith and love. May we glorify you
with one mind and one voice. We ask this through
Christ our Lord. Amen
(from the Liturgy of St. James)

Song
"There Is One Lord" by Damean Music, North American Liturgy Resources, 1981.

REFLECTION QUESTIONS

1. Isaiah 56:7 says, "I will bring you to Zion, my sacred
   hill, give you joy in my house of prayer, and accept
   sacrifices you offer on my altar. My temple will be
   called a house of prayer for the people of all nations."

   Describe what you visualize as you read this passage. How is this "house of prayer" like our church?
   How is it different?

2. Jesus' life was dedicated to drawing all men together
   in his love. He tried to break down walls and build
   up relationships. Are my actions imitations of his?
   Am I walling in or walling out other people?

THEMATIC PRESENTATION

Theme
How does the Catholic Church view those outside the
Catholic faith—those of other religions?

Outline

I. The Gospel story is a parable of Jesus' efforts to
break down walls and to draw all people to him.
   A. Jesus is in pagan territory. He has persisted in
   his travel through this land trying to break
   down the barriers between Jews and Gentiles—to make all people one.
   B. "Dogs" was a term used by Jews to refer to
   Gentiles.
   C. Jesus concluded this passage with a statement
   and action that says to us that those who are far
   away and alienated will be drawn near to him.
   D. Faith is the key to Christ's response to the
   woman. Her origin and Gentile state is of no
   consequence in the end.

II. Isaiah speaks of "a house of prayer for all peoples"
(Is 56:7).

III. The Church's teaching about our relationship to
other faiths is clearly stated in Vatican II documents.
   A. Declaration on the Relation of the Church to
   Non-Christian Religions, paragraphs 1–5.
   B. Decree on Ecumenism—a teaching on the va-
   lidity of baptism outside of Catholicism is ad-
   ressed. "Baptism is then the sacrament bond of
   unity, indeed the foundation of communion
   among all Christians."

IV. Emphasis on ecumenism is growing. We are emphasizing our commonalities rather than our differences.
   A. Give some personal stories of the growth and
   change in the Church in this area—ecumenism.

V. How does this view by the Church challenge me to
live differently? How can I be a part of the movement toward unity?
   A. What is the message of today's readings regarding the diversity within our nation and our
   Church?

INTEGRATION QUESTIONS

1. What can I do to promote the Gospel values in our
readings?

2. In my living, am I a sign of unity of faith or do I often alienate?

3. Read the following excerpt from Robert Frost's "The Mending Wall":

> Before I built a wall I'd ask to know
> What I was walling in or walling out.

Have I built any walls lately? Was I "walling in or walling out"?

What can I do to help "tear the walls down"?

CLOSING PRAYER

Read the following reflection: "One House of God"

Jesus had left Galilee for a non-Jewish region around the towns of Tyre and Sidon. According to Mark he wanted to be alone with his disciples. Then suddenly a woman who had an uncontrollable possessed daughter locked up at home sees him. She recognizes him and she starts to shout.

She shouted: "Sir," and then she added: "Son of David." Just take the situation. He was in a foreign country, a stranger, a Jew, and now this lady addressed him not with his name but with the name of the people he belonged to. She shouted: "Hey, Jew."

If I were walking down a street and someone called behind me: "Hey, mzungu, hey, white man," I would be upset too. And if you walked in a strange region and they shouted behind you: "Hey, Luo," or "Hey, Kikuyu," I am sure you wouldn't like that either.

Jesus did not react; he just walked on, trying to get rid of her, but she continued following him, and the situation became positively embarrassing, and the disciples said: "Please do something about her. Give her what she wants."

Jesus did stop and she came to him and, falling at his feet, she changed her tone and said: "Lord, please; help me!" He then said those words almost unbelievable from his mouth: "It is not fair to take the children's food and throw it to the dogs." The woman must have understood what went wrong. She must have understood that it was she who had divided humanity in groups and cities, that she herself had drawn lines that should not have been drawn, that she herself had used categories that should not have been used, and she said: "Sir, don't dogs have rights in your house?"

Her daughter was healed at that moment. The evil spirit that had been terrorizing her left at the moment that that other evil spirit terrorizing her mother and the whole of humankind left the woman.

As long as she spoke discriminatory, fascist language, Jesus could not communicate with her, but when she spoke in terms of the one family of God he spoke to her immediately.

It is that one house of God that is mentioned by Isaiah: the house of God, a house of prayer, for all peoples, a home for us all, a home that should be established already here on earth among us so that all racism, discrimination, nepotism, apartheid, and fascism will disappear from our streets and a shout like "Hey, Jew" will no longer be heard anymore. The woman went home and the girl she had left screaming in her house was screaming no longer. She was sitting peacefully on her bed: another devil humanity got rid of. Let it be, oh, let it be!

by Joseph G. Donders
(excerpts from *The Peace of Jesus, Reflections on the Gospel*, Orbis, 1983, as printed in *Maryknoll*, February 1985)

Sing an appropriate song.

Doctrinal and Pastoral Issues: Ecumenism, Salvation Outside the Church, Universality, Non-Christian Religions, Baptism

Khris H. Ford

21st Sunday in Ordinary Time

Isaiah 22:15, 19–23
Romans 11:33–36
Matthew 16:13–20

GATHERING PRAYER

Listen to "Who Is He? He Is Jesus," by Terry Talbot, *On Wings of the Wind*, Sparrow Records, Inc.

Psalm 63 as a responsorial:
Response: My soul is thirsting for you, O Lord my God.

Listen to "Do You Really Love Me?" by Rev. Carey Landry, North American Liturgy Resources, *Glory and Praise*, Vol II. 1980.

REFLECTION QUESTIONS

1. Gather several pictures of Jesus depicted in different ways: as teacher, as consoler, as forgiver, as friend, as lover, etc. If possible, show these on either an overhead projector or a slide projector. Along with each picture read a Scripture reference and brief reflection. After all have been presented ask the participants to decide which one they most identify with. Answer the question: Who do you say that I am? Then have them share their responses in small groups.

   Pictures may be obtained from *Romans Eight*, Argus Communications, Texas.

2. Complete the following statement:
   Christ is most present to me _____.

3. What is it that we have in common with Peter and the other apostles?

4. How was the leadership of Christ different than that of the "leadership" image we typically have?

THEMATIC PRESENTATIONS

Theme 1

Who do *you* say that I am?

Outline 1

I. Who do people say the Son of Man is?
   A. Prior to today's Gospel we have been dealing with the rejection of Jesus by his own people.
   B. Jesus asks: "Who do people say the Son of Man is?" The answers are indicative of the lack of understanding of the mystery of Jesus.
   C. Today's world might well answer Jesus' question similarly, with little understanding of his mystery.
      1. We must be wary of accepting the "world's" view of Jesus.

II. Jesus asks us, "Who do you say that I am?"
   A. Give a personal statement of who Jesus Christ is for you. Relate some ways in which Christ has revealed himself to you.
      1. Scripture
      2. Prayer
      3. People
      4. Sacraments

Theme 2

What was Peter's role in the foundation of the Church?

Outline 2

I. Christ called the twelve apostles.
   A. Apostles are witnesses of the resurrection.
   B. Jesus traveled through only a relatively small part of the known world and spoke to comparatively few people. It was the job of the apostles to work out the best way to carry his message to others, with the Spirit as their guide (Mt 28:18–20).
   C. The apostles were to share in Christ's work as prophet, priest, and king.
      1. They were to teach with Christ's authority (Lk 10:6, Mt 18:18).
      2. They were to continue Christ's work in offering worship to God. (Jn 20:21–23; 1 Cor 11:23–26).

II. Christ chose Peter to be the leader of the twelve apostles.
   A. Christ changed Peter's name from Simon, son of John, to Peter—meaning "rock" (Jn 1:42; Lk 6:14).

B. Peter presided over the leadership of Matthias.
C. Peter went to Rome to spread the message of Christ, and was martyred there.

III. How did the role of the Pope develop in the history of the Church?
   A. What are the titles given to the Pope, Bishop of Rome?
   B. Give a personal reflection on how you see the Church and your role in it.

CLOSING PRAYER

Lead the following prayer:

Lord, you gave your apostle Peter
the keys to the kingdom of heaven;
by a secret revelation you taught him
to acknowledge you as the living God
and Christ as your Son;
you gave him the further privilege
of witnessing to his Lord
by his victorious suffering and death.
Keep us faithful to your Son
who alone has the word of eternal life,
that he may lead us,
as the loyal sheep of his flock,
to the eternal joys of your kingdom.
We ask this through Christ our Lord. Amen

Doctrinal and Pastoral Issues: Papacy, Hierarchy, Apostolic Succession, Christology, Ecclesiology

Khris H. Ford

22nd Sunday in Ordinary Time

Jeremiah 20:7–9
Romans 12:1–2
Matthew 16:21–27

GATHERING PRAYER

Song

"Only This I Want" by Daniel L. Schutte, North American Liturgy Resources, 1981.

Lead this prayer:

Almighty, ever-living God,
you have given the human race
Jesus Christ our Savior
as a model of humility.
He fulfilled your will
by becoming man
and giving his life on the cross.
Help us to bear witness to you
by following his example of suffering
and make us worthy to share
in his resurrection.
Grant this through Christ our Lord.
Amen.
(Roman Sacramentary, Collect for Passion Sunday)

REFLECTION QUESTIONS

1. Once a person has received the gift of faith, what must he or she do to insure continued growth in faith?

2. Have you ever experienced a time of "crisis" in your faith? Reflect on this experience. What was the result of this time in your faith journey?

3. What does it mean to "offer" ourselves as "a living sacrifice"?

4. How can you share in the death and resurrection of Jesus Christ?

THEMATIC PRESENTATIONS

Theme 1

Can doubt and true faith exist within our lives?

Outline 1

I. In the first reading, Jeremiah experiences doubt and faith.
   A. Jeremiah expressed that he had been deceived, that to proclaim God's message brings destruction and persecution.
   B. Jeremiah's faith and desire to spread the message is so strong that he cannot remain in silence.

II. In the process of faith doubt must occur. Faith is a living relationship and living things are susceptible to growth.
   A. Kahil Gibran said, "We can forget those we have laughed with, but we can never forget those we have cried with." Faith matures through crises.
   B. Doubts cause us to look at and redefine our relationship with God. It is in this process of redefining that we grow and mature in faith.
   C. Relate a personal experience of doubting in an area of faith. What growth occurred as a result of this?
   D. The key to the co-existence of doubt and faith is the continued ability to hear the challenge of Jesus in our doubting. We must continue to hear him calling us to follow him once again. Then, we must respond in renewed faith.

Theme 2

What does it mean to take up your cross? to lose one's life in order to save it?

Outline 2

I. The meaning of Jesus' death is life for the Christian.
   A. Through his death on the cross, Jesus put to death all that might separate us from God.
   B. Jesus did this by the total giving of himself to the will of his Father.
   C. It is only through Christ's death and resurrection that we have the promise of "resurrection"—new life in Christ.

II. Jesus tells us, "If anyone wishes to come after me, he must deny his very self, take up his cross, and follow in my steps."
   A. First, we must deny ourselves; we too must

surrender ourselves to the will of the Father.

1. We may need to let go of our pride, our selfishness, our dependence on material things, whatever the Father calls us to do.
2. Our relationship with the Father is an intimate friendship. In any good friendship there is mutual self-giving. Jesus gave the ultimate gift of himself, in death on the cross.
   a. Discuss a time when you were called, in friendship, to give of yourself in some way. What were the results in your relationship?

B. We must follow in his footsteps. That is, we must strive to imitate Christ in all our thoughts and actions.
   1. In living the Christ-style of life we may be ridiculed and we may need to make substantial sacrifices. In doing this, we carry the cross. We carry the cross whenever we put the will of God first in our life and renounce sin in our life.

III. Just as we share in the cross of Christ, we also share in his resurrection.
   A. Jesus said, "I am the resurrection and the life." So, as we follow his steps and carry the cross, we must always remember the promise of new life in Christ.
   B. When we follow Christ and the will of his Father, we find inner joy and peace.
   C. The promise of Christ offers us hope in times of great difficulty and darkness.
   D. Our experience of daily life is one of an ongoing death-to-resurrection cycle.
      1. Give a personal example of this. Tell about a time when dying to self yielded new life for you. Even the cycle of the seasons in nature is an example of death and resurrection.
   E. Particular focus is placed on this death/resurrection cycle during the season of Lent. We concentrate on death to self so that we may truly celebrate resurrection with our risen Lord.
      1. Talk about a particular meaningful experience of Lent and Easter. How did this cycle play a part in that?

IV. Sharing in the daily cross and resurrection is but a taste of the eternal life Christ promises us.
   A. There is a vital link between our life with Christ on earth and our life with him in God's kingdom after death.
   B. Because of our relationship with Christ, Christians should share in the hope of the power of the resurrection.
      1. This doesn't mean that Christians don't fear death and the circumstances of it. Even Jesus was fearful as he faced his death. Remember his words in the garden of Gethsemane.
      2. But underlying the fear must be an attitude of hope and expectation. This is true not only in our attitude about our own death, but also in our attitude as we face the deaths of those whom we love.
      3. Share something about your own attitude toward death—your own and that of others. Have you had an experience with death? If so, how did your belief in the resurrection help you through this time of difficulty? Have you seen any change in your attitude toward death as you have matured in your faith?

INTEGRATION QUESTIONS

1. Growth in almost any area of our life requires some sacrifice. Tell about a time when you experienced discomfort, pain, and/or sacrifice in order to grow.

2. Do you believe that times of doubt and crisis in faith are necessary for growth? Explain.

3. Jesus calls us to take up our cross each and every day? How is he calling you this day? In what areas of your life must you "die to self"?

4. Is there an area of your life that seems dark and without hope? Reflect on this area in light of Christ's promise of resurrection. Write down your thoughts as you consider the hope that he offers us.

CLOSING PRAYER

Song

"Prayer of St. Francis." This prayer/song blends our call to self-giving with the "fruit" that it will bear in the eternal.

OR

Prayer

Almighty, ever-living God,
you have given the human race
Jesus Christ our Savior
as a model of humility.

He fulfilled your will
by becoming man
and giving his life on the cross.
Help us to bear witness to you
by following his example of suffering
and make us worthy to share in his resurrection.

Grant this through Christ our Lord.
(Roman Sacramentary, Collect for Passion Sunday)

OR

Listen to "Hear my Prayer, O Lord," Terry Talbot and
Joe Bellamy, *A Song Shall Rise*, 1981.

*Doctrinal and Pastoral Issues: Sacrifice, Hope, Paschal
Mystery*

Khris H. Ford

Introduction to 23rd Sunday in Ordinary Time to Christ the King

The format for these sessions is divided as follows:

Opening Prayer
Reflections
Closing Prayer

Each parish will have to adapt the local situations such as scheduling coffee breaks or the arrival of the sponsors (if they join the session after the Mass).

The prayer sessions are designed to offer a variety of models and experiences to the catechumens. A number of the examples are taken from the blessings for the catechumens from the Rite. Others are from the sacramentary. Another category is familiar Catholic prayers, such as the Act of Hope and the Prayer of Saint Francis. It is suggested that nice copies of these prayers be given to the catechumens with a folder so that they can be saved and used again and again. They could be written in calligraphy and duplicated on parchment paper, for example. One other type of prayer is the litany, either of petitions or thanksgiving. The leader is encouraged to invite spontaneous participation.

On occasion, music is suggested in the form of a tape recording. Of course, this is not a substitute for a song leader and instrumentalist. Other arrangements of the environment are not specified. The person responsible for the session is encouraged to prepare the arrangement of the room so that it is welcoming and hospitable. If it could reflect the sanctuary in an echo of color, light (candles), texture, and smell (flowers) it would be good. There should be a nice copy of the lectionary, open to the readings of the Sunday. It should be placed in a fitting location.

The reflection section is divided into two or three themes, each of which is divided into paragraph "a" and paragraph "b". The first part is a statement of the theme. The catechist should introduce the theme in his own words, or by reading the statement.

The second portion of each theme suggests a variety of ways to begin the discussion and sharing. The catechist can begin by relating an experience of his own and then asking for stories of similar situations, or he can directly ask a question. A significant amount of time should be spent in this sharing. Adults come to faith by integrating their personal experience with mystery. No one can do this for them. The catechist is the guide. The catechist can make connections and can relate the immediate experience of the local church, the immediate neighborhood, the people who are known to the catechumens and candidates.

After the sharing by the members of the group, the catechist should summarize the theme. If needed, the catechist can move the exploration of the theme to a deeper or broader level. For example, after rooting and grounding the theme in personal expeience, thought can be given to historical or contemporary situations beyond the immediate experience. Catechists should research these areas ahead of time. At the end of each reflection section two or three issues of doctrine, morality, and ecclesiology are listed. These can act as guides or chapter headings for the catechist during the preparation time. The presentation of these should not be academic and detached, but should always be framed in the reflection by the catechists and catechumens and candidates.

23rd Sunday in Ordinary Time

Exodus 33:7–9
Romans 13:8–10
Matthew 18:15–20

OPENING PRAYER

Leader: Let us pray and be mindful of these words
of Jesus to us:
"Love one another as I have loved you."

All Pray: If I have been the cause of pain to another,
if I have forgotten others' needs in my
hurry
to serve my own, I am sorry.
May the words of Jesus be a lamp for me to
examine my recent life.

(Silent pause for reflection)

All Pray: My God, I willingly forgive all who have
injured me and ask their forgiveness
at the end of this day. May your divine absolution cleanse me of any sin
or failing.

(Bow our heads and pause for reflection)

All Pray: Surrounded by your divine presence,
in union with all whom I love and all who
love you,
I enter into stillness.

(Bow our heads and pause for reflection)

Leader: Loving God, we join our voices to ask for
forgiveness in Jesus' name. Amen.

(Adapted from *Prayers for Domestic Church* by Edward M. Hayes, Kansas, Forest of Peace Books, 1979,
p. 138)

REFLECTIONS

1. Loving others involves responsibility. In relationships, it is often difficult to tell another person that
he or she is hurting me by his or her actions. If a
person admits his or her hurt, he or she becomes
vulnerable. On the other hand none of us want to be
confronted with how we hurt or are unjust to others.

Name a time when you told another that you were
being hurt by that person's attitudes or behavior.
Reflect on that time. What happened? What did you
learn in your vulnerability? Did you expect and experience healing or justice? Reflect on a time when
someone told you that you were hurting others.
What happened? What does Christian love demand
in these circumstances? What is my responsibility
for the actions of others that cause hurt and injustice?

2. In the Gospel, Jesus asks us to respond to the faults
of others. But often we refuse to accept responsibility for ourselves. We refuse to accept ourselves
when we don't face our faults, our problems, our
weaknesses, our angers, our sense of inadequacy.
Even worse is blaming our problems on others, de-
nying we have any, or insisting that we need to be
perfect. Every doctor and psychologist in the country sees the effect of that in their offices every day.

We all have things we need to forgive in ourselves
or face in ourselves. We have things we know we
ought to ask forgiveness for from someone else but
pride and stubbornness hold us back. These things
become a barrier betwen us and the community, a
hot stone in the pit of the stomach, a block to real
happiness. And nothing is going to get better until
we face them.

Question: What would you like to accept in yourself?
What particular situation should you be asking forgiveness for from someone else?"

(Excerpted from *Psalm Journal Book II*, by Joan
Chittister, O.S.B., Kansas City, MO, Sheed &
Ward, 1985)

3. God's graciousness is a constant presence. God is
present here in this time and place with each of us.
Reread Matthew 18:18–20 (slowly). A leader will ask
participants to become comfortable. By relaxing
their bodies, slow rhythmic breathing and closing
their eyes, or by other brief relaxation exercises, he
or she begins this meditation. (The phrases are spoken slowly.)

Imagine God coming to you. What is your image?
This gentle tremendous lover touches you. God
asks, "What is it that you need?" You reflect. Name
it and ask God in your words for what you need.
Talk with God. How does God respond? You listen.

God says, "Where two or three are gathered in my name, there I am in your midst."

(Allow participants to open their eyes and return to a brief discussion.)

CLOSING PRAYER

A litany of petitions. . . . .

Leader: Creator, we remember the words of Jesus that if we pray for anything, it shall be granted. We place our needs before you.

(Encourage catechumens and others to ask the community present to pray for their needs, the needs of their family, church and the world using the simple formula below)

I pray. . . . .

To each petition, all respond: Grant our prayer.

All pray this closing prayer:

We ask this with heartfelt voices in the name of Jesus, our Brother and Redeemer. Amen.

Doctrinal and Pastoral Issues: Christian Love and Responsibility, Social Sin, Self-Discipline, God's Graciousness, Prayer, God's Mercy

Joseph P. Sinwell

24th Sunday in Ordinary Time

Sirach 27:30—28:7
Romans 14:7–9
Matthew 18:21–35

OPENING PRAYER

(Read aloud, thoughtfully and slowly. Pause after the invitation to pray and again before the closing of the prayer.)

Leader: Let us pray.

Lord God, through the cross of your Son you reconcile us to you. Open our hearts, that we will grow in union with Christ, in faith, and in action.

Guide our thoughts now to our own experiences of your love in times of forgiveness. Bring to our minds the people with whom we have known forgiveness.

Guide our reflection and sharing.

We ask this in the name of Jesus, your Son and our Lord. Amen.

REFLECTIONS

1. Forgiveness is the underlying characteristic of our relationship with one another when we live in relationship to God. We learn to be forgiving by receiving forgiveness.

   Tell a story of forgiveness: Were you the one forgiven? Whom did you forgive? Was forgiveness freely given? How were you different after the forgiving? These will be stories of family life and relationships, and of the workplace. There may be an international scale: a story of an encounter with someone whose nation we call "enemy." Listen to each one. Listen for the incomplete stories. Listen for the actions that accompany the forgiveness.

2. Actions of forgiveness and reconciliation symbolize the reality that is taking place. Life in the Church is continually experienced in actions of reconciliation.

   Tell a story of baptism: someone will have been present at the baptism of a child or a friend's child. If there are candidates for full communion in the catechumenate process, one may recall baptism. Listen for the actions other than those that accompany the water bath, for example, gathering of family and friends, anointing and signing.

3. The act of incorporation into the Church is an incorporation into the life and death of Jesus. We become one with the saving, forgiving, reconciling life of Jesus. Each catechumen is signed with the sign of the cross as he or she enters the community of the Church.

   Return to the story of today's Gospel. Reread the Gospel. Ask each one to recall the stories of forgiveness. How often do we need mercy? Where was mercy shown? What form did it take: were charges dropped, was a gift given? Listen for specific details. Summarize the patterns or differences that develop. Reflect on the incidents and people of the last week and the coming week. How will this Gospel of mercy change my actions and relationships? Write in a journal one thing that each will keep before himself or herself in relation to mercy.

CLOSING PRAYER

We live in the recognition of our dependence on God for mercy. The following prayer is based on another section of the Gospel, a passage called the Beatitudes. It is a prayer for mercy. After each section please respond: "Have mercy on us."

Leader: We are signed with the sign of the cross of the Lord Jesus and we carry his example throughout life.
Let us pray.
Lord Jesus Christ, you said:
"Blessed are the poor in spirit, for theirs is the kingdom of heaven."
Yet we are preoccupied with money and worldly goods and even try to increase them at the expense of justice.
Lamb of God, you take away the sin of the world.

Have mercy on us.

Lord Jesus Christ, you said:

"Blessed are the gentle for they shall inherit the earth."
Yet we are ruthless with each other, and our world is full of discord and violence.
Lamb of God, you take away the sin of the world:

>Have mercy on us.

Lord Jesus Christ, you said:
"Blessed are those who mourn, for they shall be comforted."
Yet we are impatient under our own burdens and unconcerned about the burdens of others.
Lamb of God, you take away the sin of the world:

>Have mercy on us.

Lord Jesus Christ, you said:
"Blessed are those who hunger and thirst for justice, for they shall be filled."
Yet we do not thirst for you, the fountain of all holiness, and are slow to spread your influence in our private lives or in society.
Lamb of God, you take away the sin of the world:

>Have mercy on us.

Lord Jesus Christ, you said:
"Blessed are the merciful for they shall receive mercy."
Yet we are slow to forgive and quick to condemn.
Lamb of God, you take away the sin of the world:

>Have mercy on us.

Lord Jesus Christ, you said:
"Blessed are the clean of heart, for they shall see God."
Yet we are prisoners of our senses and evil desires and dare not raise our eyes to you.
Lamb of God, you take away the sin of the world:

>Have mercy on us.

Lord Jesus Christ, you said:
"Blessed are the peacemakers, for they shall be called children of God."
Yet we fail to make peace in our families, in our counry, and in the world.
Lamb of God, you take away the sin of the world:

>Have mercy on us.

Lord Jesus Christ, you said:
"Blessed are those who are persecuted for the sake of justice, for the kingdom of heaven is theirs."
Yet we prefer to practice injustice rather than suffer for the sake of right; we discriminate against our neighbors and oppress and persecute them.
Lamb of God, you take away the sin of the world:

>Have mercy on us.

Lord Jesus Christ,
you chose the cross as the path to glory to show us the way to salvation.
May we receive with joyful hearts the word of your Gospel and live by your example as heirs and citizens of your kingdom, where you live and reign for ever and ever. Amen.

(The above prayer is taken from the Rite of Penance, Appendix II, Number 41, with the opening and closing adapted to the catechumenate.)

Doctrinal and Pastoral Issues: Baptism—Incorporation into the Death/Resurrection of Jesus, Forgiveness—Basis of Relationship, Mercy—Virtue of Christian

Elizabeth S. Lilly

25th Sunday in Ordinary Time

Isaiah 55:6–9
Philippians 1:20–24, 27
Matthew 20:1–16

OPENING PRAYER

Leader: Let us pray.

Reader 1:   Lord we turn to you in your word. We recognize our dependence on you and we pray to learn of you and to live in you.

Reader 2:   "Seek the Lord while he may be found, call to him while he is near."

Reader 1:   Lord, teach us of your timelessness.

Reader 2:   "Turn to the Lord for mercy, to our God, who is generous in forgiving."

Reader 1:   Lord, teach us of your compassion.

Reader 2:   "See, the Lord's thoughts are not your thoughts, nor his ways, your ways.

Reader 1:   Lord, teach us of your presence.

Reader 2:   "Live in the Lord, the Creator of life and death."

Reader 1:   Lord, teach us of your wisdom.

Reader 2:   "Trust in the goodness of the Lord."

Reader 1:   Lord, teach us of your power.

Leader: Lord, Creator of all, we ask this in the name of Jesus, your Son. Amen.

(This prayer should be read with at least three voices, one for opening and closing, one for the scriptural passages, and one for the petitions. There should be a moment of reflective silence between the quotations and the petition.)

REFLECTIONS

1. Generosity is the attribute of the God of mercy and forgiveness. Last week we explored our stories of forgiveness and our own need for mercy. We had already established that forgiveness and mercy are relational: one forgives, the other is forgiven. Basically, there is a giver and a receiver.

Tell a story of giving and receiving. Think of specific people. For example, do you know people who will not accept a dinner because they cannot reciprocate and do not want to feel indebted? Do you know a time when someone gave you something that you did not deserve? How is a gift different from something that is evenly traded? Which is more difficult—giving or receiving? Can you give or receive a compliment?

2. Justice and charity are closely related to generosity through mercy and forgiveness. These are the foundations of peace, yet we often want the result without the foundation.

What happened in the last week in forgiving and in being merciful? What familiar situations arose? Were any changes made? What surprising things happened? Did you receive more that you gave? What new circumstances gave opportunities for mercy? What is fair? Reread the Gospel. Retell it in a contemporary setting. Can you? Set the scene in your family or your office or your group of friends. What is encouraging to you in this story? What in your life and our culture needs examining in light of the story of these latecomers—the unemployed, the immigrants, the financially secure, the church members, or the inquirers? Invite a member of your parish social justice committee to be present and to share in the general discussion.

3. Receiving is the counterpart of generosity.

Name a time that you found it easy (or difficult) to receive something. Which was it, easy or difficult? What was given: time, material goods, food, shelter, faith, hope?

CLOSING PRAYER

(The leader should introduce the closing prayer at the end of the summary of the dicsussion.)

As we close today, we reflect on the generosity of God and on our growing dependence on God's presence in our lives combined with our difficulty in opening ourselves to God's grace. This is not unique to each of us. Our prayer is known as the Prayer of St. Ignatius Loyola.

Let us pause a moment and then pray this
aloud together.

Take, Lord, and receive
all my liberty, my memory,
my understanding, and my entire will,
all that I have and possess.

You have given all to me.

To you, Lord, I return it.
All is yours.
Dispose of it wholly according to your will.
Give me your love and your grace
for this is enough for me.

(This is also available on tape or record, by the Saint
Louis Jesuits, *Glory and Praise*, NALR)

*Doctrinal and Pastoral Issues: Justice and Charity,
Mercy and Forgiveness*

Elizabeth S. Lilly

26th Sunday in Ordinary Time

Ezekiel 18:25–28
Philippians 2:1–11
Matthew 21:28–32

OPENING PRAYER

(The following prayer is one of the prayers of the cate-chumenate called the Minor Exorcisms, #373. The catechist should read the prayer following the directions in the Rite of Christian Initiation of Adults, #109–112.)

Leader: Let us pray.
Lord Jesus Christ,
loving Redeemer of mankind,
you alone have the power to save us.
In your Name every knee shall bow
in heaven, on earth, and under the earth.

We pray for these servants of yours
who worship you as the one true God;
send your light into their hearts,
protect them from the hatred of the evil
   one.

Heal in them the wounds of sin,
and strengthen them against temptation.
Give them a love of your commandments
and courage to live always by your Gospel,
and so prepare them to receive your Spirit,
for you live and reign for ever and ever.
   Amen.

REFLECTIONS

1. Free will is the basis for our abililty to choose God, to choose to do good rather than evil, to choose right over wrong. Any action that one takes must be based in that individual freedom. Freedom is a gift from God.

   When you became catechumens or entered the cate-chumenate, you gave reasons for your choice of the Church. Can you recall those reasons? How clearly was there a distinct choice in your life? How aware were you of moving from one way of life to another? If there has been some time (weeks, months) since the celebration of the Rite of Entrance, how have your choices changed in the meantime? (The catech-ist should listen for language that describes an interior change, a growing openness to the Gospel, the way of God.)

2. Conversion is the task of everyone confronted with the will of God. In other words, hearing the word of God always calls one to choose again and again to follow in the way of Jesus. Baptism is the celebration of the initial conversion in a person's life. For the initiated Christian, conversion is the way of life.

   The prayer we closed with a couple of weeks ago was originally written for use in a celebration of the sacrament of reconciliation, a sacrament of repentance. What is your definition of the word repent? What are the positive aspects of repentance? Write in your journals an action of repentance based on forgiveness or generosity or mercy that you have experienced in the last couple of weeks. Have any of these actions involved a noticeable change in your attitude and or behavior?

3. We have the ability to respond to God and to choose to follow in and through Jesus.

   Reread the Gospel. How do we hear invitations to follow the will of God? How often do we change our minds?

CLOSING PRAYER

(The following prayer is adapted from the "Penetant's Act of Sorrow" from *Outline of the Catholic Faith* published by the Leaflet Missal Company, 419 W. Minnehaba Avenue, Saint Paul, Minnesota, 55103. Make a copy of the prayer for each member of the group to keep in a folder.)

Leader: Let us pray.

All: My God,
I am sorry for the times that I have deliberately chosen
to disregard your will for mine.
In choosing to do wrong, and in failing to
   do good,

I close myself off from your life-giving
    grace.
I intend, with your help,
to repent, to change my ways,
to open my heart to your word more and
    more.
Our Savior Jesus Christ suffered and died
    for us.
In his name, my God, have mercy on me.
Amen.

*Doctrinal and Pastoral Issues: Free Will, Conversion,
Penance, Virtue of Humility*

Elizabeth S. Lilly

27th Sunday in Ordinary Time

Isaiah 5:1–7
Philippians 4:6–9
Matthew 21:33–43

OPENING PRAYER

Leader: We believe that God is present in his word, and among us here. We believe that God has created us to follow his will. Let us now put into words that for which we are thankful, and also those people and things that we feel are in need of God's grace.

For our families, that they may be enriched by the conversion journey of the catechumenate, we pray to the Lord:

We pray to the Lord.

(Invite petitions from others. Wait; give people time to formulate the words that are in their hearts.)

Leader: For these and all our needs and the needs of your people everywhere, we pray in the name of Jesus, your Son, our Lord. Amen.

REFLECTIONS

1. Jesus taught that the kingdom of God is at hand. One of the signs of the kingdom is the rich harvest, the good yield.

   We have just prayed for the things for which we are thankful. Are these signs of the kingdom? Review them—good relationships, harmony, growth, community, good work. Have you also prayed for our needs? How are these signs of the kingdom not yet fulfilled? Review them—war, unemployment, disease, strained relationships.

2. The reality of our lives involves both glimpses of the kingdom and the tension of its absence. One of the virtues of a Christian is hope. If we had all that we need we would not need hope. We ground our hope in the death and resurrection of Jesus.

   What are your stories of death and resurrection—rejection from one job, only to find a better one; change from an independent living style as a single to the new life of interdependence as a couple; death of someone close to you; birth of a child; passing of the seasons? How much pruning and trimming and dying do we need in order to become all that we could? What disciplines do we choose? What disciplines does the Chrisian community impose on itself?

CLOSING PRAYER

(Hope is one of the three theological virtues. The Christian's prayer always is centered in hope. Distribute copies of the Act of Hope so that all may recite the prayer together.)

Leader: Let us pray.

All: O my God,
trusting in your infinite goodness and
   promises,
I hope to obtain pardon of my sins,
the help of your grace,
and life everlasting,
through the merits of Jesus Christ,
my Lord and Redeemer. Amen.

Doctrinal and Pastoral Issues: Prayer, Kingdom of God, Eschaton, Virtue of Hope, Centrality of the Death and Resurrection of Jesus

Elizabeth S. Lilly

28th Sunday in Ordinary Time

Isaiah 25:6–10
Philippians 4:12–14, 19–20
Matthew 22:1–14

OPENING PRAYER

(The opening prayer for every Sunday Mass is chosen from two options. One of the prayers today focuses on love as the foundation of our lives. The other highlights the journey or pilgrimage aspect of the life of faith. Below is the second option.)

Leader: Let us pray.
Father in heaven,
the hand of your loving kindness
powerfully yet gently guides all the moments of our day.
Go before us in our pilgrimage of life,
anticipate our needs and prevent our falling.
Send your Spirit to unite us in faith,
that, sharing in your sevice,
we may rejoice in your presence.
We ask this through Christ our Lord.
Amen.

REFLECTIONS

1. One of the images of the Church is that of a people on a pilgrimage, a people with a destination. One of the attributes of the pilgrim is an openness to the invitation to move out of the familiar toward the unknown. The willingness to risk is based on faith.

   Reread the first half of the Gospel, the parable about the banquet. Ask someone present to retell the story in contemporary terms. What are the excuses today for not answering and accepting the invitation of God? Ask for stories of times when the invitations were accepted, when someone did respond to another in spite of a busy schedule or personal desires. The catechist can give some examples of the challenges that are before the Church today. For example, in the community, name the places for the unemployed and the hungry? Do you know that they exist? On a wider scale, tell how the Church is involved in the sanctuary movement, or Bread for the World, or Pax Christi. How can we become a people on the way of the Gospel today?

2. When one responds to the call of the Gospel, there will be changes. One must choose, one must decide to live the values of the Gospel. Paul speaks of some of the changes he has encountered. In summary, he speaks of the willingness of others to share with him.

   Introduce the catechumens and candidates to the work and life of Mother Teresa. Tell the story of St. Francis of Asissi (his feast day may have just passed). One of the catechists could prepare information about a local person. Someone in your community could come to share a personal story of choice and change in the name of the Gospel. Some examples could be a person from a Catholic Worker House, a member of a religious community, a youth minister, or a missionary. Allow time for the catechumens and candidates to share the joy or the tension that the Gospel presents to them.

3. God is always present. When we are self-satisfied and complacent we risk not trusting in his wisdom and his way.

   Reread the second part of the Gospel. Whenever and wherever in our lives we have accepted the invitation to follow God, we must always adjust and adapt. We do not do this alone, but with God's grace.

CLOSING PRAYER

(Perhaps, today, there is an uneasiness with knowing in what direction to turn. We hear the Gospel, but do not yet see what we need to do and where we need to go. The following prayer is adapted from a prayer for catechumens, RCIA #123. It is adapted precisely to reassure the catechumens and candidates that being on a faith journey is part of being Church.)

Leader: Let us pray.

All-powerful God,
help us to deepen our knowledge of the Gospel of Christ.

May we come to know and love you
and always do your will with generous
hearts and willing spirits.
Guide us as we welcome our brothers and
sisters into a life of holiness,
and count them among your Church
so that they may share your holy mysteries
here on earth
and in the everlasting joy of heaven.
We ask this through Christ our Lord.
Amen.

Doctrinal and Pastoral Issues: Models of Church—Pilgrim, Life of Christian Service, Grace

Elizabeth S. Lilly

29th Sunday in Ordinary Time

Isaiah 45:1,4–6
1 Thessalonians 1:1–5
Matthew 22:15–21

OPENING PRAYER

Leader: Let us pray.
Lord God, we direct our thoughts to you;
quietly, we ponder your presence with us,
your loving care for us, before we knew
you.
We recognize ever more clearly that we
are yours.

(Sing or play a recording of "I Have Loved You" by Michael Joncas from *Eagles' Wings*, NALR)

Grant that we may grow in love for you,
our Creator,
through Jesus Christ. Amen.

REFLECTIONS

1. God is the author of life. God acts and we respond.
The readings today reflect upon God's initiative and
our response. First, let us recall the times in which
we have become aware of God's presence in our
lives.

In what events, associations, or actions of the last
few weeks have you recognized God's presence?
Where have you touched or been touched by birth
or death in the last month? How has your life been
affected by this awareness? What choices have you
made or will you make because of this?

2. A few weeks ago we discussed freedom and free will.
We have just now been thinking about choices.
Paul, in his letter, gives an excellent summary of the
life of a Christian. The Christian's decisions are
rooted in faith, hope and charity. These are so
closely related to our relationship with God that
they are called the theological virtues.

Reread the letter of Paul. The catechist or a sponsor
could paraphrase Paul and speak about the catechumens of the local church concerning growth in faith,
love, and hope. It will be good for the catechumens
and candidates to hear, as did the Christians of
Thessalonica, from one observing them. This will
model a discerning process. Then each could write
in a journal personal reflections on growth in faith, a
need for hope, and a possibility for charity.

3. We know God in the mystery of the Trinity. Look
again to Paul for this pattern: know God, in Jesus,
through the Holy Spirit.
We began the reflections today speaking of God's initiative and our response. That we are able to respond at all to God is the action of the Spirit in us.
We are already participating in the life of God when
we respond according to his will.
The Christian, acting in faith and hope and love, in
the relationship of the Trinity, is free to respond to
the world. There are responsibilities to government
and family that each one has. However, our faith
tells us that we are made in the image of God, so our
most appropriate behavior is to form ourselves according to his will, discerned within the Christian
community. There is no Christian without the present and past tradition of the Church, the Christian
community.

Describe at least one new activity or association that
you do or have made with the Christian community.
How is the Church supporting and forming you?

CLOSING PRAYER

(The following Prayer of St. Francis should be available
for each person to have a copy to keep.)

All: O Lord, our Christ, may we have your
mind and your spirit.
Make us instruments of your peace:
where there is hatred, let us sow love;
where there is injury, pardon;
where there is discord, union;
where there is doubt, faith;
where there is despair, hope;
where there is darkness, light
and where there is sadness, joy.

O divine master grant that we may not so
    much seek
to be consoled as to console;
to be understood as to understand;
to be loved as to love;
for it is in giving that we receive,
it is in pardoning that we are pardoned
and it is in dying that we are born to eter-
    nal life. Amen.

*Doctrinal and Pastoral Issues: Theological Virtues,
Trinity, Church*

Elizabeth S. Lilly

30th Sunday in Ordinary Time

Exodus 22:20–26
1 Thessalonians 1:5–10
Matthew 22:34–40

OPENING PRAYER

(Last week we talked about the three virtues of faith hope, and love. Our opening prayer today is called the Act of Love. Give copies for the prayer books.)

All: O my God, I love you above all things,
with my whole heart and soul,
because you are all-good and worthy of all my love.
I love my neighbor as myself for love of you.
I forgive all who have injured me,
and I ask pardon of all whom I have injured. Amen.

REFLECTIONS

1. Who is our neighbor? In the Gospel, Jesus is constantly meeting and associating with people who did not mix socially or ritually. We are called to expand our definition of neighbor and to expand our relationships with and responsibilities toward others.

   Who are the "other" people in our lives? These could be competitors in business or sports. They could be foreigners without papers or school dropouts without degrees. Contrast the stories of the "others" with stories of the times that the tables were turned and we found ourselves on the outside, the stranger. Who was our neighbor in those circumstances? Write in the journal the name of someone who could be a "neighbor." Write some action—greeting, invitation, assistance—that you will do in relation to the neighbor.

2. When we live in imitation of the Lord, our actions become visible. Faith is not a matter for the intellect alone. Rather it is an integration of personal experience and the life of Jesus. Faith calls for the re-sponse of choosing to act like Jesus, in the will of the Father.

   Take stock of where we have been. This can be described as a conversion journey. Invite all to share in the exercise of writing down in their journals a word to name where each was and then extend from that word with an arrow to a word describing the new choice. For example, one might write: I have moved from fear to trust; another could say: I was self-centered and I have moved to a greater community awareness, from death to life, from information to understanding, from Sunday morning television to worshiping with this community. Invite the group to share some of the examples. Summarize how the examples that are shared are expressions of the love of God with one's heart, soul, and mind.

CLOSING PRAYER

(The following is an adaptation of the signing of the forehead and senses of the Rite of Becoming Catechumens.)

Leader: There are several traditional postures for prayer. Today I am going to ask you to repeat three phrases after me and to join me in a gesture with each phrase. We will ask for grace in our hearts, senses, and minds, as we prayed for you when you were first signed with the sign of the cross. The heart will be signed by the crossed hands in front of the chest; the senses, by hands open and apart at waist height; the mind by the open hands raised to shoulder or head height.

Let us pray.
God our creator, savior, and life, fill us with your grace.
Come into our hearts,
(Cross hands over chest while all repeat the petition.)
—that we may love you more.
Come into our senses,

(Gesture with hands open while all repeat
    the petition.)
—that we may recognize you today.
Come into our minds,
(Raise hands while all repeat the petition.)
—that we may derive meaning through the
    mystery of your presence.
(pause)
We ask this in the name of the Father, the
    Son, and the Holy Spirit.
Amen.

Doctrinal and Pastoral Issues: Love of Neighbor, Conversion, Covenant, Golden Rule

Elizabeth S. Lilly

31st Sunday in Ordinary Time

Malachi 1:14—2:2,8–10
1 Thessalonians 2:7–9, 13
Matthew 23:1–12

OPENING PRAYER

(Make copies of this prayer for the prayer folders.)

Leader: Let us pray.

All: Glory be to the Father,
and to the Son,
and to the Holy Spirit.
As it was in the beginning,
is now, and ever shall be,
world without end. Amen.

REFLECTIONS

1. The readings today give us a glimpse of the Trinity—God the Creator, Father of all; God the Son, the Messiah and Teacher; God the Spirit at work within those who believe. Last week we focused on God's grace in our minds and hearts and whole being. Today we move in our reflections to consider how each of us is, becomes, and enlivens God's presence in others in our interrelationships.

    Reread the last two verses of the first reading. What has happened in the last week, or recently, that has brought you to a new or deeper awareness of God in your life? These could be a visit with a friend, a talk with a child, a smile from a clerk, a diagnosis from a doctor. Is what you hear today in the Scripture causing you to continually re-evaluate your values and actions? How do others help you by their faith, their example, or their hope?

2. The word for what we are talking about is catechesis—sharing faith. That is what being Church is, what being Christian is. We are so made that there will be outward signs of our interior disposition.

    A way to broaden the discussion is to ask: "Who is a catechist for you?" "For whom are you a catechist?" Catechumens, candidates, sponsors, and leaders may reflect how the others are sharing their faith. This could be an affirmation exercise during which each person listens to others tell how their faith is formed by the faith of each, one at a time.

3. Good liturgy strengthens faith. The liturgy is the important sign of unity. Our prayer in the name of Jesus forms unity and nurtures faith. A person who disassociates from the liturgy of the Church on Sundays is estranged from the Church.

    How is our communal worship a service to each other? How do we, a parish community, pray together? Invite the catechumens and candidates to describe the liturgical actions that are prayerful and faith-forming. A member of the parish liturgy committee could be present to participate and listen.

CLOSING PRAYER

(Paul thanks God constantly for the growth in faith of the Thessalonians. The following prayer is a litany of thanksgiving. Please invite all to add to the list of thanks and to respond to each name with: "We thank you, Lord God.")

Leader: Let us pray.
Lord God, you continually re-create us in your image, the image of your Son who serves, your Spirit that is at work within us.
For your life and presence we give thanks.
For our families,

All: We thank you, Lord God.
For our sponsors,

All: We thank you, Lord God.
For this parish community,

All: We thank you, Lord God.

(Indicate that anyone may name someone or some situation for which we give thanks.)

Leader: For all your gifts, we thank you in the name of Jesus, the Christ. Amen.

Doctrinal and Pastoral Issues: Trinity, Incarnation, Commandments of the Church, Catechesis

Elizabeth S. Lilly

32nd Sunday in Ordinary Time

Wisdom 6:12–16
1 Thessalonians 4:13–18
Matthew 25:1–13

OPENING PRAYER

(The following prayer is taken from the Universal Prayer, attributed to Pope Clement XI. It is found in the sacramentary. It could be distributed and read antiphonally.)

Lord, I believe in you: increase my faith.
I trust in you: strengthen my trust.
I love you: let me love you more and more.
I am sorry for my sins: deepen my sorrow.

> Let me love you, my Lord and my God,
> and see myself as I really am:
> a pilgrim in this world,
> a Christian called to respect and love
> all whose lives I touch,
> those in authority over me
> or those under my authority,
> my friends and my enemies.

Help me conquer anger with gentleness,
greed by generosity,
apathy by fervor.
Help me to forget myself
and reach out toward others.

> Make me prudent in planning,
> courageous in taking risks.
> Make me patient in suffering,
> unassuming in prosperity.

Teach me to realize that this world is passing,
that my true future is the happiness of heaven,
that life on earth is short,
and the life to come eternal.

> Help me to prepare for death
> with a proper fear of judgment,
> but a greater trust in your goodness.
> Lead me safely through death
> to the endless joy of heaven.

Grant this through Christ our Lord. Amen.

REFLECTIONS

1. We have spoken of the names of the Church: the people of God, the body of Christ. Another name is the communion of saints. This image helps us expand our view to include that which is outside our dimension of time. This includes the living and the dead.

   Tell the story of the patron saint of the parish or the diocese. Ask people to describe how they were named. Often names tell family stories and emphasize our relatedness to those for whom we are named. Prepare a description of the patron saints of the people present.

2. The Church and the kingdom of God are not the same. The Church is a sign of the kingdom because it is the presence of Christ in our time, in history. Initiation into the sacramental life of the Church is an incorporation not only into the community of believers, but also into the eternal presence of God. The Christian believes in life after death and in the transformation of the body.

   We have been reflecting on conversion. This is already a transformation in our lives, a turning toward God, now. How, like the wise virgins in the Gospel parable, are you continually anticipating your union with God? When do you find your own time to pray? Do you have a particular time or place to pray?

CLOSING PRAYER

(We have Masses for special occasions, as well as Sundays and weekdays. The following prayer is one example of an opening prayer from a Mass for the Dead. If friends or relatives or particular persons have been mentioned in the discussion, they could be mentioned again in this prayer.)

Leader: Let us pray.
Lord,
those who die still live in your presence
and your saints rejoice in complete happiness.
Listen to our prayers for (name those who have died)

who have passed from the light of this
   world,
and bring them to the joy of eternal radiance.
We ask this through our Lord Jesus Christ,
   your Son,
who lives and reigns with you and the
   Holy Spirit,
one God, for ever and ever. Amen.

*Doctrinal and Pastoral Issues: Life after Death, Com-
munion of Saints, Prayer*

Elizabeth S. Lilly

33rd Sunday in Ordinary Time

Proverbs: 31:10–13, 19–20, 30–31
1 Thessalonians 5:1–6
Matthew 25:14–30

OPENING PRAYER

(The following prayer is the alternate opening prayer of this Sunday. The catechist could choose to repeat the opening prayer of the liturgy of the word or to pray the one not chosen by the presider.)

Leader: Let us pray.
Father in heaven,
ever-living source of all that is good,
from the beginning of time you promised
us salvation
through the future coming of your Son, our
Lord Jesus Christ.
Help us to drink of his truth
and expand our hearts with the joy of his
promises,
so that we may serve you in faith and in
love
and know for ever the joy of your presence.
We ask this through Christ our Lord.
Amen.

REFLECTIONS

1. Security is something on everyone's mind. We hear of national security and financial security and security blankets. True security is a gift from God and it is not earned. The Gospel challenges us to risk acting upon what we have heard.

   Invite someone from the social justice committee or peace committee of your parish or neighborhood to be present with the catechumens and candidates. Let them share their concerns for peace and security and let them give examples from your local community of people working to bring about true security. Encourage the catechumens and candidates to question and exchange ideas. Arrange for a time to work in a soup kitchen or other activity in or out of the parish.

2. There is evil in the world. We do not explain it; we acknowledge its existence. Evil is always against life. We have the choice to avoid evil, to work through evil and to remove evil from particular situations. We are confronted by evil.

   How, in a practical way, do you make choices for good? Name examples of moving through evil such as being with a terminally ill person, a victim of a natural disaster, etc. We live in the midst of many temptations to find our security by our own inventions. How are these false securities? What changes will each of us make in our investment of trust, time, and energy?

3. God is a generous giver and forgiver. We are to act the same. As we are forgiven, so are we to forgive. It is cyclic. We come to recognize and acknowledge our own need for forgiveness as we forgive others. We trust in the love and compassion of God because of Jesus.

   It has been a while since we shared about forgiveness in our lives. Has there been a new occasion to extend forgiveness to a "neighbor"? Have you received forgiveness from someone unexpected?

CLOSING PRAYER

(The leader should recollect the false securities and strengths of the power of evil that have been brought forth in the discussion. These will form the petitions of the following prayer. Ask all to respond to the petitions with: "Lead us not into temptation.")

Leader: Let us pray.
Father of mercy and compassion,
we turn to you in hope.
When we are tempted to call another "enemy" rather than "neighbor",

All: Lead us not into temptation.

Leader: When we are tempted to trust weapons of destruction to secure peace,

All: Lead us not into temptation.

Leader: When we kill the defenseless through our negligence or apathy,

All: Lead us not into temptation.

Leader:	When we refuse to let others help us because of our pride,
All:	Lead us not into temptation.
Leader:	(Add situations that are timely and appropriate for your community.)
All:	Lead us not into temptation.
Leader:	For these and all that which is evil and draws us away from your love, we ask that you deliver us, through your Son, Jesus. Amen.

Doctrinal and Pastoral Issues: Social Justice, Evil, Forgiveness

Elizabeth S. Lilly

Christ the King

Ezekiel 34:11–12, 15–17
1 Corinthians 15:20–26, 28
Matthew 25:31–46

OPENING PRAYER

(The following prayer is from the concluding prayers of the Rite of Penance, number 208.)

Leader: Lord God, creator and ruler of your kingdom of light,
in your great love for this world
you gave up your only Son for our salvation.
His cross has redeemed us, his death has given us life,
his resurrection has raised us to glory.
Through him we ask you to be always present among your family.
Teach us to be reverent in the presence of your glory;
fill our hearts with faith, our days with good works,
our lives with your love;
may your truth be on our lips and your wisdom in all our actions,
that we may receive the reward of everlasting life.
We ask this through Christ our Lord.
Amen.

REFLECTIONS

1. The images of king and shepherd are frequently used in the Bible. They may not be familiar to us in our increasingly urban republic. Let us look again at the description of the actions of the shepherd in the first reading.

   Collect the words of healing, comfort, rescue. Look for a figure, or persons today who could also be described by these words. From Mother Teresa to the nurse in the local convalescent hospital, from the known to the unknown, there are many examples of shepherds in our midst.

2. Judgment is not an isolated act, detached from the way one lives. Reread the Gospel. Pause after each activity. These are called the corporal works of mercy. Christians are called by the Gospel to work to alleviate pain and suffering and injustice in the world.

   Recall a time when you were able to do something for another, and in the act of giving found that you actually felt that you received more than you gave.

3. The reflections of giving and serving illustrate how the Christian is always converting knowledge about Jesus to understanding of the life of Jesus in the spirit in us now. Our understanding of the kingdom of God grows in every choice of life over death that we make. We deepen our dependence on God as we come to realize that we are the hungry and thirsty, desiring more than the material satisfactions that we can provide.

   When you entered the catechumenate, we prayed that the Christian Church would support you in your quest for faith. In what ways is the Church welcoming, comforting, and satisfying? In what ways do you challenge the Church and yourselves, now, to act more decisively?

CLOSING PRAYER

(The following is modeled on the Prayer of the Faithful. Explain that after an introduction, anyone may name something for which we pray.)

Leader: We hunger and thirst for the satisfaction that your life can bring to us.
We want to be a sign of your love in the world, removing barriers that make us strangers to one another.
In and through your presence, we want to comfort one another.
We pray for these needs and others that we particularly name:
For a world beyond war,
We pray to the Lord,

All: Lord, hear our prayer.
For just distribution of the world's resources,

	We pray to the Lord,
All:	Lord, hear our prayer.
	(other petitions)
Leader:	Father, we trust in your mercy, and hope in your kingdom. We ask these in the name of Jesus, your Son, our Lord. Amen.

Doctrinal and Pastoral Issues: Judgment, Kingdom, Hospitality, Healing, Service

Elizabeth S. Lilly

HOLY DAYS

Mary and the Saints

By Eugene A. LaVerdiere

Besides all the other feasts and solemnities which we have already seen, the liturgical year includes two great feasts of Our Lady and the feast of All Saints. For this last, the Gospel reading is Matthew 5:1–12, the Beatitudes, which we have already examined on the Fourth Sunday in Ordinary Time.

The feasts of Mary are that of the Immaculate Conception, which comes on December 8, during Advent, and that of the Assumption, which we celebrate on August 15, during Ordinary Time. The readings for these feasts are from Luke's prologue.

The Promise

With the Feast of the Immaculate Conception we celebrate the story of God's promise of salvation, from the first covenant to the fulfillment of the covenant in Christ. The story is epitomized by the person of Mary through whom God's life and word became flesh. Mary also embodies the vocation of the Church and of every Christian.

The reading for the feast is Luke 1:26–38, the story of Gabriel's annunciation that Mary would be the mother of the Son of god. Touched by grace, she was open to the Holy Spirit and accepted her role as the servant of the Lord. In such a life and commitment, there is no sin. The Church is called to the same selfless service and to bring forth the life of God into the world. Unlike Mary, we are not sinless, but we do have her as an ideal expression of what humanity ought to be. Mary is the vision of humanity's fulfillment in the reign of God. As such she stretches our hopes beyond the horizon of our personal lives and beyond history itself.

The Fulfillment

With the Feast of the Assumption we celebrate the story of how God's promise is fulfilled over and over again throughout history. It is because we have seen the promise fulfilled so often that the promise is a source of hope for us. The story of fulfillment, like the story of the promise, is epitomized in the person of Mary, whom Elizabeth greeted in the name of the entire Old Testament as well as in our own name as the Mother of the Lord.

The reading for the feast is Luke 1:39–56 which includes the Magnificat, Mary's song of praise, in which her rejoicing sings of how God is glorified in what has been done through her person. Her song is also the prayer of the Christian fulfillment. All that we pray for in the Lord's Prayer is celebrated in anticipation as already fulfilled. No longer need we pray that God's name be hallowed. His name is hallowed. His reign is established in the reversal of worldly values. The lowly have been raised up and the mighty toppled from their thrones, and the hungry have been filled with good things. Thus it is that in the person of Mary we celebrate both the promise and the fulfillment of life and history.

Introduction to the Assumption, Immaculate Conception and All Saints Day

The sessions for these feasts are arranged like those of the season of Lent. They contain the following parts:

Opening Prayer
Reflection
Integration
Closing Prayer

For further explanation of this method, please refer to the introduction to Lent.

Feast of the Assumption

August 15

Revelation 11:19; 12:1–6, 10
1 Corinthians 15:20–26
Luke 1:39–56

OPENING PRAYER

Opening Song

"Lift Up Your Hearts," (*Glory and Praise*, NALR, or similar song of praise)

Leader: Happy are they who believe the promises of the Lord will be fulfilled.

All: Happy are they who believe the promises of the Lord will be fulfilled.

Leader: For God has called us out of darkness into light.

All: Happy are they who believe the promises of the Lord will be fulfilled.

Leader: And God has chosen us as special and holy.

All: Happy are they who believe the promises of the Lord will be fulfilled.

Leader: Truly god has blessed us with the hope of our future.

All: Happy are they who believe the promises of the Lord will be fulfilled.

Leader: Let us remember each other's needs: (spontaneous prayer)

All: Happy are they who believe the promises of the Lord will be fulfilled.

Leader: Let us pray.
Good and gracious God,
happy indeed are we who believe
that all you have promised us will be ours.
Give us the wisdom to see more clearly
your guidance and support in these days.
Give us tongues to sing out and proclaim
your goodness
everywhere we go.
Give us the conviction, like Mary your servant,
to entrust our lives into your hands.
We make this prayer in the name of Jesus,
who is both Redeemer and Brother,
through the power of your Spirit. Amen.

REFLECTION

(Material for leader to develop)

"The sun will come out tomorrow; bet your bottom dollar that tomorrow, there'll be sun." So goes the song "Tomorrow" from the Broadway musical *Annie*. Sometines we live only for tomorrow, placing our hope and trust in the many tomorrows that lie before us. We dream dreams and plan our lives out. For many of us, today is only bearable because there is a tomorrow for us. And just maybe that tomorrow will make things different.

Tomorrow can be a vision of hope. But more often than we would like to admit, tomorrow becomes an escape. Scarlet O'Hara from *Gone with the Wind* captures the sentiment in her closing words: "I just can't think about it now; it'll drive me crazy. I'll think about it tomorrow. For tomorrow is another day." Tomorrow can become the motivation to "close up shop" today and not care, not take action, not respond, bury our head in the sand, become immobile.

INTEGRATION

(Choose appropriate exercise/discussion questions)

1. Share some experiences when you were waiting for "tomorrow." Was there a sense of anticipation? of wonder? of excitement?

2. Discuss why some people might be truly longing for tomorrow, such as victims of war who wait for the relief tomorrow may bring, or the starving who pray tomorrow may bring food.

3. What are some concrete ways in which tomorrow can be an escape?

4. Try and remember some "escapes" into tomorrow. What seemed to be driving you? What were you

hoping for? Were you satisfied when tomorrow came?

REFLECTION CONTINUES

The celebration of the Feast of the Assumption is a celebration of tomorrow, God's tomorrow: the full and final kingdom of God. The kingdom of God is God's reign of compassion, justice, peace, love. Inaugurated in the person and life of Jesus, the Christ, the kingdom will be fully realized when all creation is drawn up into the fullness of God's embrace of love, i.e., when all creation has allowed itself to experience the gratutitous gift of God's love which transforms and redeems.

INTEGRATION

(Choose appropriate exercise/discussion questions):

1. Share with each other the important parts of Jesus' message that you think make a difference. List these qualities. Do they have anything to do with the kingdom of God?

REFLECTION CONTINUES

Choosing to live with the kingdom of God as one's vision means to live God's tomorrow today. The kingdom of God is at hand! It is not choosing to stand back and let life go by with the hope that someday God will come and take us away from it all. Rather, it is a call to be immersed in life now, to truly live life now, to be about God's values now so that all creation will be touched by God's values now. And the depth of this challenge reaches out to all people, to social institutions, to all of creation. God's kingdom is not a private possession we hold onto. It is not a private privilege you or I hope to have fully someday. God's kingdom is the community of God's people gathered together. This is present in root form today as the new creation, and this has profound social implications. Mary's canticle of praise in today's Gospel bears witness to the call to justice. This beautiful hymn, patterned after Hannah's song in 1 Samuel 2:1–10, is a proclamation of God's unending love and compassion which calls us to justice and fellowship today because we have been touched by God.

INTEGRATION

(Choose appropriate exercise/discussion questions)

1. Recall a time when the vision of tomorrow strength-

ened you at that time. How did that affect how you lived then? Did you desire the vision of tomorrow any differently after that?

2. What are some of the excuses we use to avoid confronting evil and injustice? How often is tomorrow one of them (i.e., I'll help them tomorrow)?

REFLECTION CONTINUES

Mary's assumption is a symbol of our hope that we too will be raised to glory with God. This feast celebrates Mary who shares our destiny, our future. She touches our deepest longings and desires for completion and fulfillment in God. All of this is brought together for us in the resurrection of Jesus, the Christ. The focus is God's activity, not Mary. God has raised Jesus from the dead. Mary, because of her obedience to God by living in fidelity to God's continual call in her life, now shares in the fullness of God's presence. Mary becomes the symbol of all we will be in Christ. (Cf. Corinthians text)

Talk of resurrection raises the important notion of the body. Is the resurrection a "spiritual" matter, and hence the "soul" is raised? Mary's assumption offers an important clarification to the discussion of the resurrection. The tradition holds that Mary was assumed "body and soul," i.e., one complete person. Salvation is for the whole person. Hence, Mary's assumption becomes an affirmation of the worth and goodness of the material. We are called upon to examine our vision of our bodies, our sense of material goods, our use of resources. The doctrine of the resurrection affirms that "all will be made new," i.e., we will be raised in our transformed bodies (this is not the corpse). Jesus has redeemed us fully: the whole person and not only the "spiritual" dimension.

INTEGRATION

(Choose appropriate exercise/discussion questions)

1. How do you view your body? What are some images or words which describe your body to you? How might you appreciate your body more?

2. Discuss the importance of being balanced, of moving toward wholeness on all levels: emotionally, physically, psychologically, intellectually, spiritually, etc. Take a brief inventory on how faithful you are to your whole person, i.e., how do I care for myself and how do I not care for myself? Choose life this day.

CLOSING PRAYER

Leader: Let us pray.
Creator God,
it is you who are our beginning and our
end.
You are the source of life, and to you all
life is drawn.
Help us recognize the deep hunger we
have for you.
Give us the strength and courage needed
to allow ourselves
to listen deeply to your word proclaimed.
And transform our hearts by this same
Word
so we might be men and women of conviction and justice.
May we sing out in praise of you as did
Mary as she prayed:

All: My soul proclaims the greatness of the
Lord . . .
(continue with the Canticle of Mary)

*Doctrinal and Pastoral Issues: Eschatology, Justice and
Peace, Resurrection, Assumption*

Thomas H. Morris

Feast of all Saints

November 1

Revelation 7:2–3, 9–14
1 John 3:1–3
Matthew 5:1–12

OPENING PRAYER

Song

"For All the Saints" (or similar song) (Traditional melody)

Recite the psalm response of the day (Psalm 24) with the antiphon "We Praise You, O Lord" (Dameans) between strophes.

REFLECTION

(Material for leader to develop)

Heroes and heroines—everyone has them. In fact, the contemporary cry is that we don't have enough heroes and heroines to meet the new demands of our times. Yet for many of us, we grew up with our heroes and heroines right there by our side. We knew them from literature, or from the silver screen, or from government. Sometimes our models were local town folk, maybe even someone in our family. But more often than not, our heroes and heroines were people we had not met but who touched us and inspired us. Be they a Hemingway, a Hepburn, a Roosevelt, a Garbo or even a Linus van Pelt, heroes and heroines helped form our lives, gave us vision.

Sometimes we make our heroes and heroines unreachable, untouchable, and hence unreal. We create their story to be larger than the person—and we lose touch with the special quality such a person brings to our lives: their own expression of humanity. If we are not careful, our heroes and heroines become our new gods: we fill them with such mystery and awe that we catch ourselves saying things like: "Oh, I worship the ground he walks on" or "I simply adore her." Then our heroes and heroines become distorted and we lose sight of their valuable contribution to human living: the fidelity with which they lived life and used their gifts for the creation of a more human world. But if we allow our heroes and heroines to be human, to experience pain and doubt, to make mistakes, then we can appreciate them more fully, see them more clearly, and be inspired more profoundly because they chose to live life from their gifts.

INTEGRATION

(Choose appropriate exercise/discussion questions)

1. Name some of your childhood heroes and heroines. Why were they important to you? How have your heroes and heroines changed since your childhood? What makes the difference now?

2. What can happen when we idolize our heroes and heroines? What happens to us because of this?

REFLECTION CONTINUES

Today's great feast is about heroes and heroines. Today we celebrate the many men and women who chose to live life from their gifts in response to a call from God, a call each of us is given. The Church sets them aside and holds them as models of Christian life. And this is so not because they led extraordinary lives (though the popular tales about the saints seem to suggest this), but rather because in their very ordinary lives they lived faithfully the Gospel way of life. They struggled and sinned and sought forgiveness; they prayed and experienced darkness and reached out for light; they embraced the cross and allowed God to transform them. They were like you and me, ordinary people who believed that the cross of Jesus Christ made all the difference. And it did.

INTEGRATION

(Choose appropriate exercise/discussion questions)

1. Do you have a favorite saint? Tell your favorite story about this saint. Why is he or she special to you?

2. Can you relate to your favorite saints as friends, fam-

ily, neighbors, or do you behold them from afar and gaze at them?

REFLECTION CONTINUES

We are called to be saints, to be holy. But how can we become holy? How can we make a difference? Today's Gospel spells out the way of life for those who choose to follow Jesus. The Beatitudes reflect a new code of living. And what rises as fundamental is not so much the actions we take (or don't take) but the attitude which grounds these actions. We all know people who are charitable for the praise they can get, and people who are just because their profit is at stake, and people who are helpful because they want you to repay their kindness back a hundredfold. And perhaps these people are us. But the Beatitudes point to a different way of living life, different attitudes which form and direct our actions.

INTEGRATION

1. Reread today's Gospel slowly. In small groups, discuss the various attitudes which the text invites us to develop. Restate the text for contemporary men and women using these attitudes.

2. How can we live from these Beatitudes? How do you undersand purity of heart (single-heartedness, to desire one thing: God and God's will, to see all creation as part of God's will, to focus on the way of life Jesus models, etc.)?

3. How do the Beatitudes relate to God's vision?

REFLECTION CONTINUES

"Oh, when the saints go marching in, when the saints go marching in. How I want to be in that number, when the saints go marching in." Yes, we do want to be part of that number, and we can. Today we celebrate not only the great men and women of our tradition who lived in fidelity to the Gospel call, who lived the attitudes of the Beatitude life, but we also celebrate our destiny, our heritage, our own way of living life. We are invited to reflect on the quality of our lives, the patterns we have chosen, and ask the hard questions. Then we too will be counted among those "who have survived the great period of trial; they have washed their robes and made them white in the blood of the Lamb" (Rev 7:14).

INTEGRATION

1. What does it mean for me to be a saint? How can I live a holy life while still being involved in my work, family, career? What will make the important "difference" in all of this?

CLOSING PRAYER

Leader: Good and gracious God,
with great love and devotion we celebrate
our sisters and brothers who have witnessed to your love.
We thank you for them and for the life they have led.
We are grateful that we have known some of them
as family, friends, colleagues, members of our community.
May we continue to be inspired and empowered
by their way of life of self-sacrificing love.

Litany of Saints: sung response: "Pray for us."

(Be careful not to drag the litany. It is meant to be a mantra chant, and should move gracefully and crisply)

Holy Mary, Mother of God . . .
St. Peter and St. Paul . . .
St. Mary Magdalene . . .
St. Stephen . . .
St. Perpetua . . .

(continue with names of catechumens and other saints you wish to mention)

St. Elizabeth Ann Seton . . .
Pope John XXIII . . .
Dorothy Day . . .
Thomas Merton . . .
All holy men and women of God . . .

Close with exchange of peace.

Doctrinal and Pastoral Issues: Communion of Saints, Intercession, Beatitudes

Thomas H. Morris

Feast of the Immaculate Conception

December 8

Genesis 3:9–15, 20
Ephesians 1:3–6, 11–12
Luke 1:26–38

OPENING PRAYER

Opening Song

"Glory and Praise to Our God" (or similar praise song)

Leader: Let us give thanks to our God.

All: For God's love endures forever!

Leader: Let us sing praise to the One who has loved us.

All: For God's love endures forever!

Leader: Let us rest in confidence in God's providence.

All: For God's love endures forever!

Leader: Let us remember the needs of each other (silence).

All: For God's love endures forever!

Leader: Let us pray . . .
Good and gracious God,
we gather to break open your word
so that we might be nourished and fed.
Open our hearts and minds
that we may gently receive the gift of this day.
Help us to ponder the wonder of your servant, Mary,
as her life models for us the call to obedience.
We make this prayer
in the name of Jesus,
who is both Redeemer and Brother,
through the power of the Spirit. Amen.

REFLECTION

(Material for leader to develop)

Beginnings. Beginnings seem to intrigue most of us.

People are often in search of their roots, their family tree, the foundations of a certain group or society. Beginnings attract us because they seem to contain some hidden wisdom, some simple insight as to the direction or goal of a person, family or event.

INTEGRATION

(Choose appropriate exercise/discussion questions) (Allow time for quiet reflection and small group sharing)

1. Tell a story about the beginnings of your family.

2. Why do you think people are so intrigued by their beginnings?

3. Why do you think having a sense of history is important for knowing yourself?

REFLECTION CONTINUES

The celebration of the Feast of the Immaculate Conception is a celebration of beginnings. Through Mary, God manifests the triumph of grace; the natural order is now the order of a graced nature. God surrounds Mary with the gift of God's love or grace; this is God's free choice and initiative. Mary stands as symbol of the relationship God also offers each of us: from the very beginning we have been surrounded with God's love, immersed in God's love so much so that God's love is indeed at the very core of our person. We were created as God's loved ones, "holy and blameless: to be full of love."

INTEGRATION

(Choose appropriate exercise/discussion questions)

1. Spend a few moments in silence. Create for yourself a sense of being in the womb. Create for yourself a sense of life within you. What would that experience be like? Envision this child (you) covered with bright light, feeling very good and warm, feeling welcomed and cared for. How do you think this will affect the child?

2. Reflect on stories you remember about yourself as a baby. Remember times when people loved you, cared for you. In this remembering is God's initial caring for you as you are.

REFLECTION CONTINUES

This feast also questions our awareness of our free choice to refuse life in God's love, to choose the reality of sin. It would be naive to think we live faithfully in relationship with God, choosing love as the center of our lives. We see the forces of dehumanization and degradation around us, and we need to humbly acknowledge our personal involvement in such destructive patterns of living. This is original sin: the reality that we are born into a world in which exists evil. We are not born evil and yet we find ourselves caught in the web of violence and destruction.

INTEGRATION

(Choose appropriate exercise/discussion questions)

1. What does sin look like? Try to create images that describe sin.

2. Have you ever felt "caught up" in a group experience, such as a pep rally or a football game? Describe the feeling. Can you remember similar experiences which were unhealthy, such as being caught up in a gossip circle, or other forms of violence? Describe the experience.

REFLECTION CONTINUES

The closing line of the Genesis texts links us with our Gospel account. Eve was named the mother of the living, a sign of hope of the ultimate victory of God's grace over death. Mary models the life of one who lives in fidelity to the core of a person, the grace-filled center where God is present. Great things happen in Mary because of God. She trusts who she is gifted to be and hence is open to the possibilities of life with God (rather than hiding in fear and shame). Mary is willing to entrust herself to God.

We are back to beginnings, new beginnings. Do we choose being turned in on ourselves, and hence being fearful, shamed, hiding? Or do we choose openness to possibilities? Such openness does not guarantee we will not be troubled or disturbed. But it bespeaks of a posture of life that is willing to listen to God's call, and therefore to be obedient. We can choose isolation and selfishness or we can choose a trust in God that can lead

to a healthy sense of indifference, i.e., whatever the outcome, one trusts that God's will is our well-being. The Feast of the Immaculate Conception reminds us of not only Mary's beginnings but our beginnings as well. It is not a celebration of Mary's separation from the rest of us, but rather Mary as rooted in our deepest identity: men and women graced with God's presence at the core of our being. Mary chose to live from her center. What is your choice?

INTEGRATION

(Choose appropriate exercise/discussion questions):

1. Name your gifts. Gifts are not necessarily talents such as singing, or sports. How do you discover your gifts and the gifts of others?

2. Gifts are given for all. Reread the Gospel text slowly. Note where Mary recognizes her giftedness from God. How does she respond? How are you like Mary?

CLOSING PRAYER

Leader: Let us pray.
We praise you, O God who fashioned us
and loved us with an enduring love.
You are the source of our beginnings
and you have gifted us with your very life
within us.
Give us the courage to look within
to discover the gifts of love you give us.
Help us find that our true beginning
is to start again and again as your children.
We make this prayer in the name of Jesus,
who is both Redeemer and Brother,
through the power of your Spirit. Amen.

Doctrinal and Pastoral Issues: Theology of Grace, Original Sin, Sin, Free Will, Role of Mary, Distinction Between Immaculate Conception and Virgin Birth, Stewardship of Gifts

Thomas H. Morris

Additional Catechetical Resources

Listed on this bibliography are additional resources for a catechumenate director. Books listed in the various sections of this text are not necessarily reiterated here. This is a list of additional resources. This list is also in no way meant to be the last word. There are other exceptional materials available. Hopefully, there will be many more developed in the future.

Bausch, William J. *Storytelling: Imagination and Faith*. Twenty-Third Publications, Mystic, CT., 1984.

Bergan, Jacqueline and Schwan, S. Marie. *Forgiveness: A Guide for Prayer*. St. Mary's Press, Winona, 1985.

Coughlin, Kevin. *Finding God in Everyday Life*. Paulist Press, New York, 1980.

DeBoy, James. *Getting Started in Adult Religious Education*. Paulist Press, New York, 1979.

DeMello, Anthony. *Sadhana: A Way to God*. Institute of Jesuit Sources, St. Louis, 1979.

————, *The Song of the Bird*. Image Books, New York, 1984.

Duggan, Robert, Editor. *Conversation and the Catechumenate*. Paulist Press, New York, 1984.

Farrell, Edward. *Celtic Meditations*. Dimension Books, New Jersey, 1976.

Fischer, Kathleen. *The Inner Rainbow: The Imagination in Christian Life*. Paulist Press, New York, 1983.

Forum. Newsletter of the North American Forum on the Catechumenate. Washington, D.C.

Groome, Thomas. *Christian Religious Education*. Harper & Row, New York, 1980.

Halpin, Marlene. *Imagine That*. Wm C. Brown, Dubuque, Iowa, 1982.

Hays, Edward. *Prayers for the Domestic Church*. Forest of Peace, Easton, Kansas, 1979.

Hefling, Charles C. *Why Doctrines?* Cowley Publications.

Hestenes, Roberta. *Using the Bible in Groups*. Westminster Press, Philadelphia, 1983.

Huck, Gabe. *Teach Me to Pray*. Sadlier, New York.

Ivory, Tom. *Looking at Our Faith*. Sadlier, New York.

Link, Mark. *Breakaway*. Argus Communications, Allen, Texas, 1980.

Maloney, George. *Centering on the Lord Jesus: The Whole Person at Prayer*. Michael Glazier, Inc., Delaware, 1982.

McCauley, George. *The Unfinished Image*. Sadlier, New York, 1983.

McMakin, Jacqueline. *Doorways to Christian Growth*. Winston Seabury, 1984.

Palmer, Parker. *To Know as We Are Known: A Spirituality of Education*. Harper & Row, San Francisco, 1983.

Rite of Christian Initiation of Adults. USCC, Washington, D.C.

Share the Word. Paulist Evangelization Center, Washington, D.C.

Simons, George F. *Keeping Your Personal Journal*. Paulist Press, New York, 1978.

Smith, Gregory Michael. *The Fire in Their Eyes*. Paulist Press, New York, 1976.

Wallis, Jim. *A Call to Conversion*. Harper & Row, New York, 1981.

Warren, Michael, Editor. *Sourcebook for Modern Catechetics*. St. Mary's Press, Winona, 1983.

CALENDAR: ADVENT TO PENTECOST: 1986–1999

Year	Sunday Cycle	1st Sunday of Advent	1st Sunday of Lent	Easter Sunday	Pentecost
1986–87	A	Nov. 30	Mar. 8	Apr. 19	June 7
1987–88	B	Nov. 29	Feb. 21	Apr. 3	May 22
1988–89	C	Nov. 27	Feb. 12	Mar. 26	May 14
1989–90	A	Dec. 3	Mar. 4	Apr. 15	June 3
1990–91	B	Dec. 2	Feb. 17	Mar. 31	May 19
1991–92	C	Dec. 1	Mar. 8	Apr. 19	June 7
1992–93	A	Nov. 29	Feb. 28	Apr. 11	May 30
1993–94	B	Nov. 28	Feb. 20	Apr. 3	May 22
1994–95	C	Nov. 27	Mar. 5	Apr. 16	June 4
1995–96	A	Dec. 3	Feb. 25	Apr. 7	May 26
1996–97	B	Dec. 1	Feb. 16	Mar. 30	May 18
1997–98	C	Nov. 27	Mar. 1	Apr. 12	May 31
1998–99	A	Nov. 29	Feb. 21	Apr. 4	May 23

Contributors

Ellen Bush, CSC, is Coordinator for Adult Development and Liturgy for the Diocese of Boise, Idaho. Her pastoral ministry includes work in Colorado and in Southern California. She holds a Master's in Theology from the University of Notre Dame. Sr. Ellen is a team member for the North American Forum on the Catechumenate.

John T. Butler is Director of Parish Services for the Archdiocese of Washington, D.C. He holds a degree in counseling and is presently studying at Washington Theological Union for his Master's in Theological Studies. For the past five years he has been a team member for the North American Forum on the Catechumenate and is curently a member of their steering committee.

Khris S. Ford is the Director of Evangelization and the Catechumenate for St. Elizabeth Seton Parish in Plano, Texas. She holds a Master's in Education. Mrs. Ford, a teacher for many years, is active in the RCIA Council for the Diocese of Dallas and has conducted workshops for their catechumenal teams. She is a member of the National Conference on Evangelization.

Karen M. Hinman is Director of the North American Forum on the Catechumenate. She has had extensive pastoral experience in three parishes, on a college campus, and in a prison. She is a consultant for implementation of the RCIA. Ms. Hinman holds the Bachelor in Sacred Theology, Bachelor of Science, and Master of Divinity Degrees.

Rev. Michael J. Koch is pastor of St. Philip Neri Church in Saskatoon, Canada. He received his education at the University of Saskatchewan and St. Joseph's Seminary, Edmonton. He also studied at the University of San Francisco and in Jerusalem. Father Koch is a member of the Steering Committee of the North American Forum on the Catechumenate, Washington, D.C.

Father Eugene LaVerdiere is the editor of *Emmanuel* Magazine and an associate editor of *The Bible Today*.

He holds a doctorate in New Testament and Early Christian Literature from the University of Chicago. Father LaVerdiere is the author of many books as well as audio and video cassettes. His most recent books include *The New Testament in the Life of the Church* and *When We Pray* (both Ave Maria Press).

Elizabeth S. Lilly is the Liturgy Coordinator and Director of the Catechumenate in St. William Parish, Los Altos, California. She holds a Master's in the History of Art from the University of California, Berkeley. She is a member of the Diocesan Committee on the RCIA, Diocese of Monterey.

J. Michael McMahon is Director of Liturgy and Music at Blessed Sacrament Catholic Community, Alexandria, Virginia. Mr. McMahon has a Master's in Liturgical Studies from the University of Notre Dame and a M.Div. from the Washington Theological Union, and is presently working on his doctorate in Ministry at The Catholic University of America.

Thomas H. Morris is Director of Religious Education at St. Mary of the Mills Parish, Laurel, Maryland, where he also directs the catechumenate program. He holds a Master's in Theology from the Washington Theological Union and is completing doctoral studies in Christian Spirituality at The Catholic University of America.

Joseph P. Sinwell is Diocesan Director of Religious Education, Diocese of Providence, and Co-Director of the Rhode Island Catechumenate. He is a founding member of the North American Forum on the Catechumenate and currently serves on its executive committee as treasurer. He holds Master's degrees in Religious Education and Agency Counseling and is pursuing a Doctor of Ministry degree at St. Mary's University, Baltimore.

Victoria M. Tufano is Director of the Liturgy Office for the Diocese of Des Moines. She received her Master of Divinity and Master of Arts in Liturgical Studies from the University of Notre Dame.